COWLEY
THROUGH TIME

Ken Pearce

AMBERLEY PUBLISHING

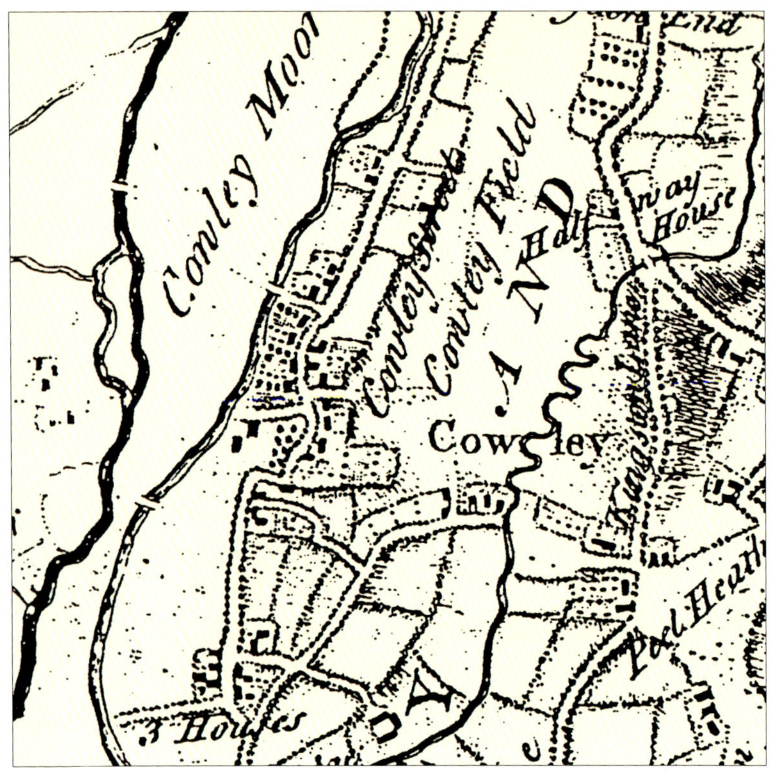

Part of Jean Rocque's map of Middlesex, 1754.

To Joyce Randall
who gave me every encouragement

First published 2010

Amberley Publishing Plc
Cirencester Road, Chalford,
Stroud, Gloucestershire, GL6 8PE

www.amberley-books.com

ISBN 978 1 84868 803 2

British Library Cataloguing in Publication Data.
A catalogue record for this book is available from the British Library.

Typeset in 9.5pt on 12pt Celeste.
Typesetting by Amberley Publishing.
Printed in the UK.

Introduction

In July 1965 a group of amateur archaeologists carried out an excavation on land in Cowley that was about to become the site of Brunel University. They uncovered part of a Roman road, about twenty feet in length. This confirmed an already existent theory that a road from St Albans had passed southwards through the area to a Thames crossing at Staines.

It seems probable that a temple for the worship of Roman gods was erected by this road, about half a mile to the south of the dig, and that the building was abandoned when the Romans left. It then presumably fell into disrepair.

A century or two later the first Christian missionaries arrived in the area and, as happened elsewhere, rebuilt it as a church. This is the best explanation we have for the position of the parish church of St Laurence. Around it developed a small community called 'the settlement of a man called Cofa'. This has evolved into 'Cowley'.

By the time of the Domesday survey of 1086 Cowley, spelled 'Couelie', was owned by Westminster Abbey. Only three people are mentioned – two villains and a cottar – which suggests a population of about twenty people only. In the centuries that followed Cowley remained a small community, totally surrounded by Colham Manor and Hillingdon parish, and with no clear boundaries.

Jean Rocque's 1754 map, a section of which is shown here, indicates that Cowley had by then developed into three main areas. There was the original settlement round the church, still small and not labelled. The largest area was now Cowley Street, on the main road from Uxbridge to West Drayton and mostly north of Iver Lane. Further south along the main road lay the '3 Houses', which later became known as Cowley Peachey, after the Peachey family who owned the manor in the fourteenth century.

In addition to these three districts the map shows a large stretch of open land reaching northwards to the fringe of Uxbridge township, and known as Cowley Field. This was actually part of Hillingdon parish, but by now Colham, Cowley and Hillingdon were 'inconveniently intermixed and separated.' That is a quotation from an Inclosure Act of 1796, which attempted to clarify the position. It was only partly successful, and it was left to the implementation of the Divided Parishes Act of 1882 to finally end the fragmentation of the area. In this book older parts of Cowley are covered, as well as the modern parish.

For centuries Cowley was a small agricultural village, with some flour-milling and brick-making. In 1801 the population was 214, by which time the Grand Junction Canal had just reached the district. A dock at Cowley Peachey promoted commercial development, especially the transportation of bricks to London, as well as a packet-boat service from Paddington.

Later in the nineteenth century there was a move away from growing corn to market-gardening and fruit-growing; and the Lowe and Shawyer cut-flower nursery gradually took over more fields.

The West Drayton to Uxbridge branch line of the Great Western Railway opened in 1856, but it was not until 1904 that Cowley Station came into service. In 1901 the population had reached 869, but the parish remained a rural community until after the 1914-1918 war.

Between the wars much house-building took place. Some of it was by Uxbridge Council, and some by builders R. T. Warren and W. S. Try. By the outbreak of war in 1939 the population was nearing 3000.

In the post-war years yet more house-building took place, and in the 1950s Uxbridge Council built nearly a thousand homes. They were constructed mostly to the south of the district on both sides of the main road. The population figure had risen to 8202 by 1961.

1958 brought the voluntary liquidation of the Lowe and Shawyer nursery, which meant that nearly 200 acres of land became available for redevelopment. Most of the site was destined to become the home of Brunel University, and today (2010) there are some 15,000 students on the campus, many of them living on the site.

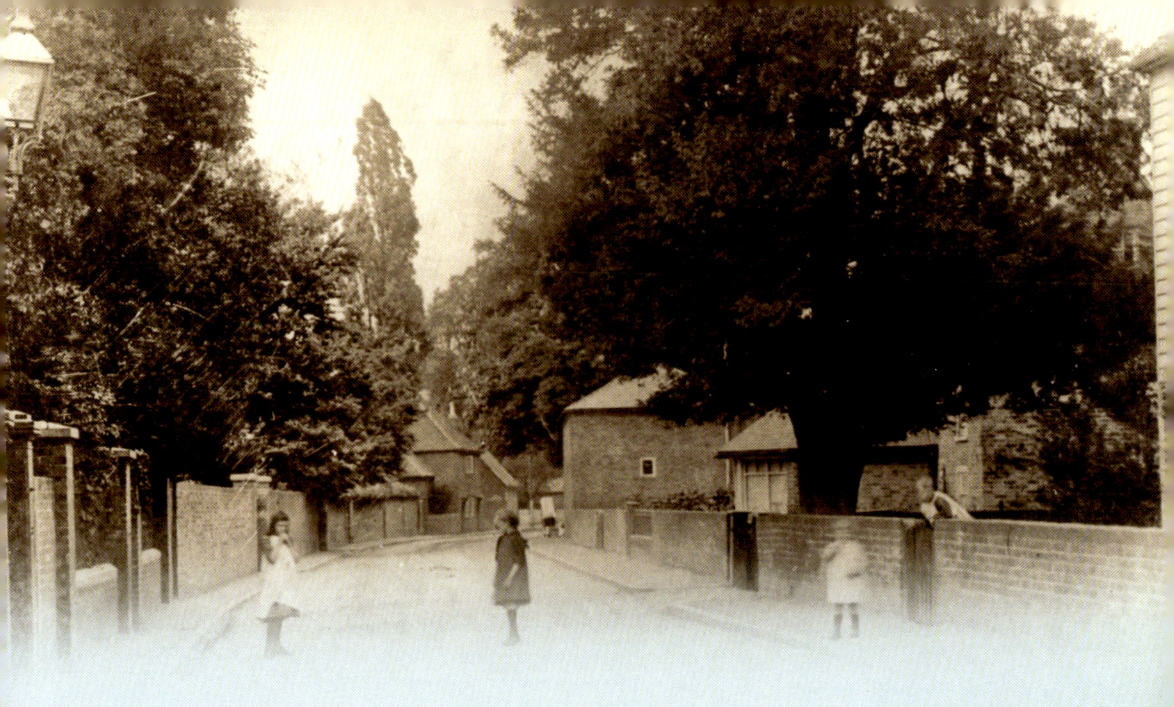

CHAPTER 1

The Village

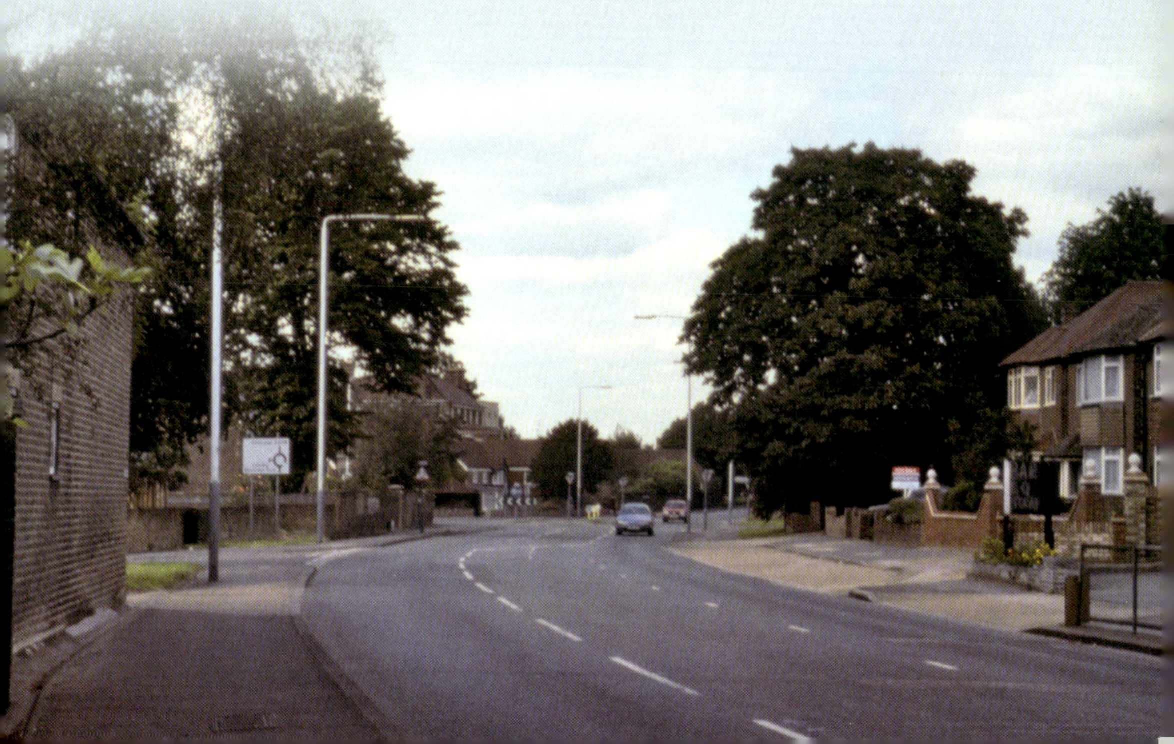

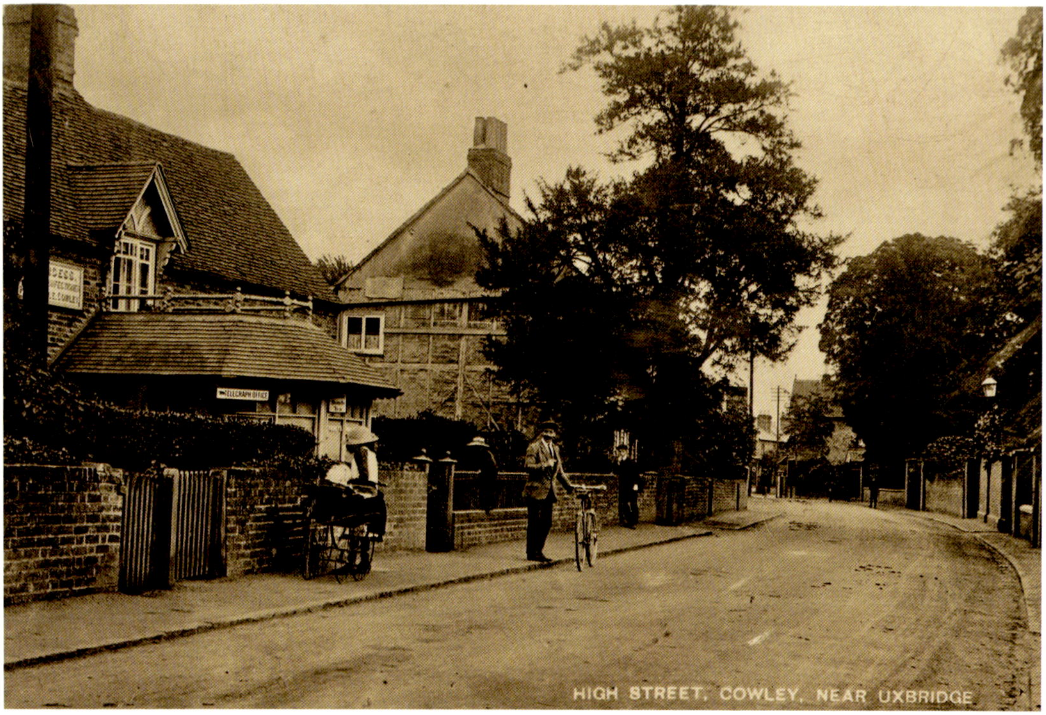

HIGH STREET, COWLEY, NEAR UXBRIDGE

The Old Post Office

It stood just north of the Crown Inn in the High Street. Originally a bakery, it became the Post Office as well, in Victorian times, and this led to the building being extended at the front. The lower picture was taken early in 1938, just before the Post Office moved to its present location in Dellfield Parade.

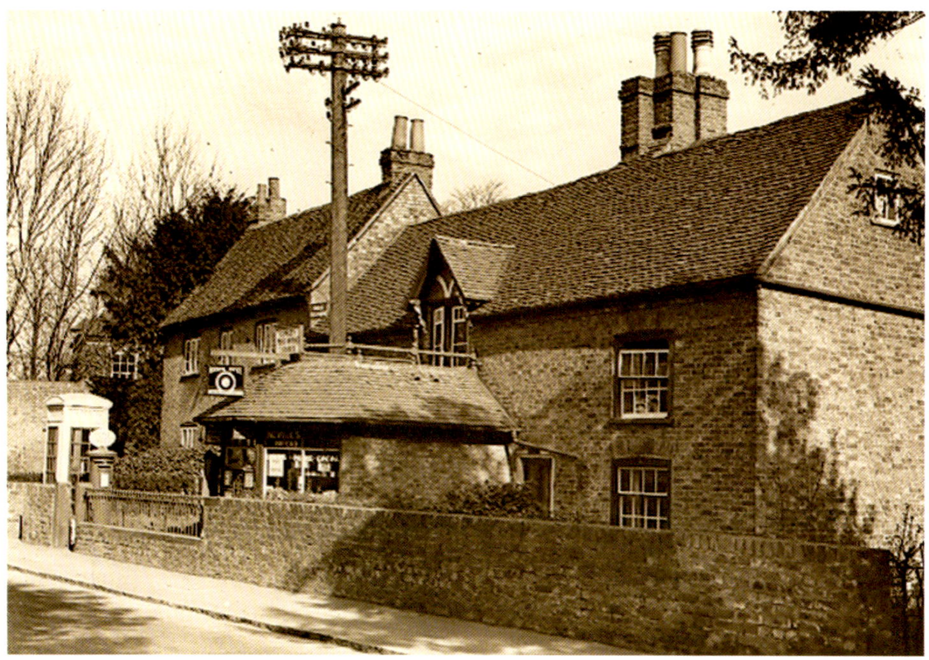

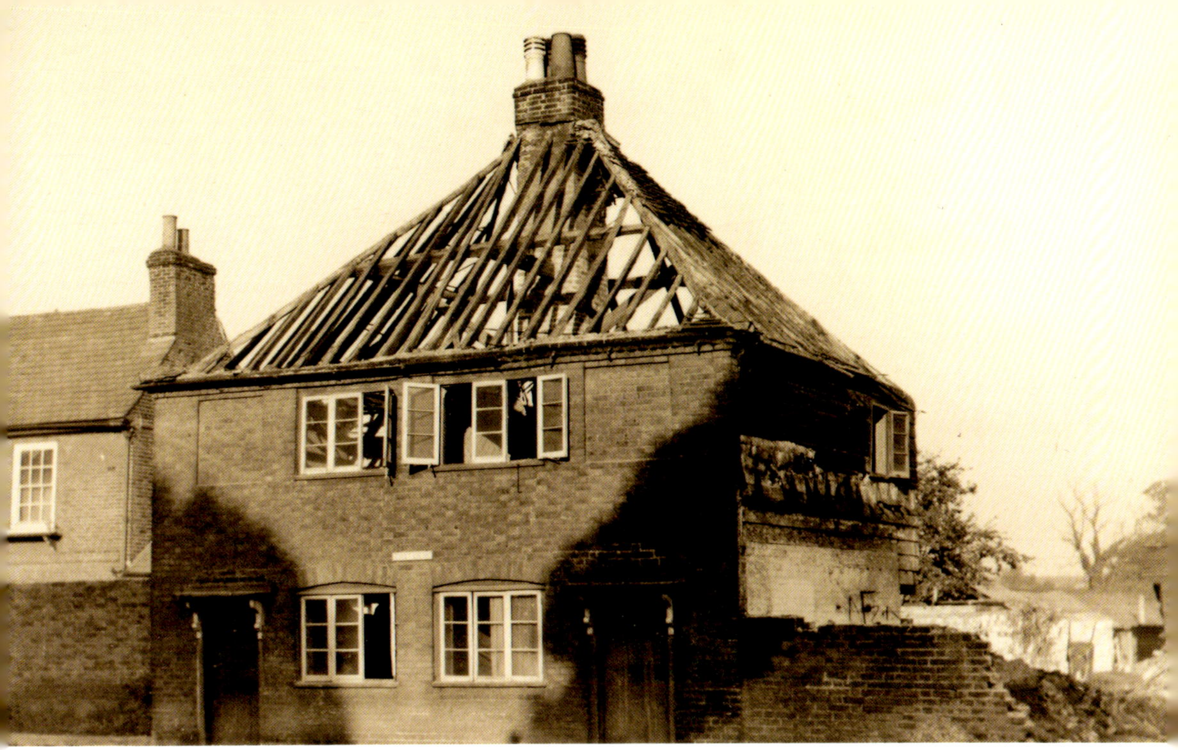

East View

The demolition of these High Street cottages in 1962. They were soon replaced by an office block for the building firm W. S. Try, but this has also now disappeared. The acquisition of additional land behind led to the opening of Cowley Business Park in 1990. Included on that site, after mergers and take-overs, are the offices of Galliford Try plc.

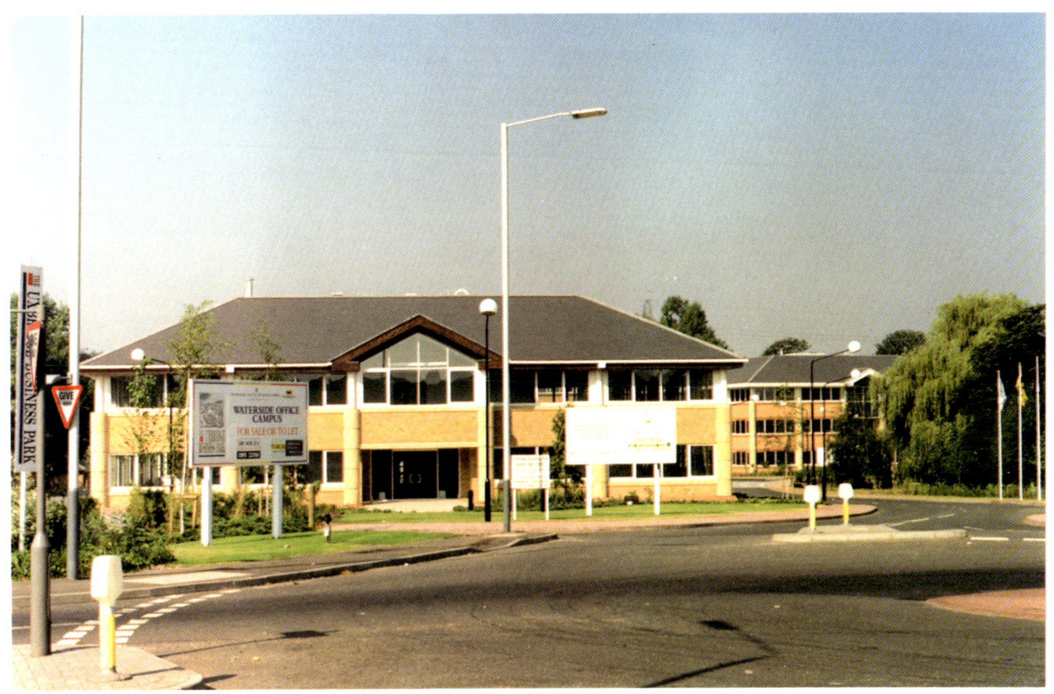

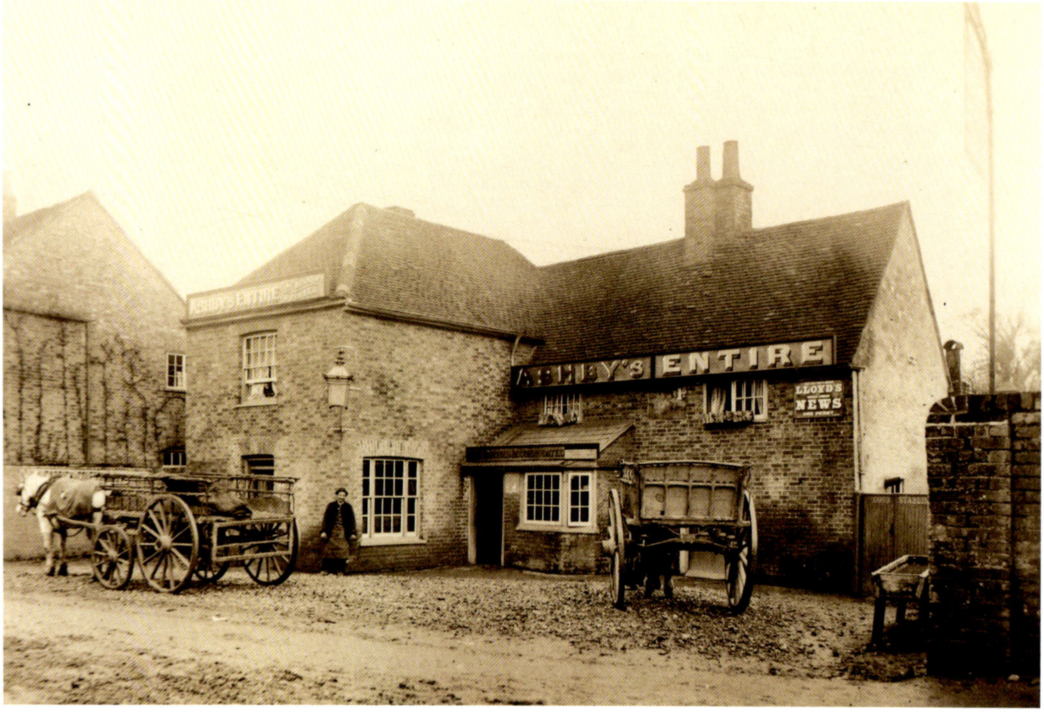

The Crown Inn

The oldest public house in Cowley by far, with parts of the building dating from the sixteenth century. This inn was one of many in the area owned by Harman's Uxbridge Brewery, but they were taken over by Courage in 1962. Clearance of houses on the north side has made space for a much-needed car park.

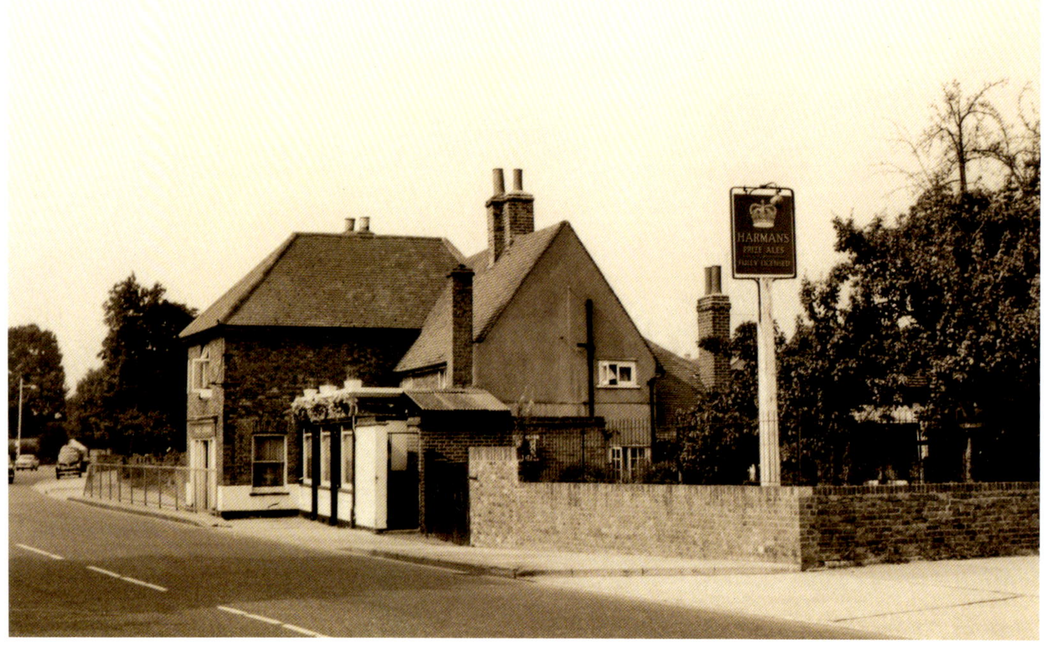

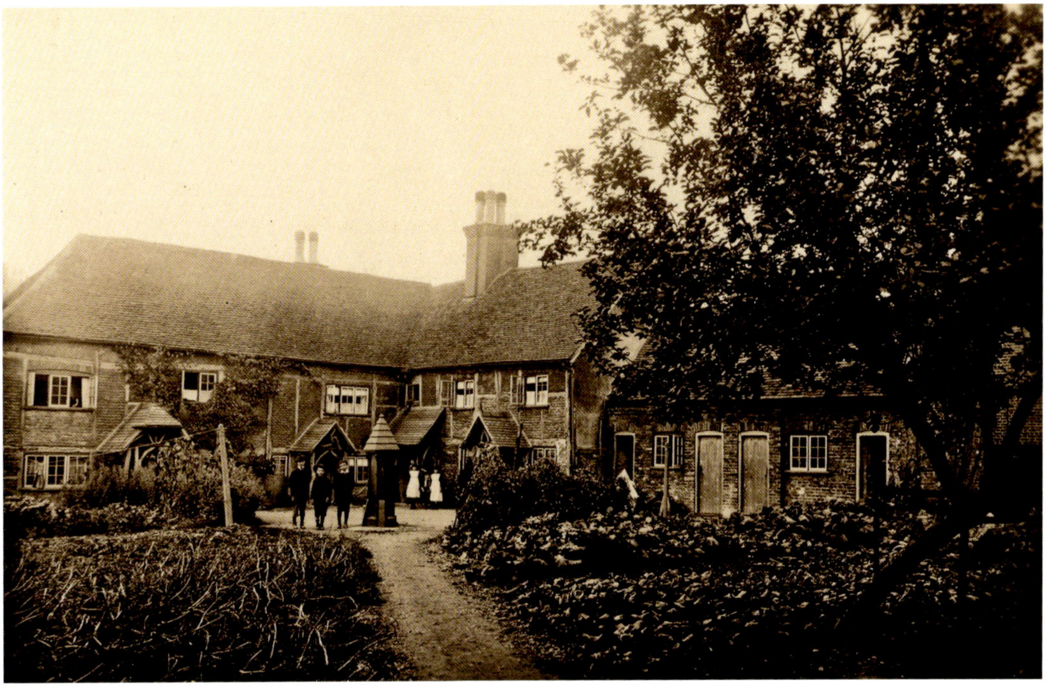

The Old Tanyard

An L-shaped group of cottages facing a communal water-pump, they stood opposite the Crown Inn. This is a clear indication that the tanning of leather, albeit on a small scale, took place here in centuries gone by. Fray's river, just behind, would have provided the necessary water. Soon after this 1900 photograph was taken the cottages were demolished. The scene today is not inspiring.

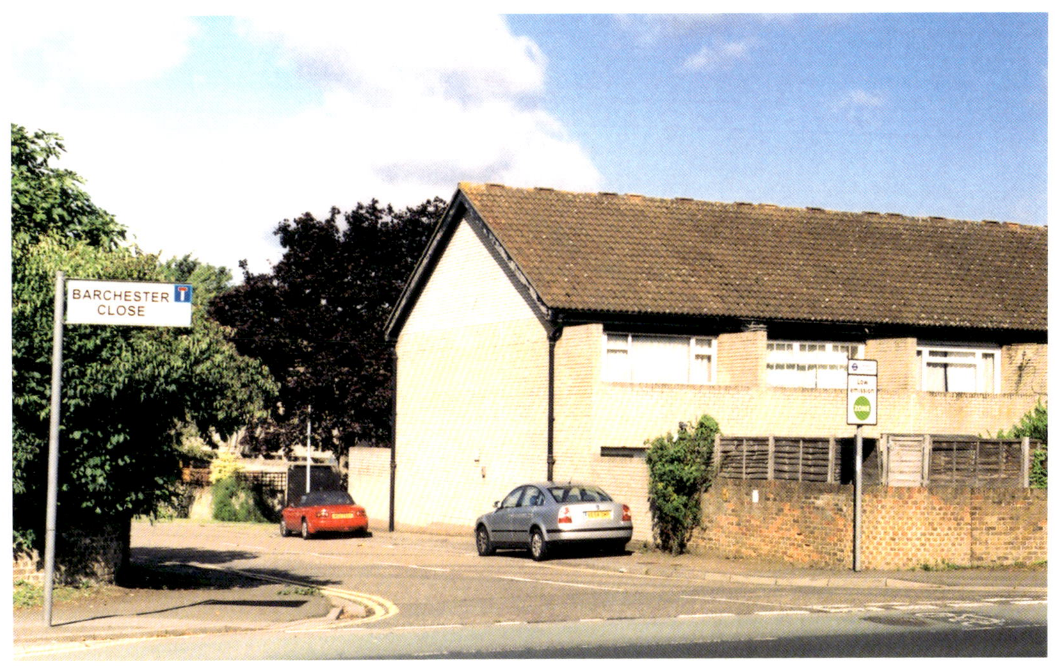

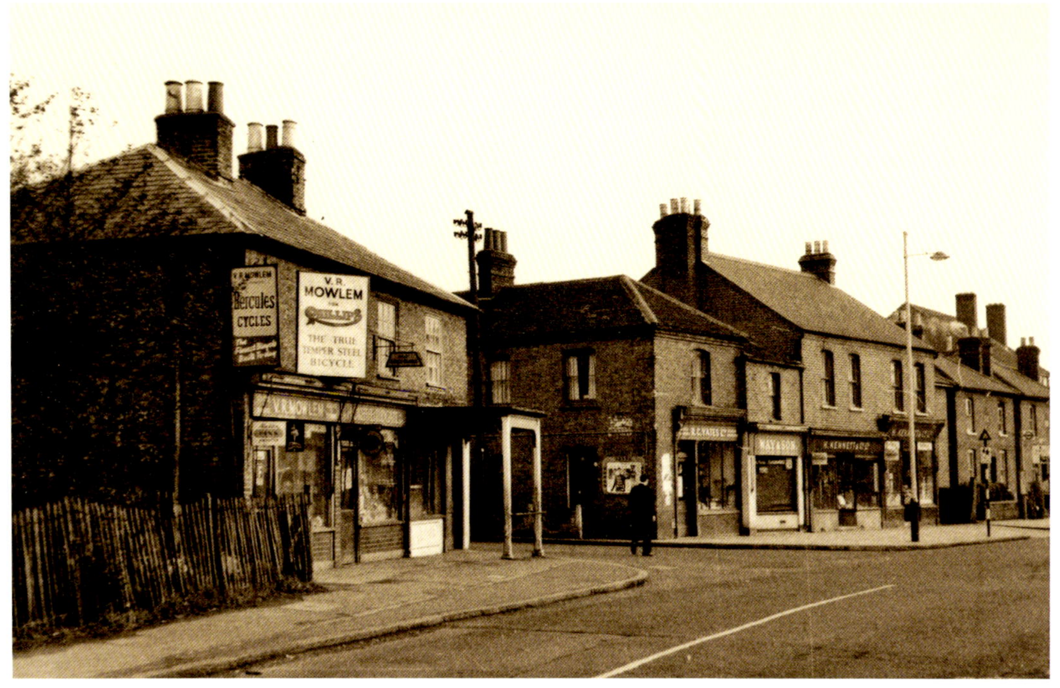

High Street/Station Road Junction

This picture was taken early in 1958, just before the nearer group of three shops was demolished. They were the cycle, radio and TV shop of Victor Mowlem, the newsagents O'Keefe and Ludgate, and the butcher's shop of Bob and Ken Darey. All three moved into the brand new shopping parade built behind. The lower scene dates from 1994.

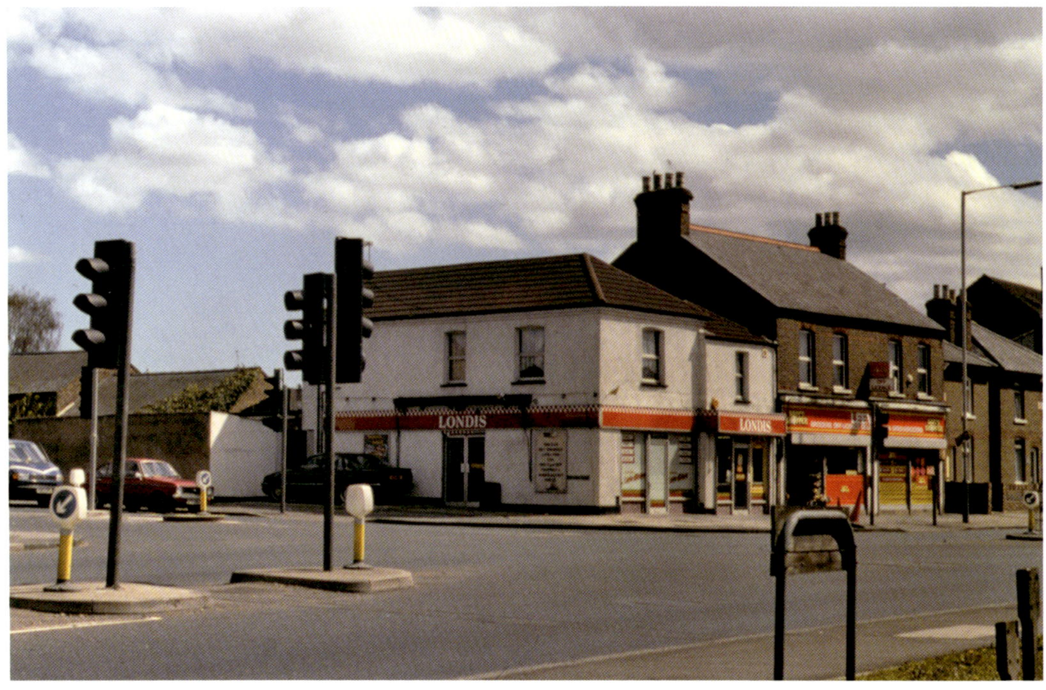

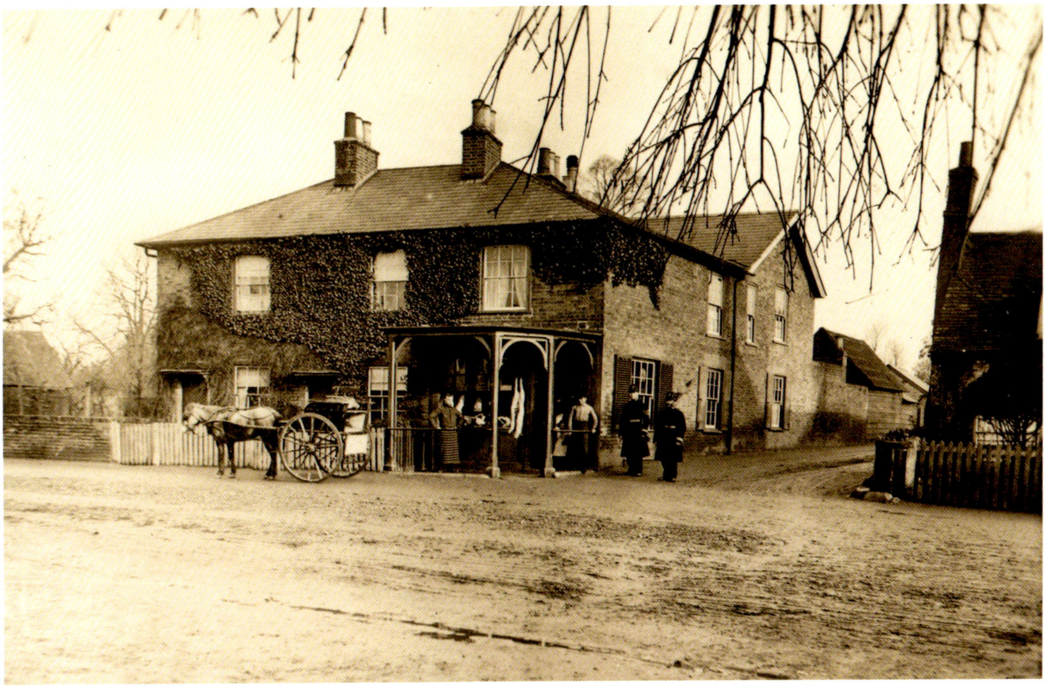

High Street/Station Road Junction

The same place in 1900, when Station Road was still named Fox Lane after the public house opposite. Two policemen can be seen in the roadway, and a canopy protects the meat hanging outside the butcher's shop. Today the road has been widened, and shops and flats are built further back off a service road.

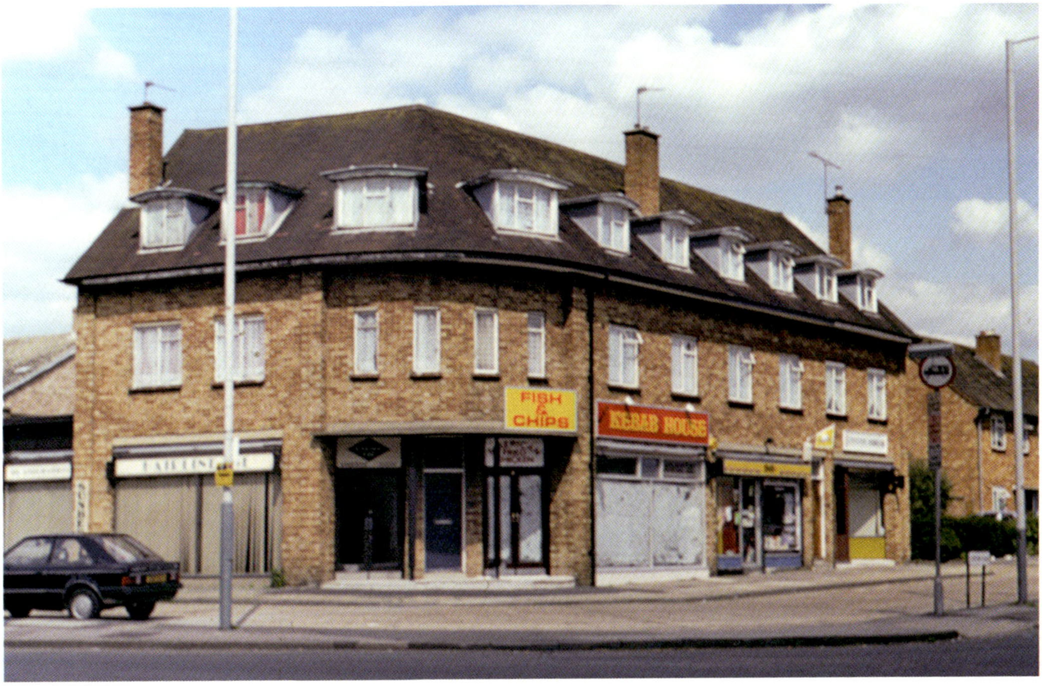

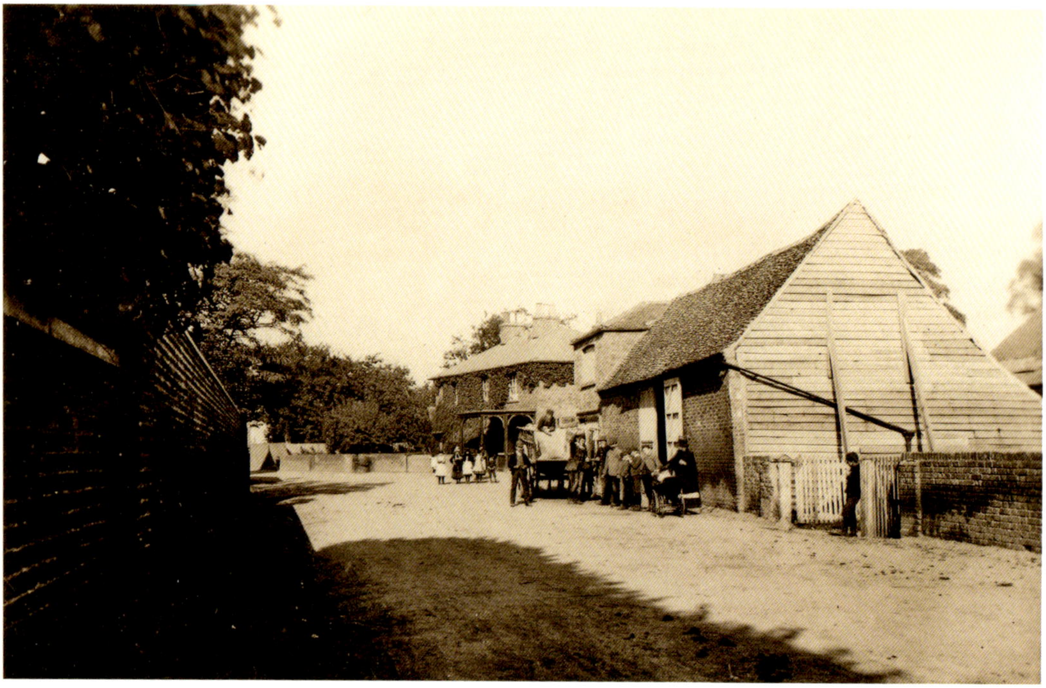

High Street/Station Road Junction

A third view of the same place, this time from the south. It seems almost incredible that there was a barn here about a century ago. Since the 1994 photo was taken, traffic lights and a pedestrian crossing have been added.

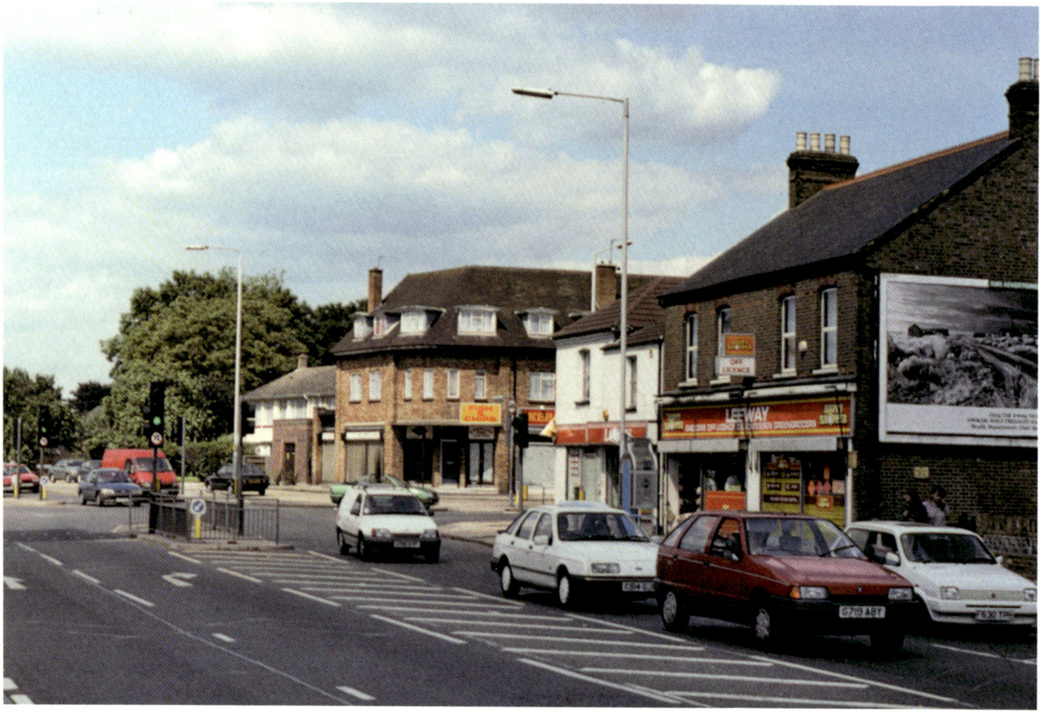

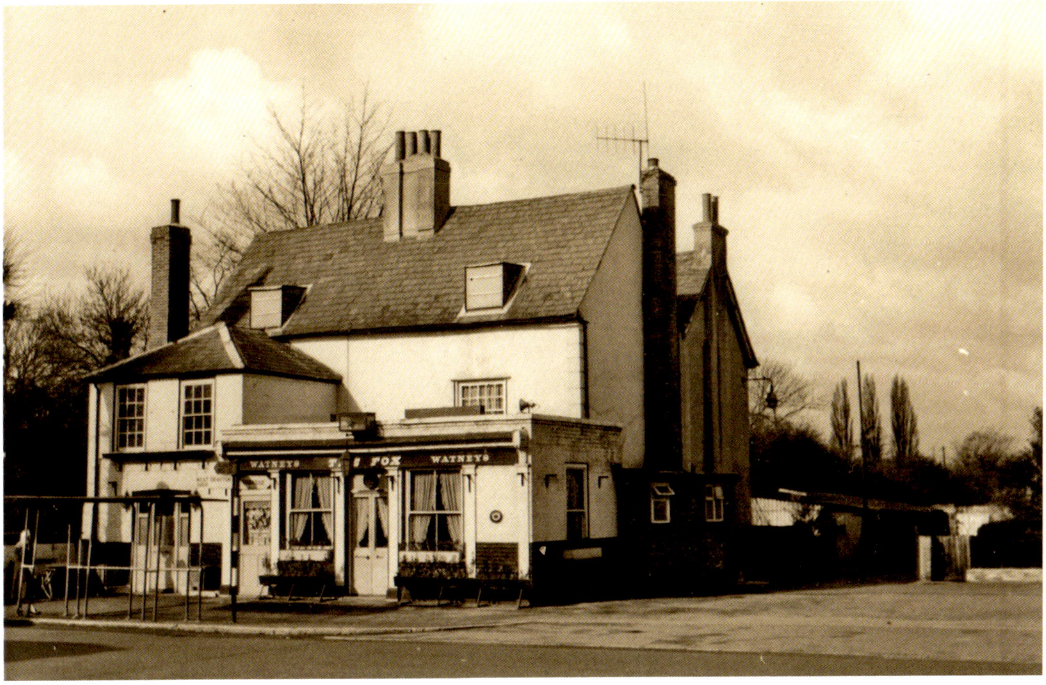

The Fox Public House

Another old Cowley pub, but a fire in the upper floor helped to hasten its closure and demolition in 1968. At the same time a large house called The Cedars, just to the south, was also cleared. A new public house was built on that site, and was also initially named The Fox. A striking all-metal sign was erected outside, designed and made by a young Polish sculptor name Walenty Pytel.

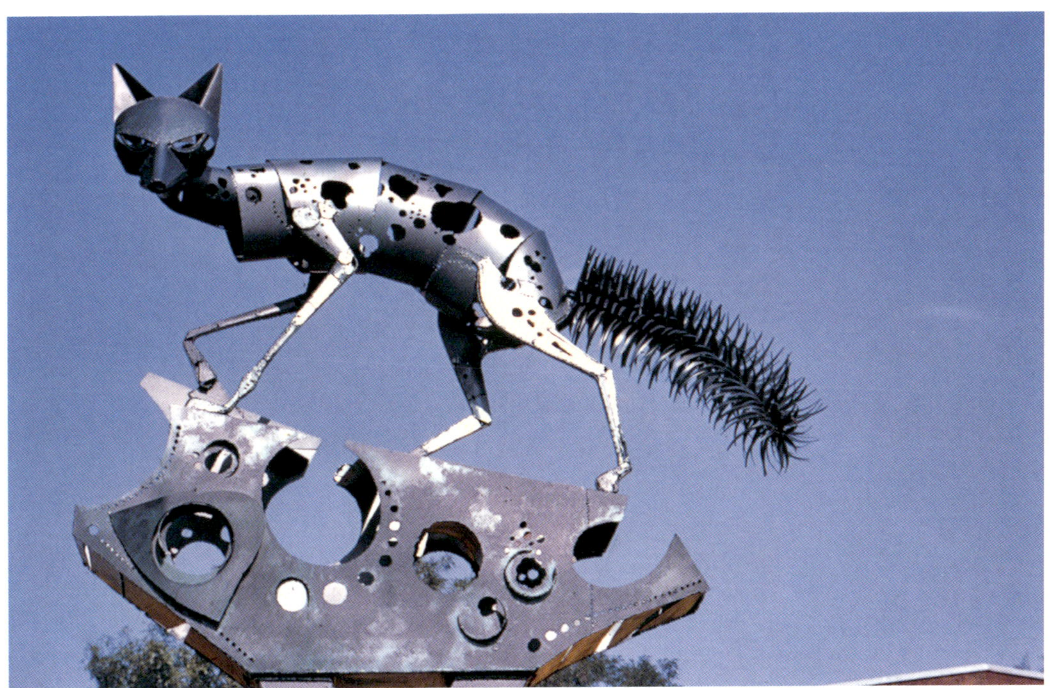

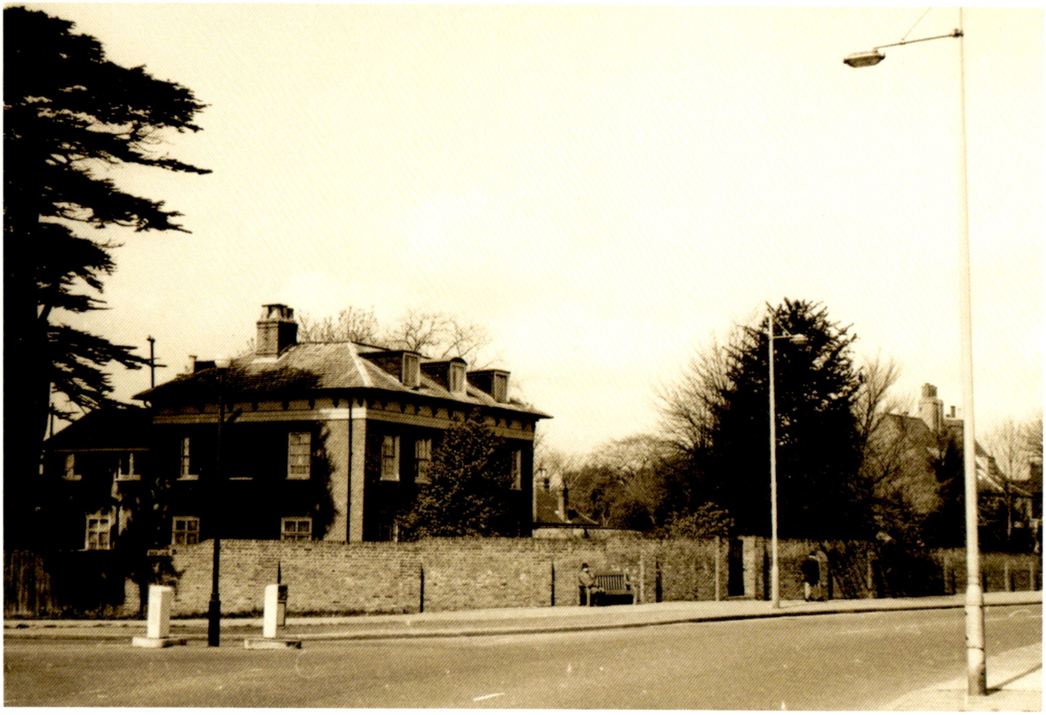

The Cedars in 1966

The Fox Inn can be seen on the extreme right of the picture. The new public house was painted bright yellow, but in its early years earned a bad reputation because of anti-social behaviour by the customers. The owners therefore decided to make a fresh start, and after refurbishment it opened under the name The Coachman's Inn.

The wonderful sign, shown on the previous page, became scrap metal.

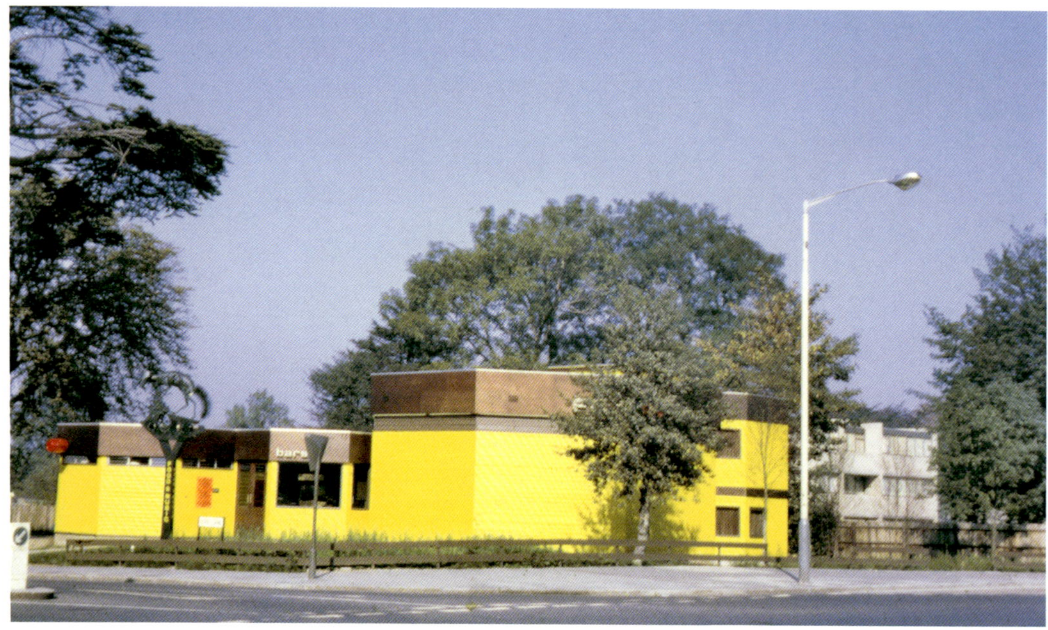

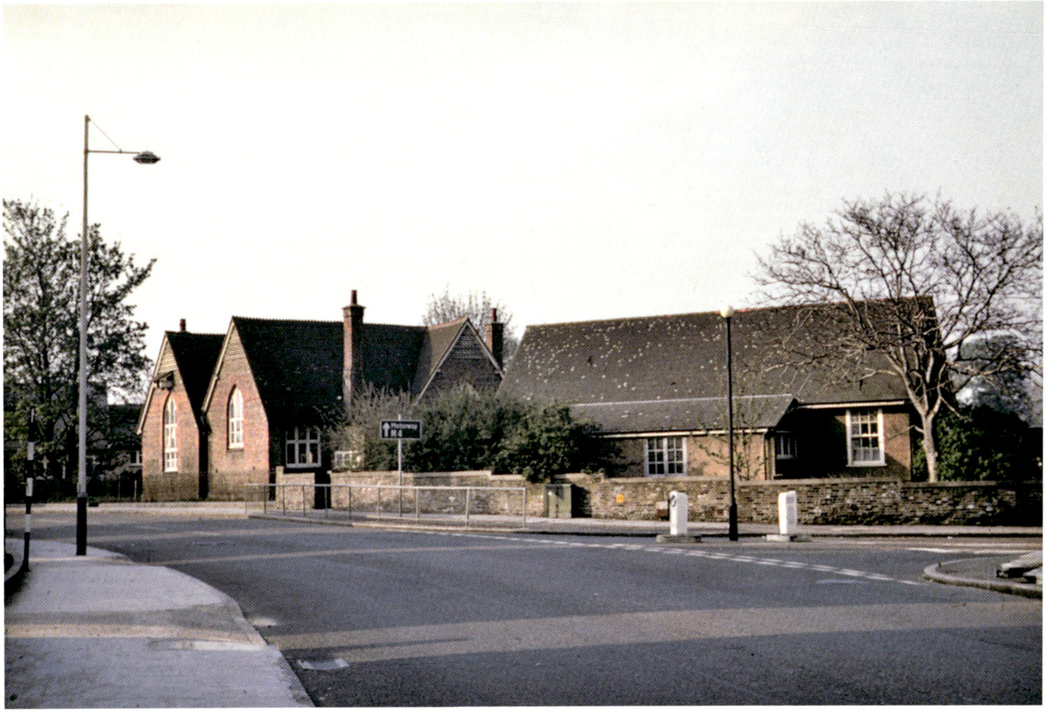

Junction of High Street and Iver Lane

The old St Laurence C of E School stands on the corner. It was abandoned in 1967, and a new Church Hall was built on the site. It can be seen behind the trees in the lower photograph. The hall was built by the firm of W. S. Try, cost £45,000, and was opened in August 1976.

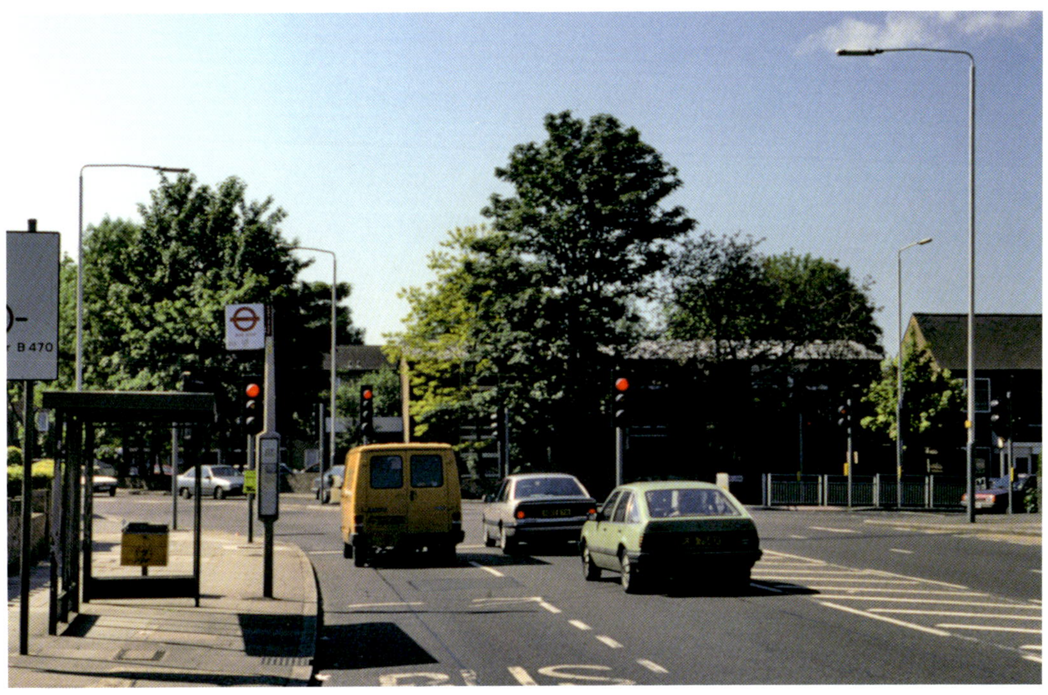

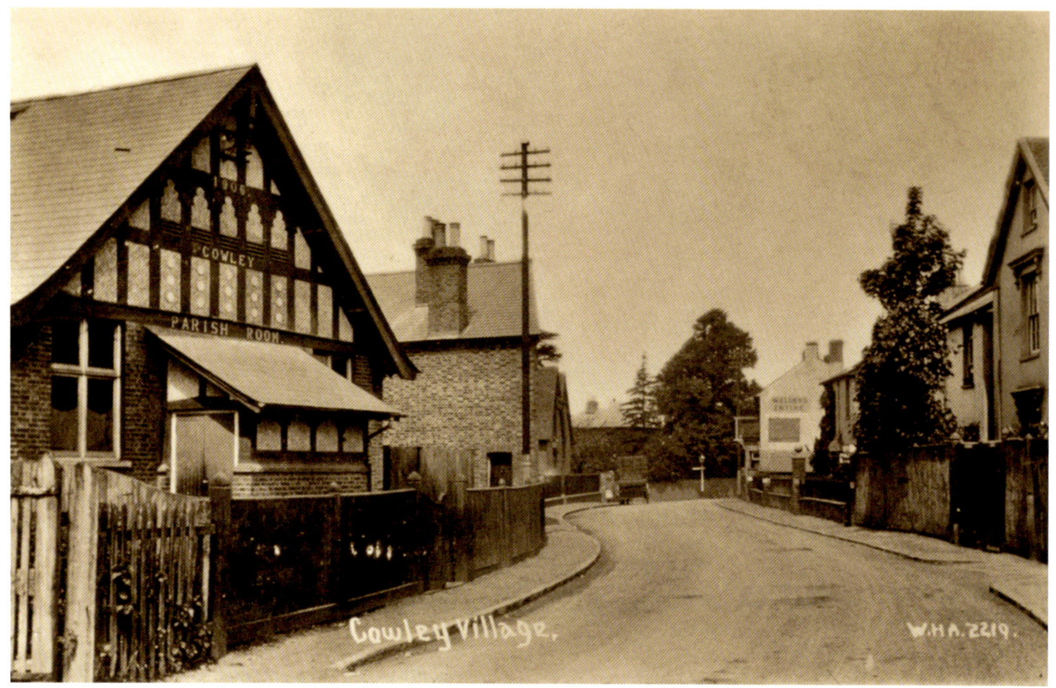

The Old Church Hall

This hall was opened in the High Street in November 1906 by the Dowager Countess of Essex, who was then living at Cowley House, and was one of the first building projects of W. S. Try. The hall was enlarged and modernised in 1932, but by 1973 when the lower picture was taken, it was inadequate for modern needs. Demolition came in 1975, and the consequent housing development called Shepherds Close gave the parish the funds to build the new hall.

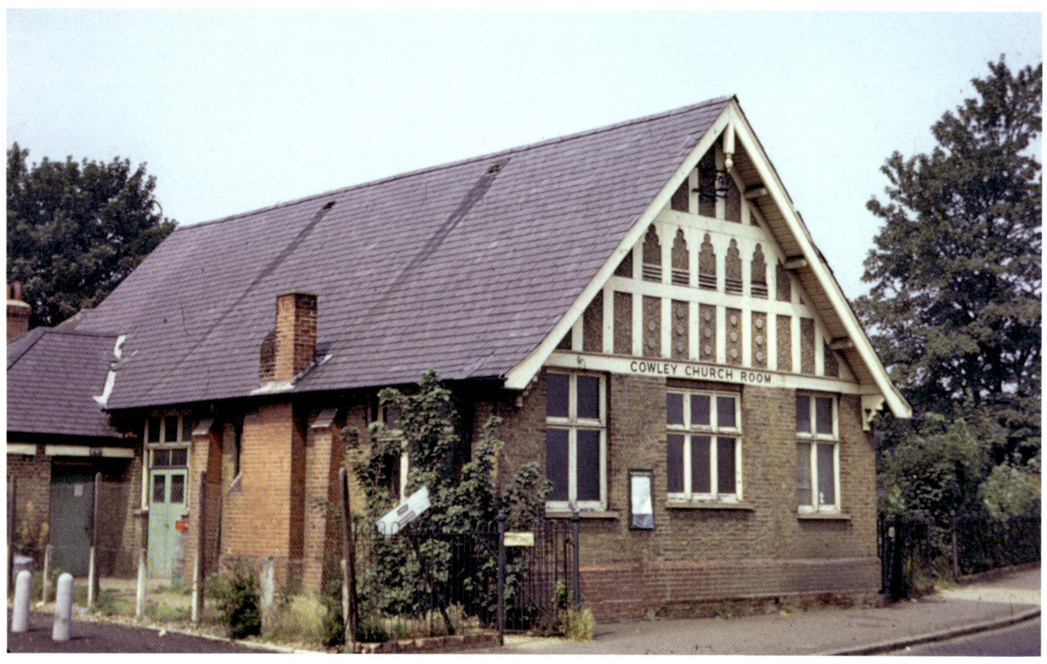

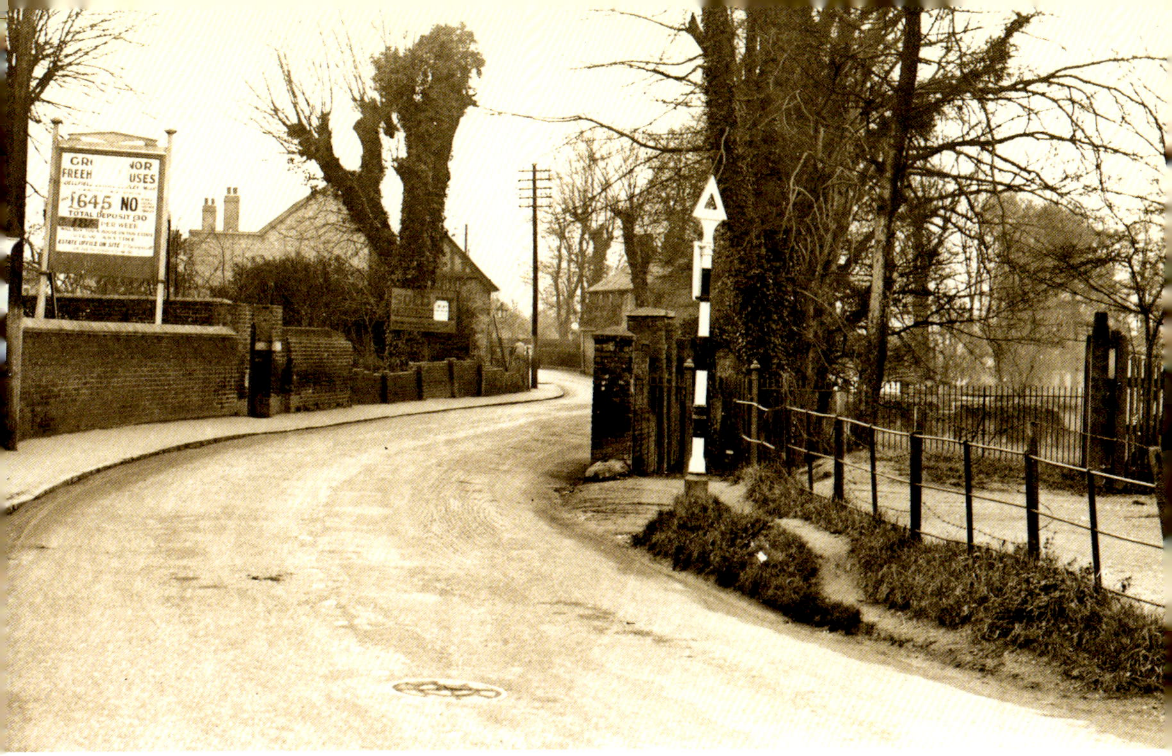

Development of the Dellfield Estate

The recreation ground can just be seen on the right of this 1938 photograph. The High Street curved a lot at this period, but in 1955 this section was widened and straightened. Houses in the new Dellfield Crescent are being advertised at £645 each.

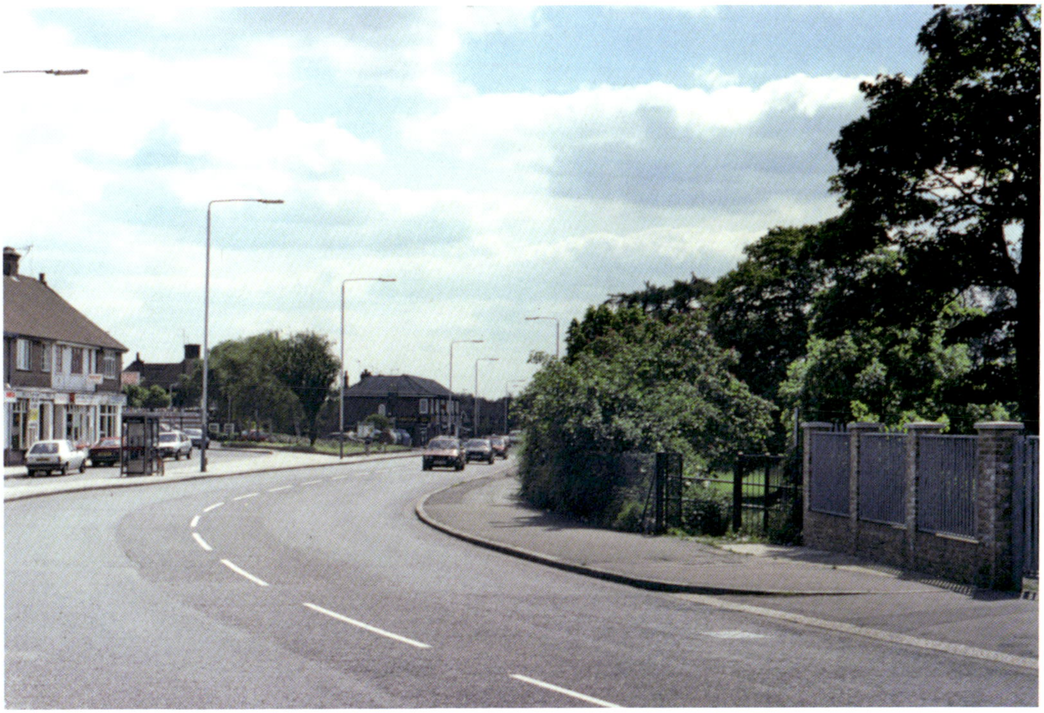

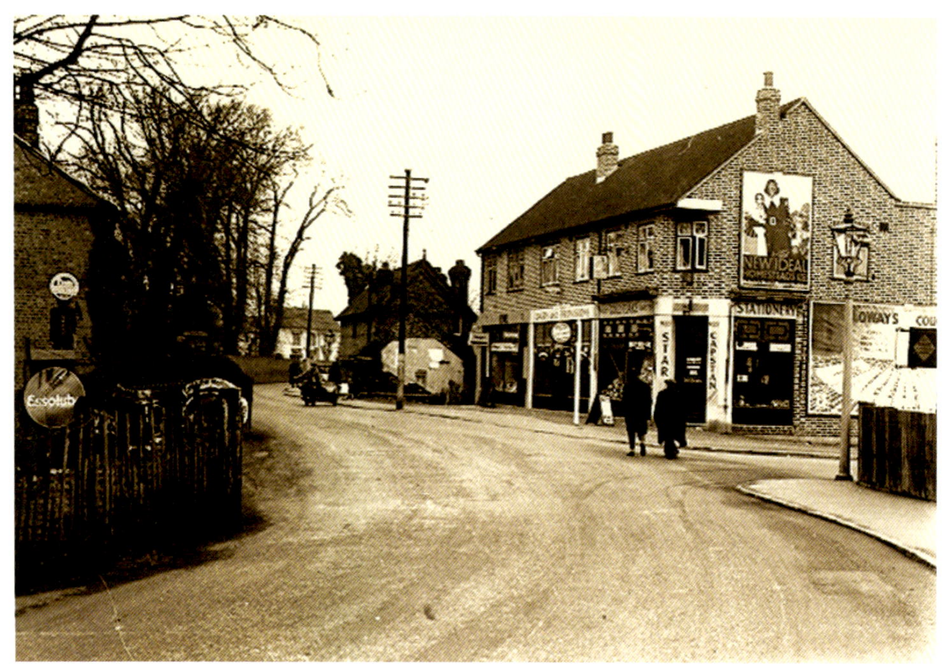

Dellfield Parade

At the same time the Dellfield Parade shops were being built on what was a serpentine High Street. On the left are the premises of a local garage owner known as 'Brassy' Briant, and he appears in the photograph on his motor-cycle combination. The former High Street is now a service road.

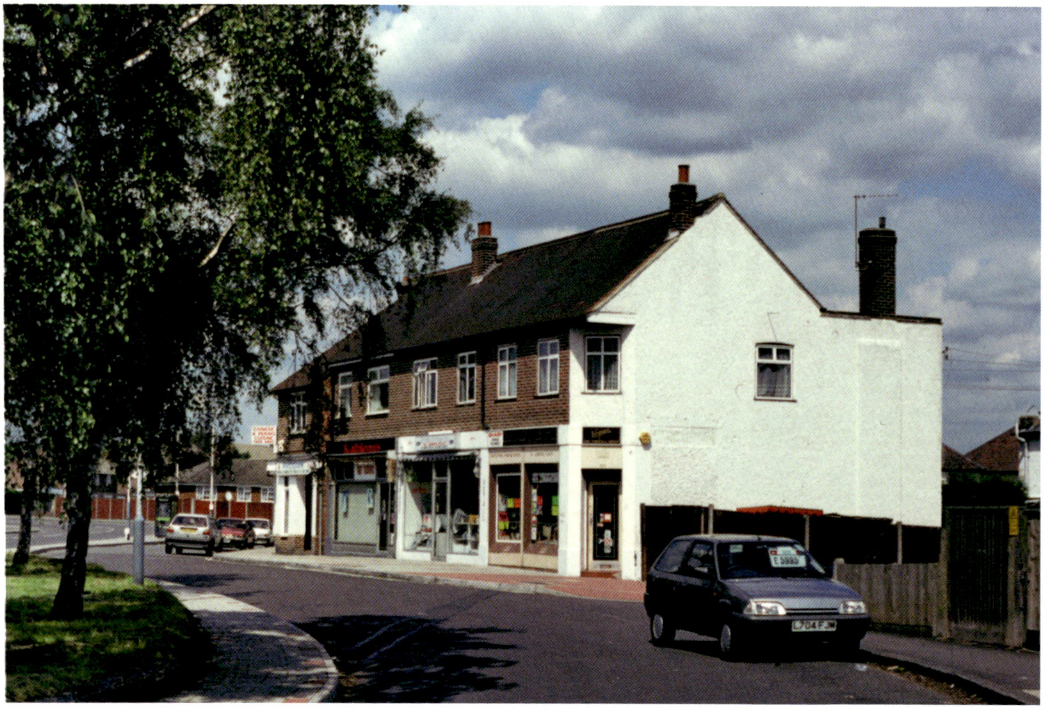

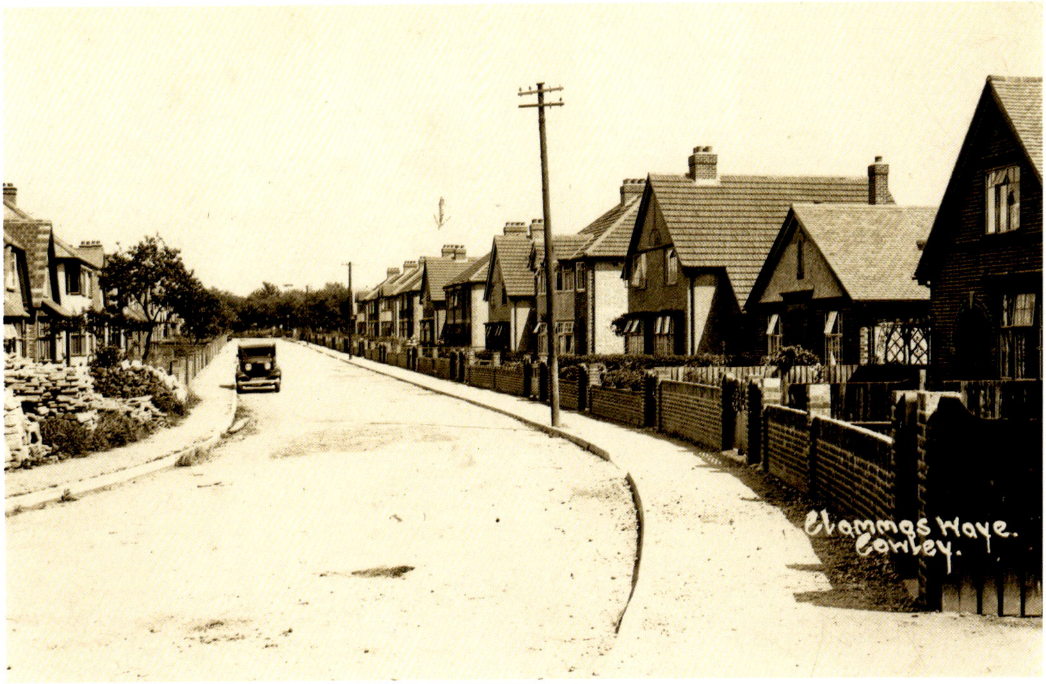

Clammas Way

A large area of Cowley, stretching from the High Street to the railway station was developed in the 1930s by W. S. Try. It included Clammas Way, Hamilton Road (named after a previous rector) and Orchard Drive. An old public house in the High Street called The Royal Oak was rebuilt at the same time. It was later renamed The Horse and Barge, but is now known as The St James.

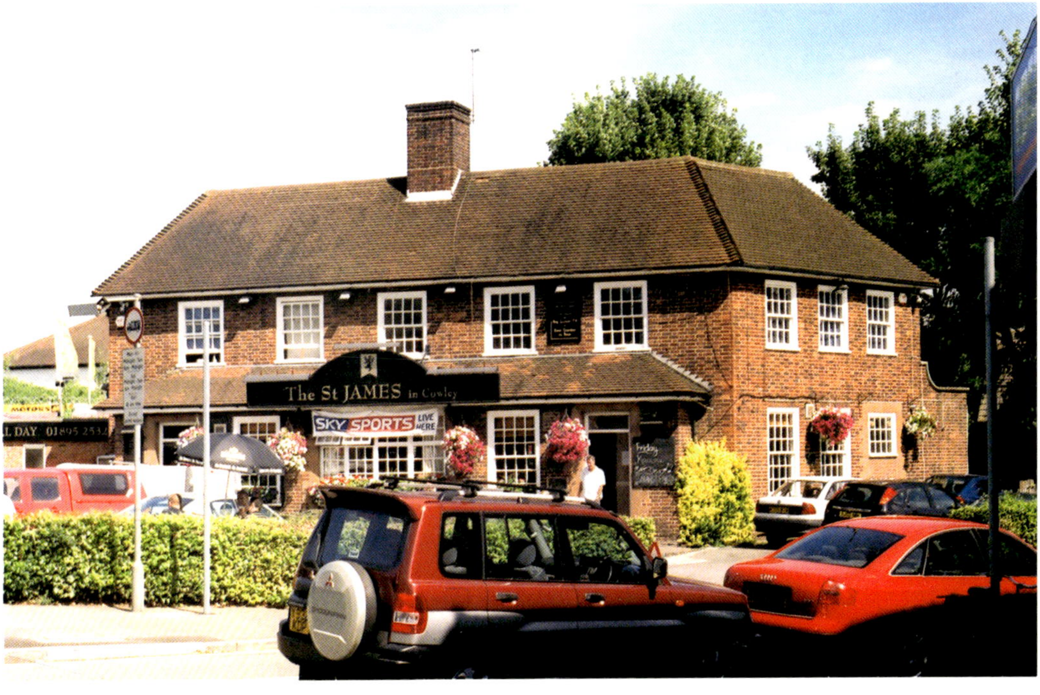

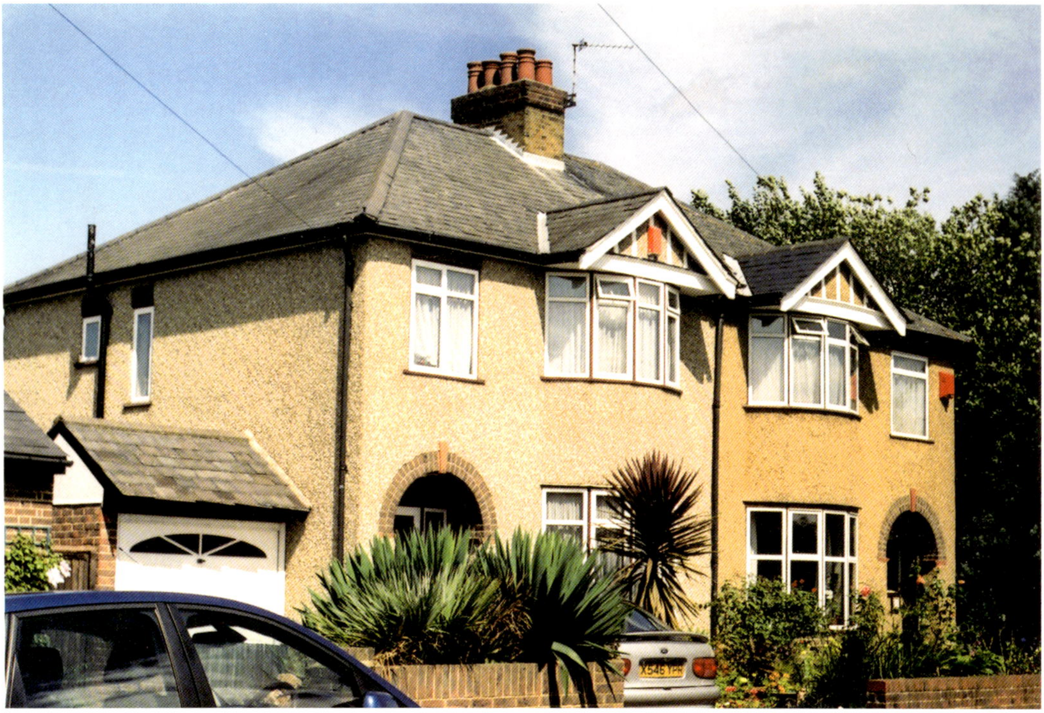

The Try Houses

When built in the 1930s these semi-detached houses in Clammas Way would have cost about £600 each, whereas the detached house below would have been priced at £900. This Try development is commendable in that there were detached and semi-detached houses as well as bungalows. They were also varied in design, rather than rows of identical properties, and are therefore of special architectural interest.

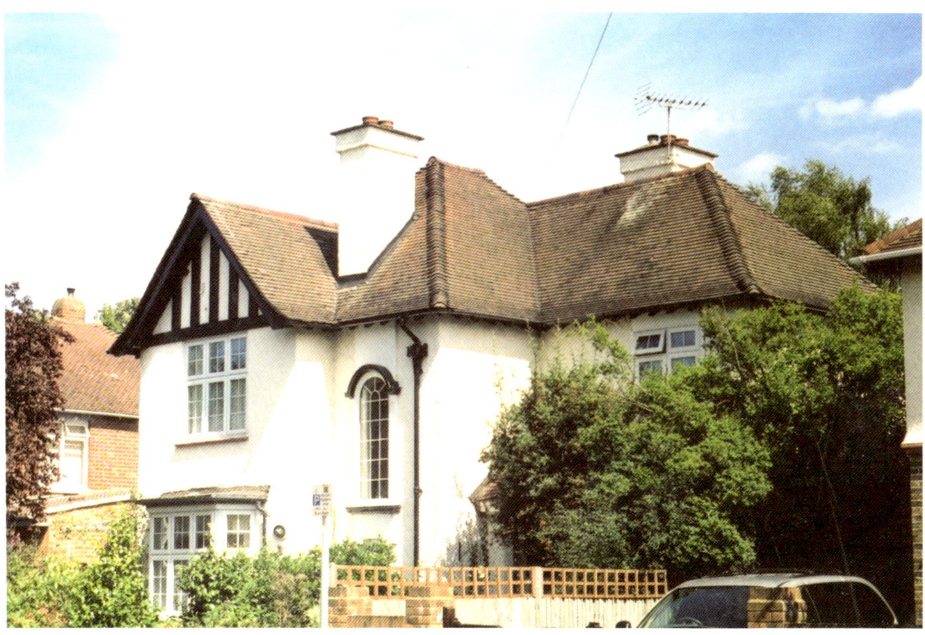

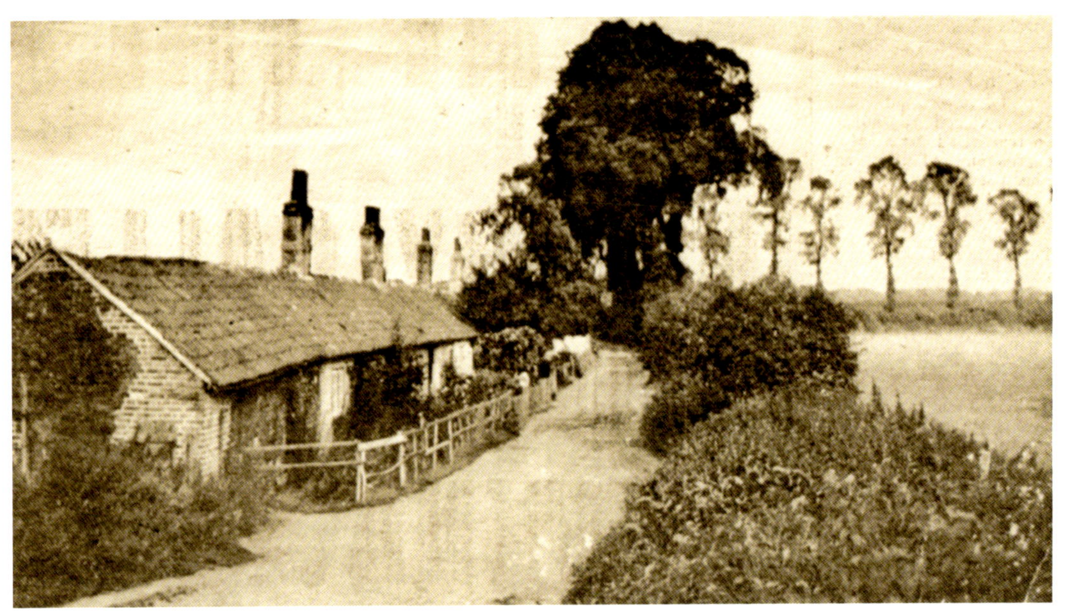

Bulldog Lane

This newspaper photograph must have been taken about 1920. On the left are cottages known as Bird Row. Water for the tenants came from a pump outside the back doors, and the privies were at the bottom of the garden. The rent was 4*s*.6*d*. per week. They were part of the Cowley Hall estate, so demolition in 1932 was followed by the construction of the Benbow Waye Council housing. The Benbow family were the last family to operate the flourmill on the other side of the canal at the end of the road.

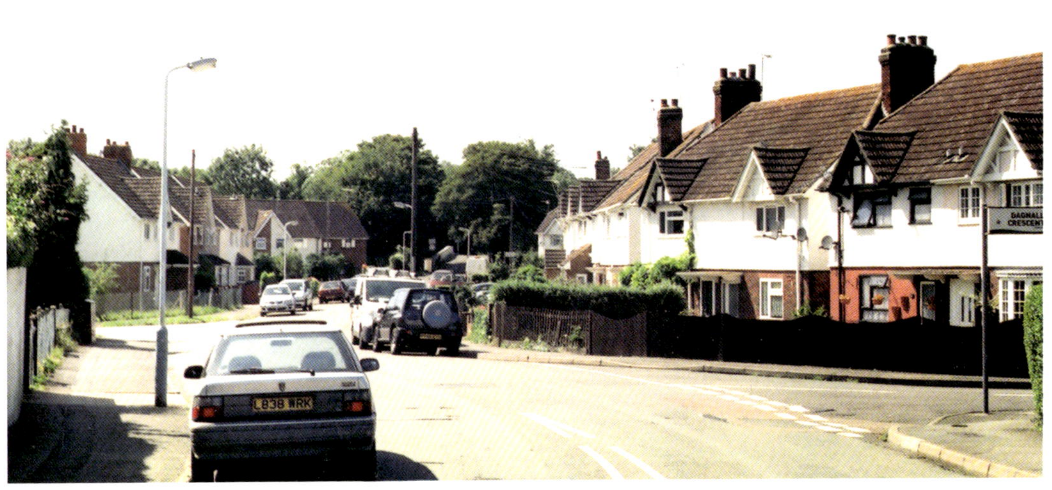

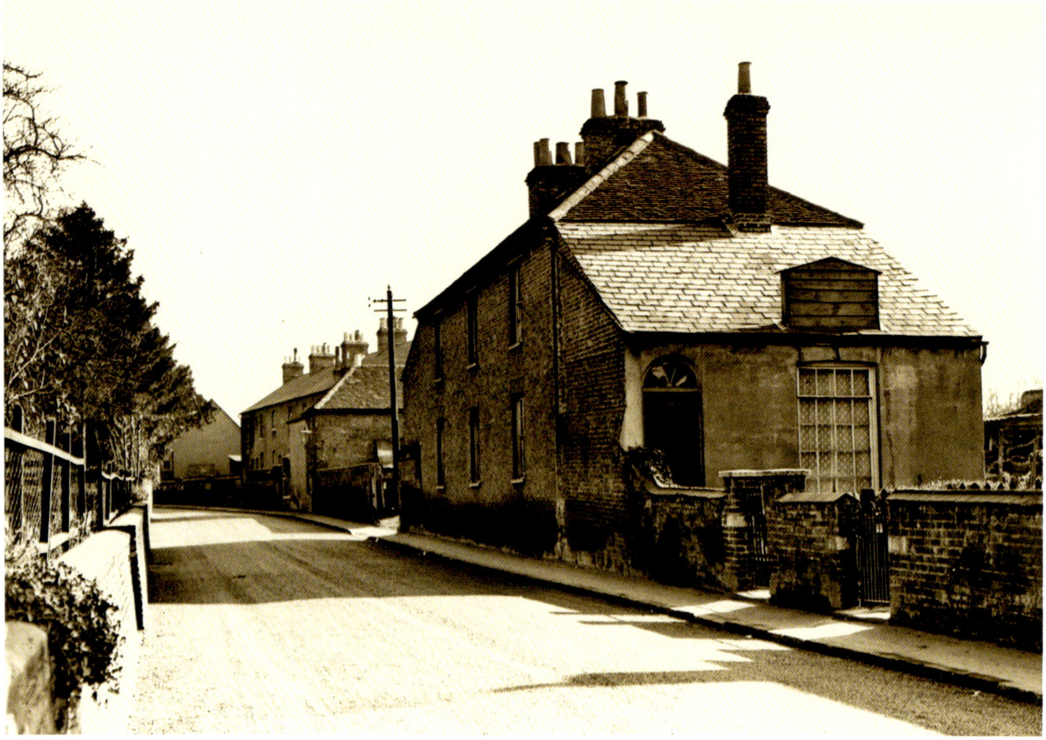

Iver Lane

We are looking towards the High Street in 1938. Only the row of cottages on the right, built by Herbert Barlee in 1892, survive today. The road has been widened, and the old buildings have been replaced by modern housing.

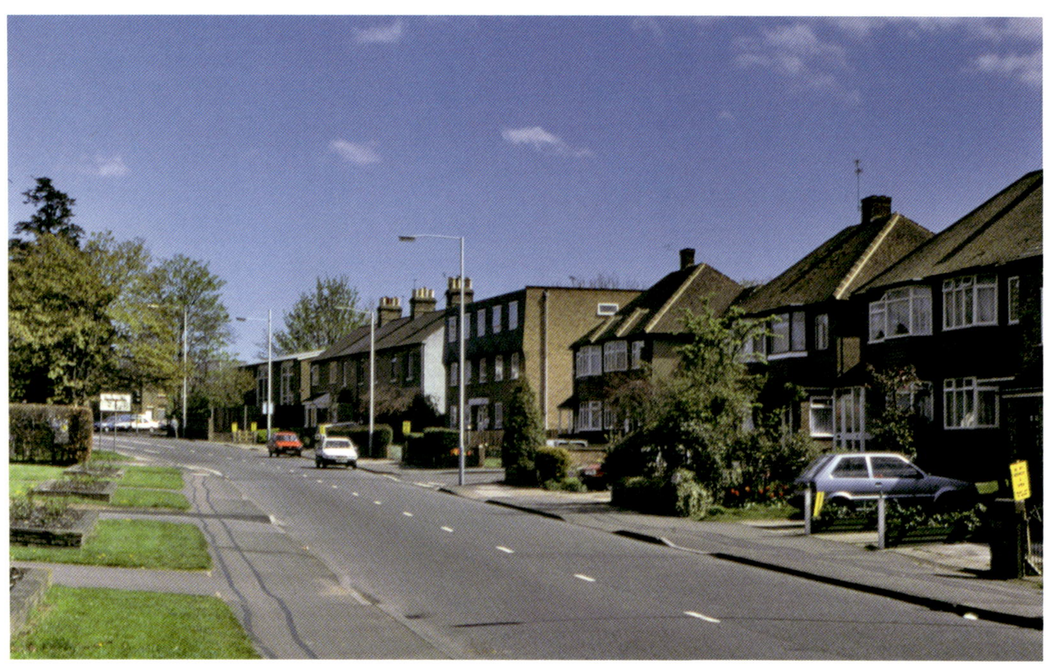

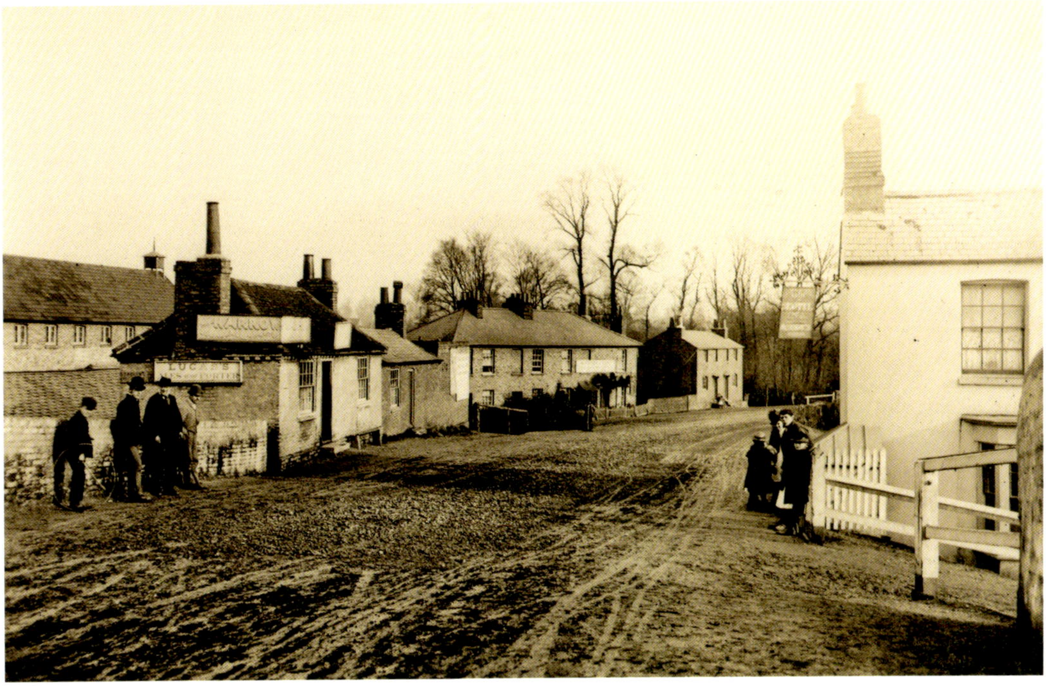

The Shovel Bridge

On the left, about 1900, is a small beer-house called The Harrow, and behind it we can just see the coconut fibre factory on Cowley Wharf. In the modern picture we notice that the front wall of the beer-house has not completely disappeared, and the highway is less muddy!

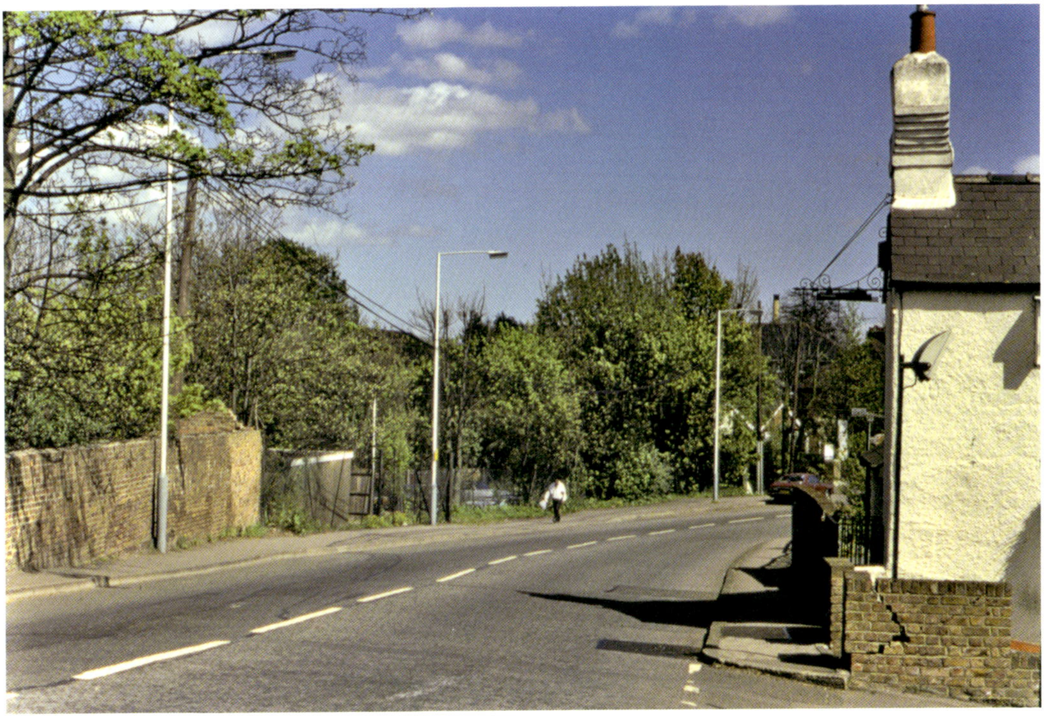

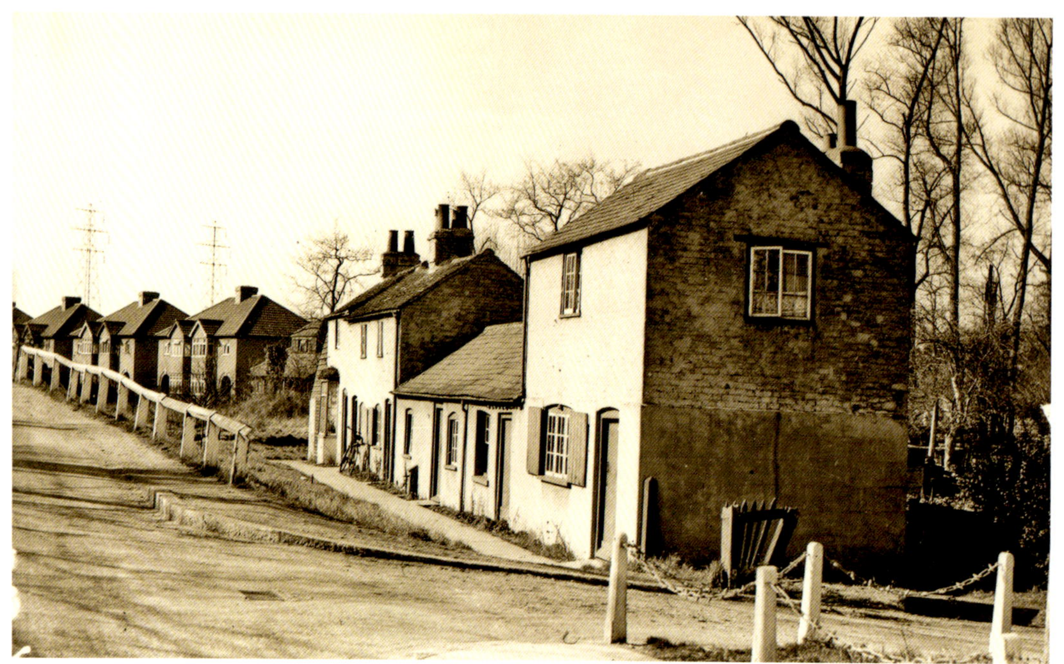

Clisby's Cottages

These cottages stood near the Colne bridge – Clisby's bridge – in Iver Lane. In this 1938 picture recently-built houses across the Buckinghamshire border in Iver can be seen. Soon after this the cottages were demolished and the site cleared. The scene below was taken in 1994, and on the right we see part of the office block of Cape Products, formerly the Uxbridge Flint Brick Company. Since then that building too has been demolished.

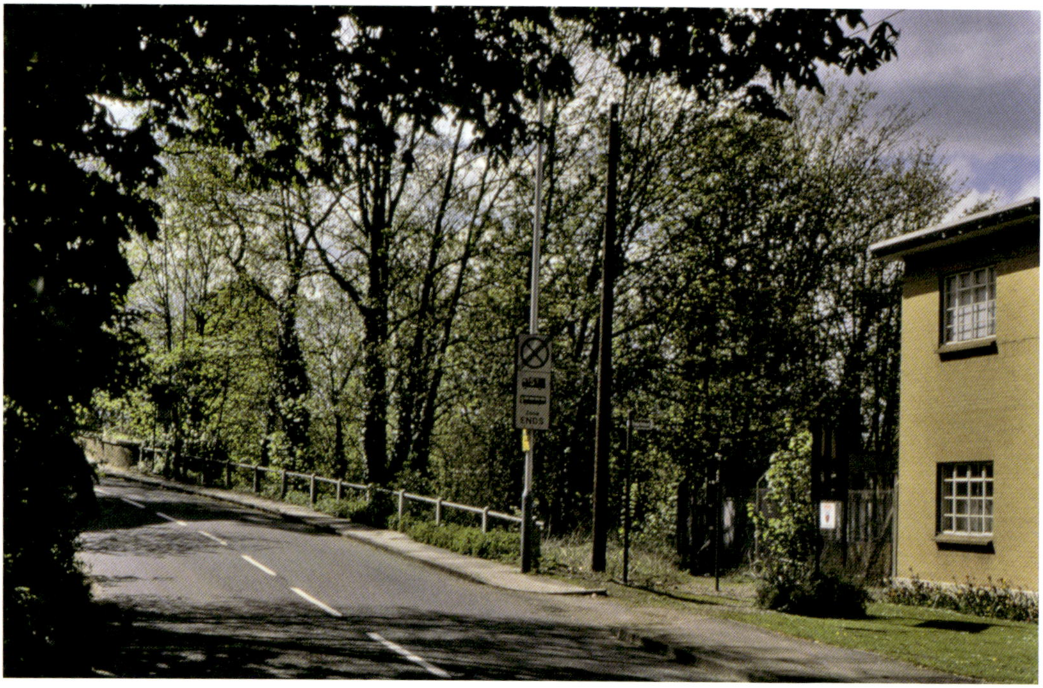

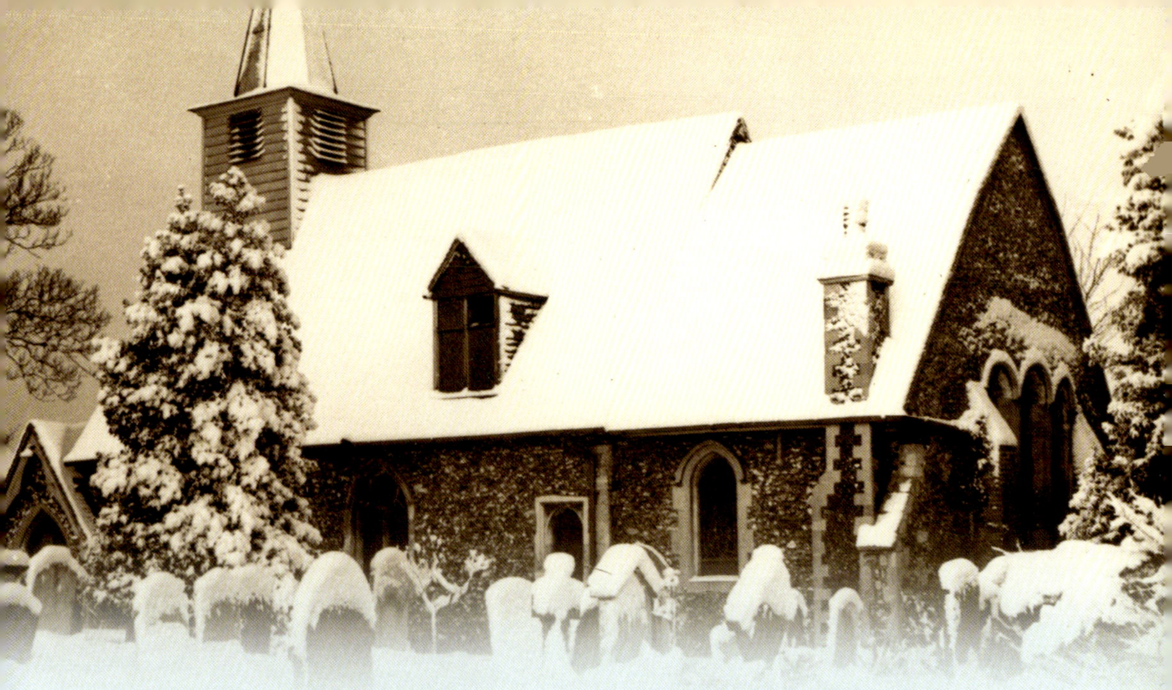

CHAPTER 2

The Church

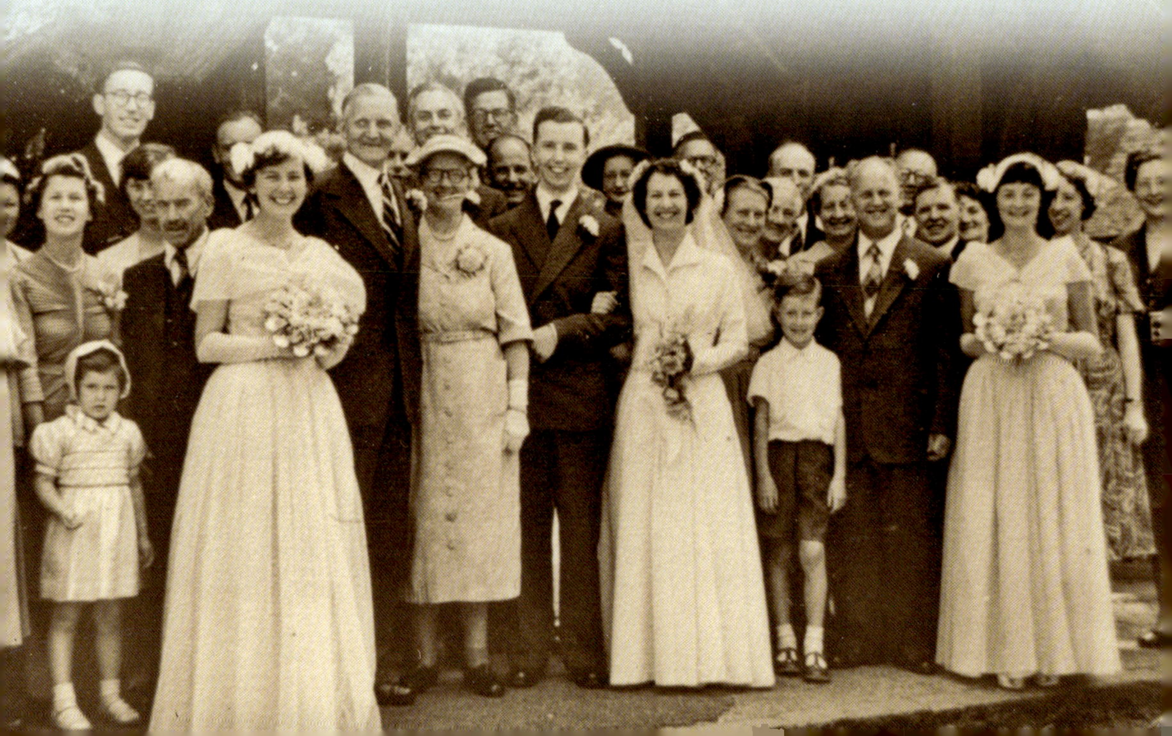

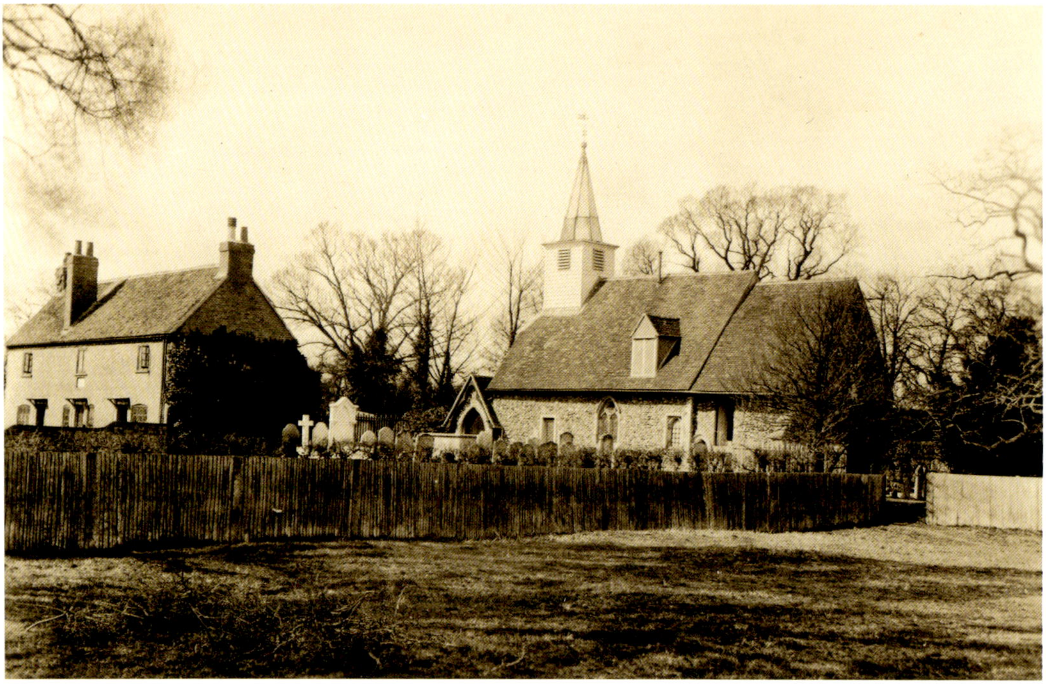

St Laurence Church

The parish church as it looked in 1900. The almshouses on the left were built in 1776, and were demolished in 1950. The land in the foreground was added to the churchyard in 1903. The lower view shows the church from the south-west. On the left is the vestry added in memory of William Sidney Try (1882-1953), and donated by his family.

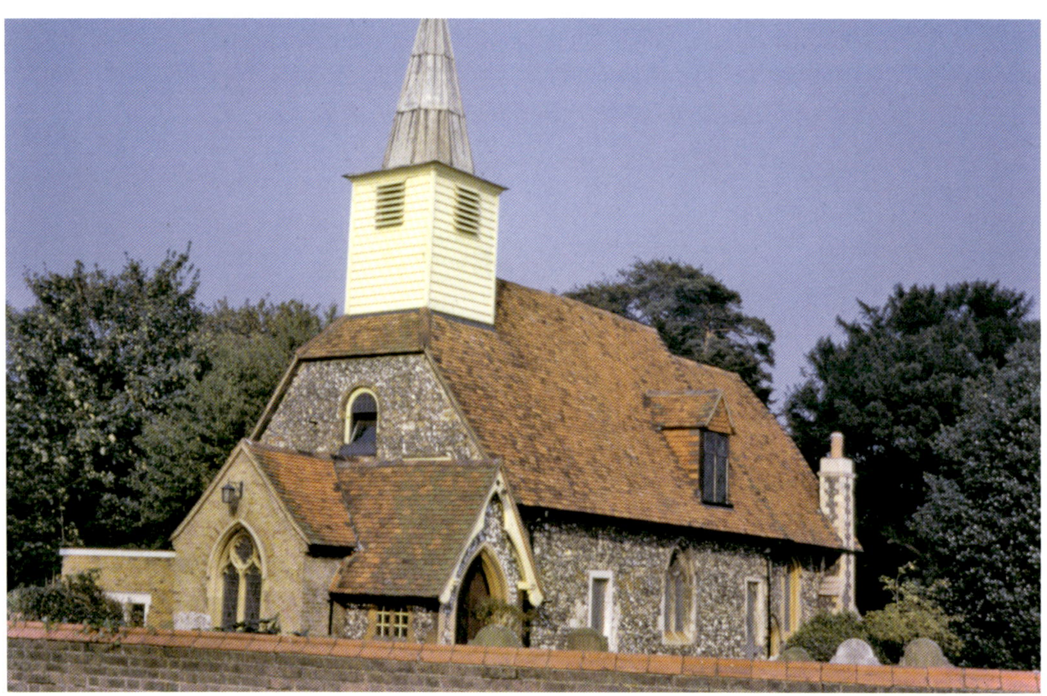

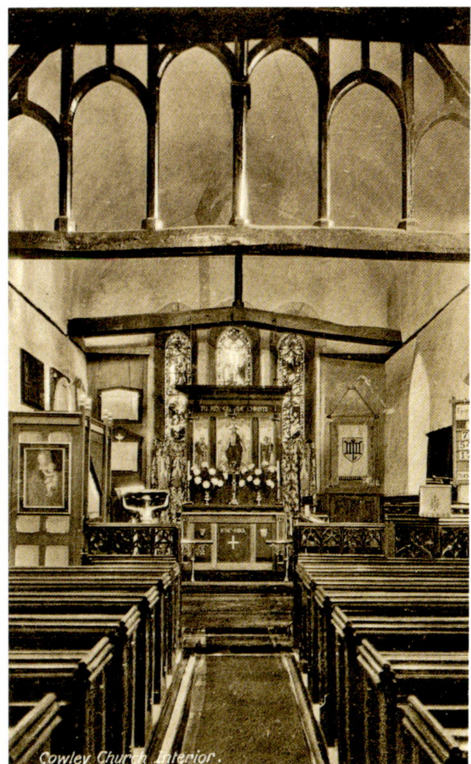

Church interior about 1920

The king-post trusses which support the roof are clearly shown here. The chancel (below) dates from the thirteenth century, and the nave from the twelfth. A small pipe organ can be seen on the left. In the 1950s the tall reredos, which blocked light from the three lancet windows, was moved back, as was the organ.

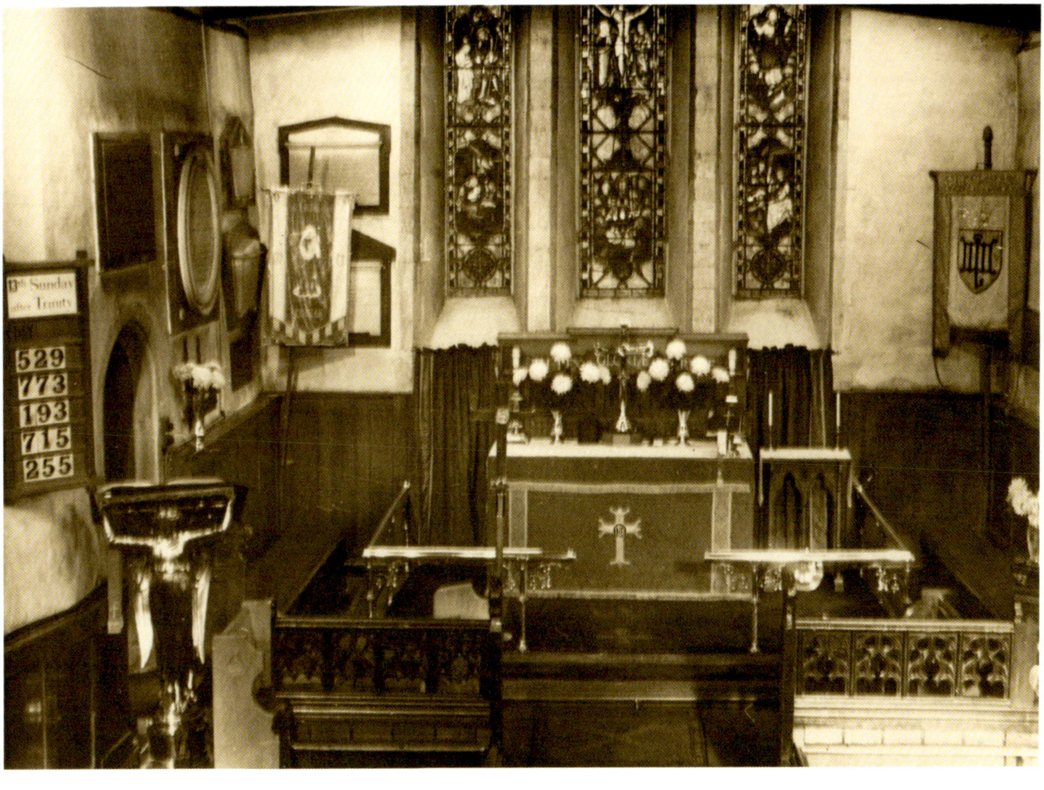

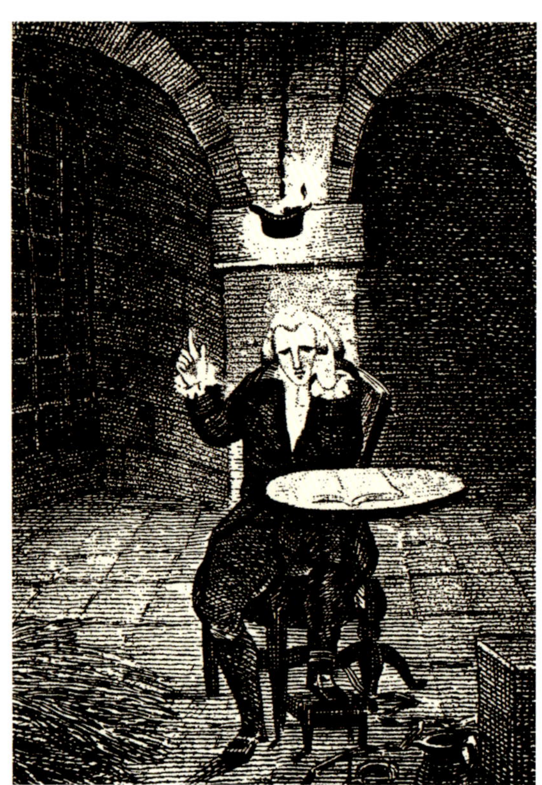

Dr William Dodd

A drawing showing Dr Dodd in Newgate prison awaiting hanging. He ruined a promising career by living far beyond his means, and eventually forged a bond for £4,200 in a desperate attempt to clear his debts. The forgery was discovered, and Dodd was sentenced to death. His body was brought to Cowley, where his brother Richard was rector, and buried in the churchyard.

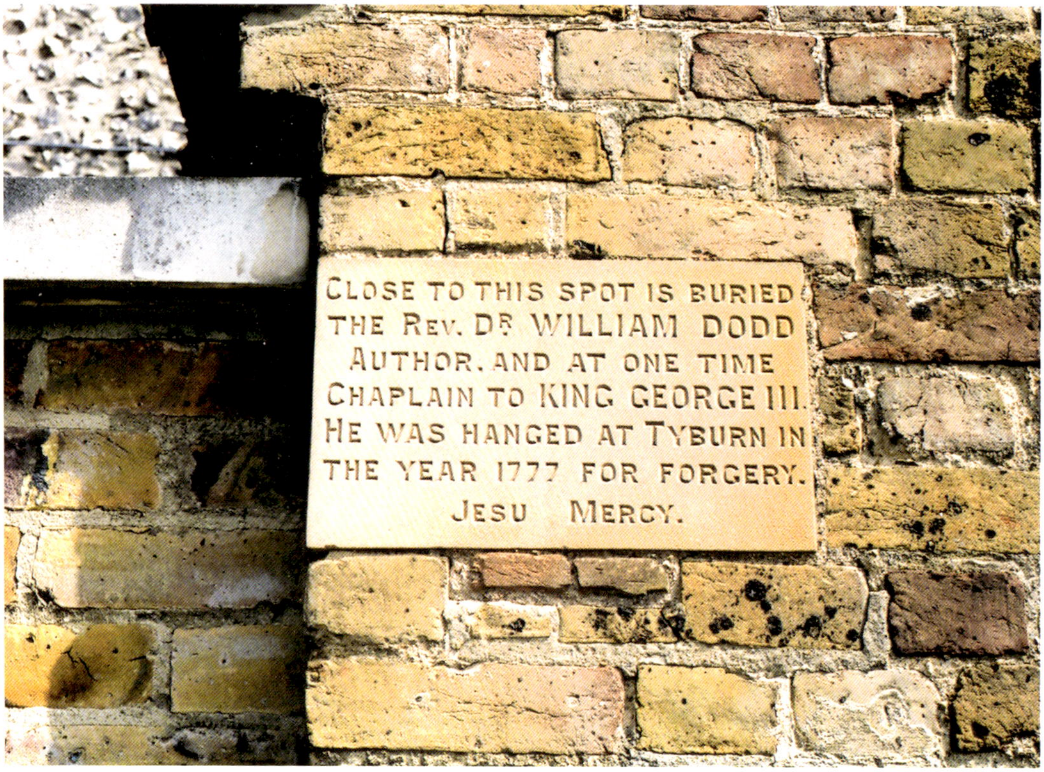

CLOSE TO THIS SPOT IS BURIED
THE REV. DR WILLIAM DODD
AUTHOR. AND AT ONE TIME
CHAPLAIN TO KING GEORGE III.
HE WAS HANGED AT TYBURN IN
THE YEAR 1777 FOR FORGERY.
JESU MERCY.

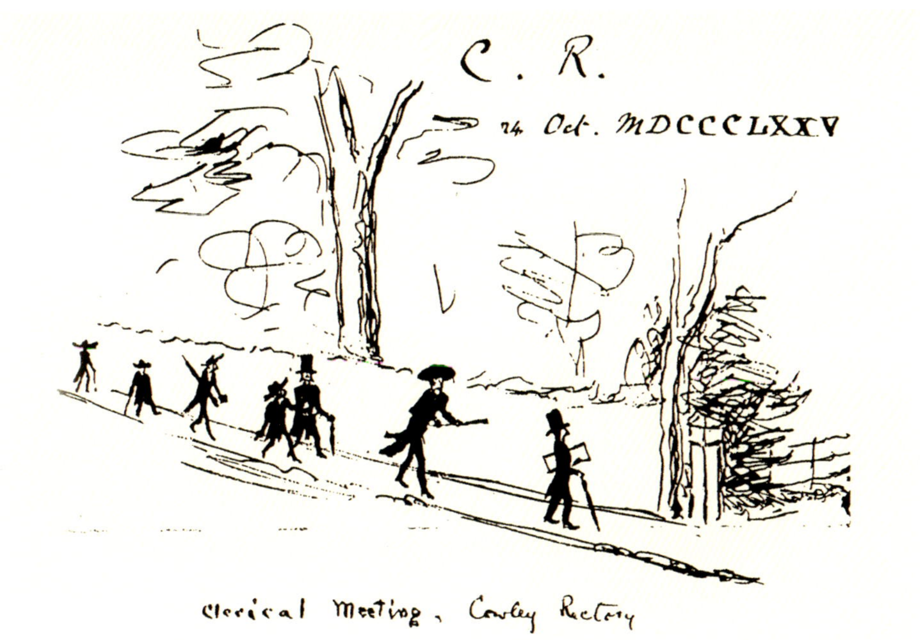

Clergy conference

This sketch of clergymen meeting at Cowley in 1875 is thought to be the work of Laurence Hilliard. He was the son of the rector, Revd John Crosier Hilliard, and his wife Mary (nee Jermyn). At this period a frequent visitor to the rectory was the author and art critic John Ruskin. In 1876 Laurence became Ruskin's secretary.

Below is the tomb of the naturalist Revd John Lightfoot (1735-88). He was the first person in England to identify the reed warbler, and it was by the river Colne. After his death his collection of plants was bought by King George III.

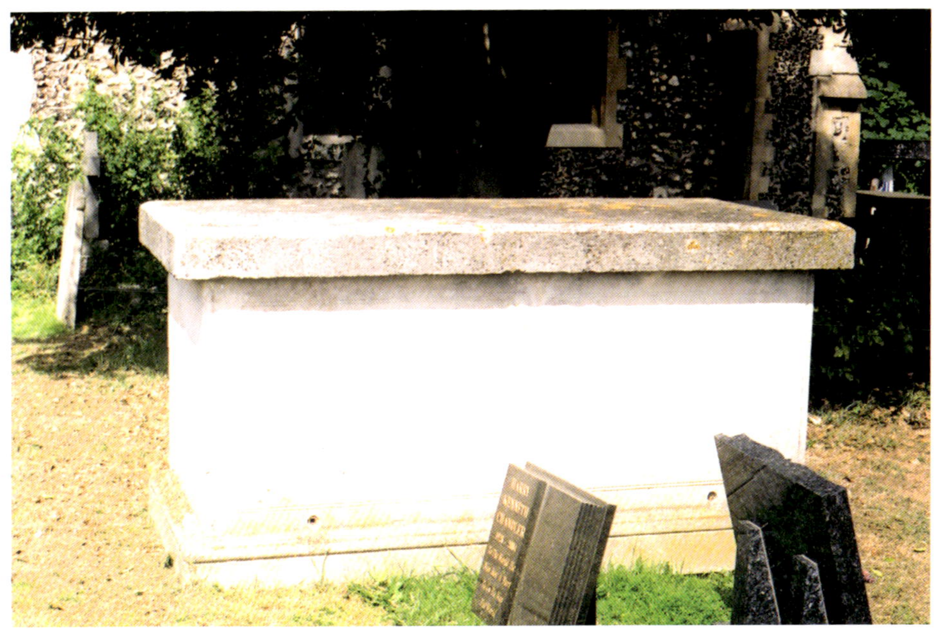

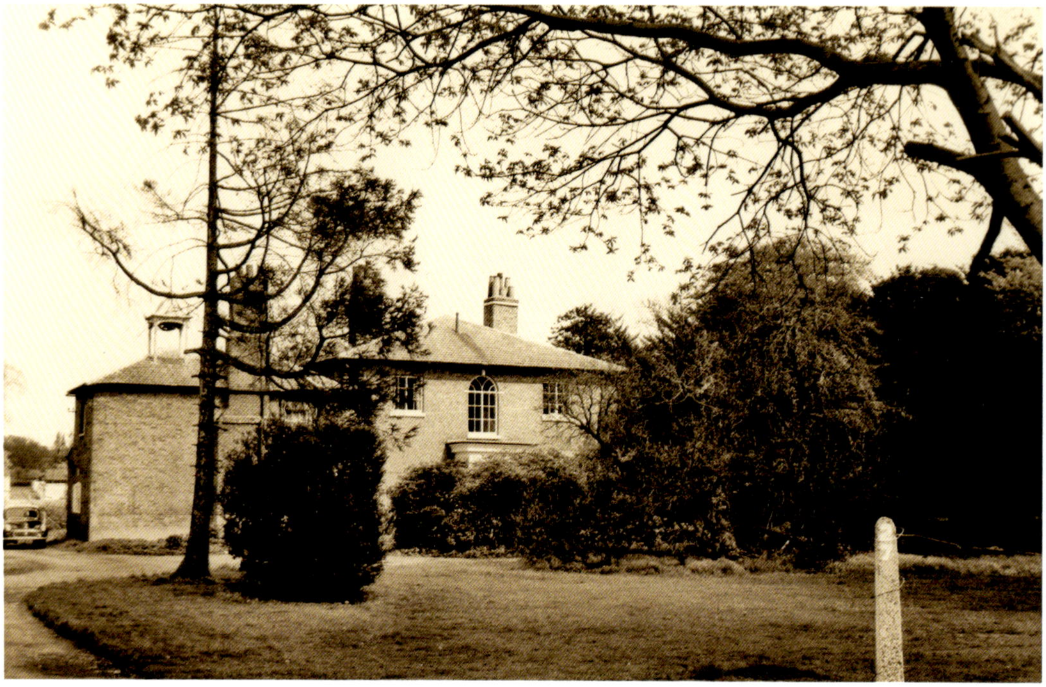

The old rectory

This building was erected by Revd John Hilliard soon after he took up his duties in 1807. (Three generations of the Hilliard family were rectors for a period of ninety-five years.) The bell in the turret on the left, perhaps from an earlier rectory, bears the words, 'Come away. Make no delay. 1737', and was doubtless used to summon the household to prayer. The present rectory dates from 1970.

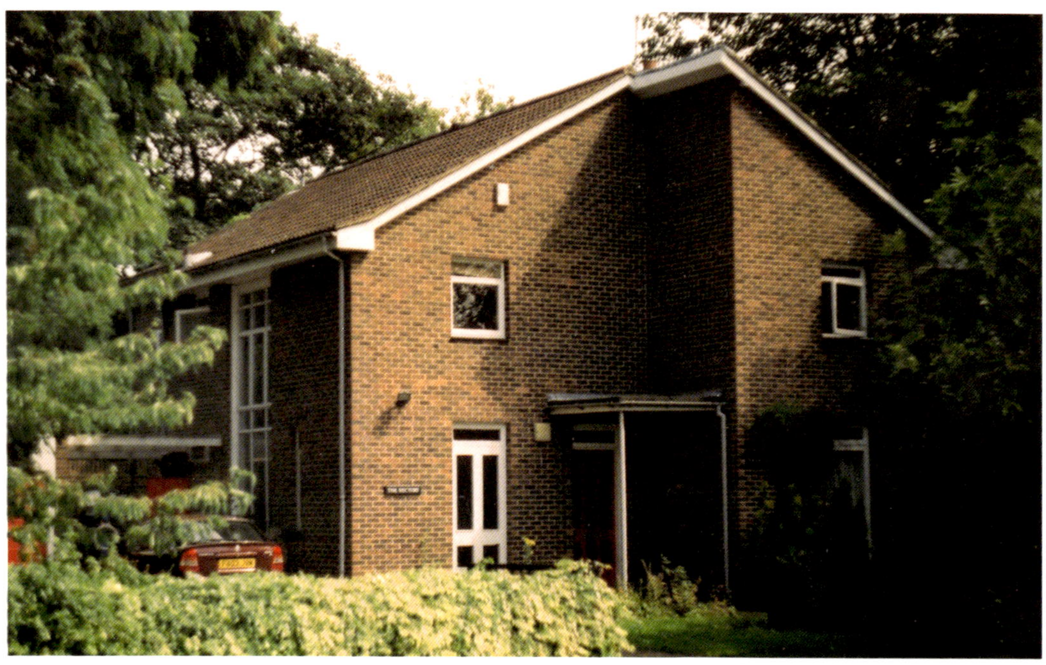

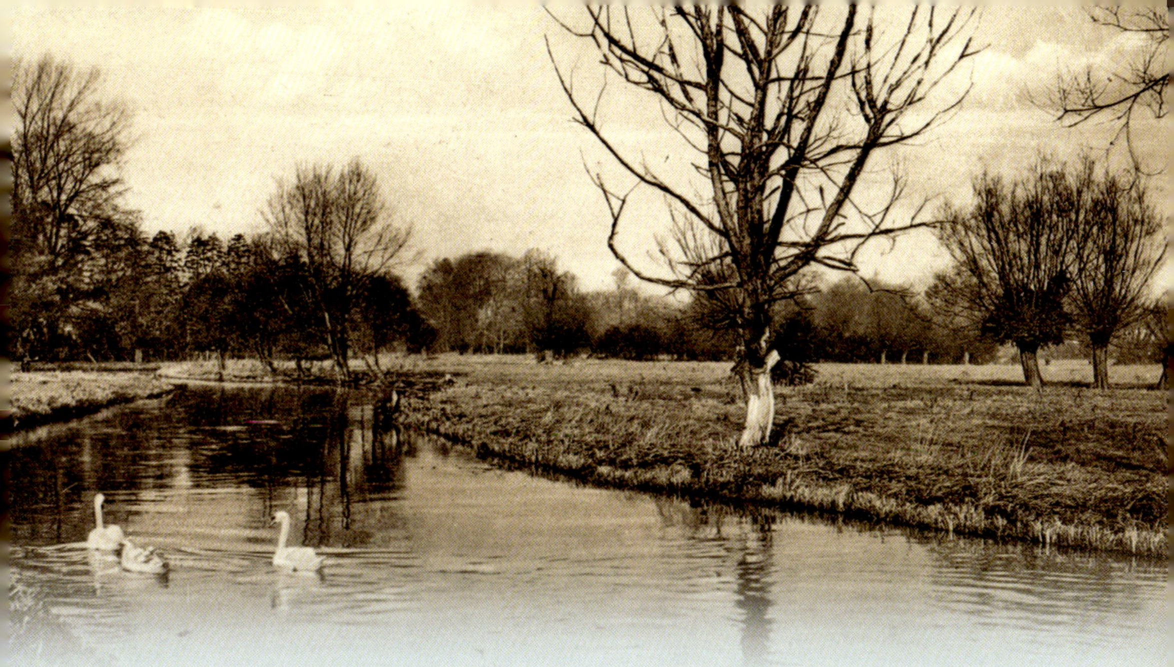

CHAPTER 3

Waterways

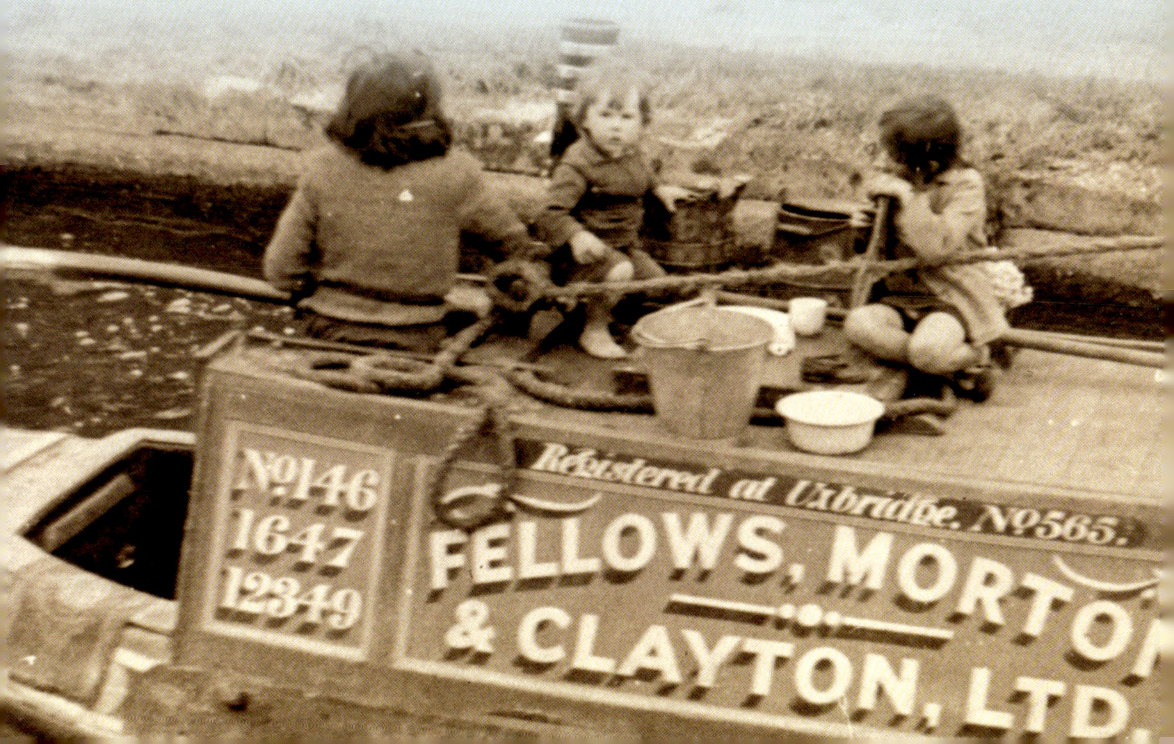

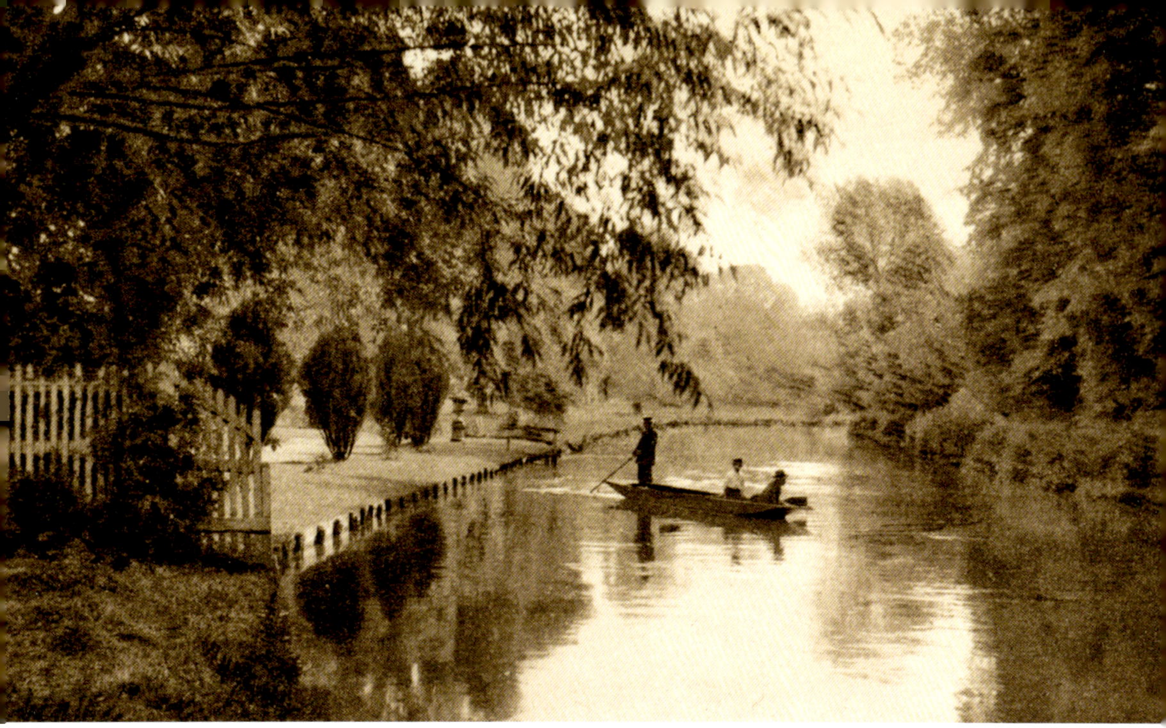

Punting on the river Colne

This river, on the western side of Cowley, forms the boundary between Middlesex and Buckinghamshire. It is a tributary of the Thames, and was navigable as far north as Uxbridge in medieval times. The lower view was taken at the point where the river and Little Britain lake conjoin.

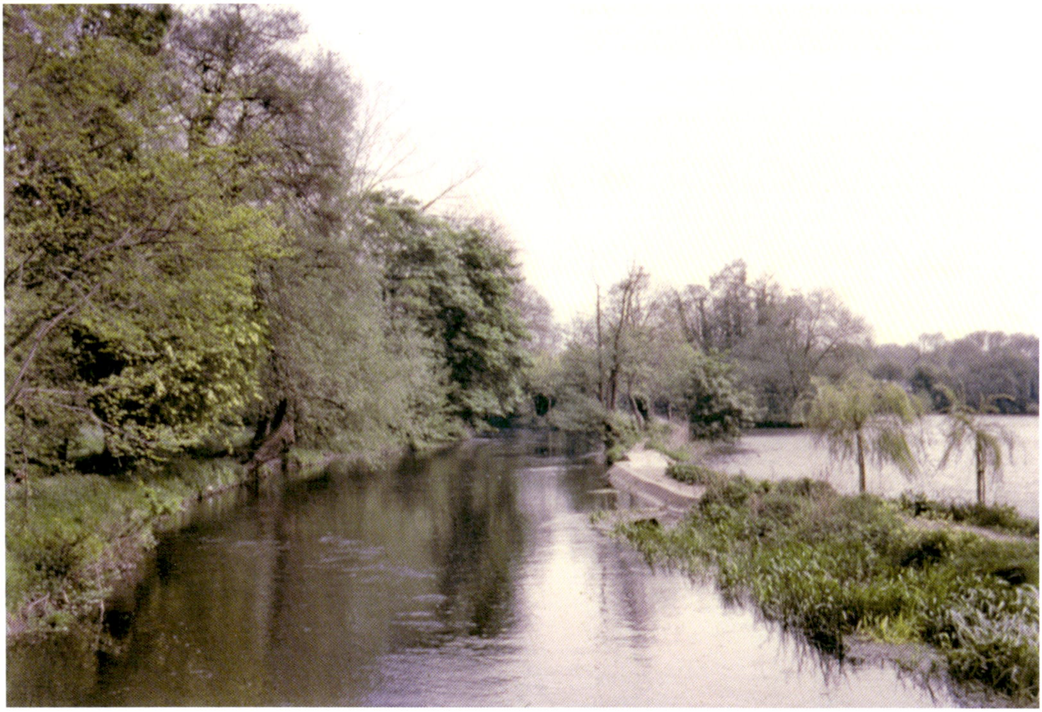

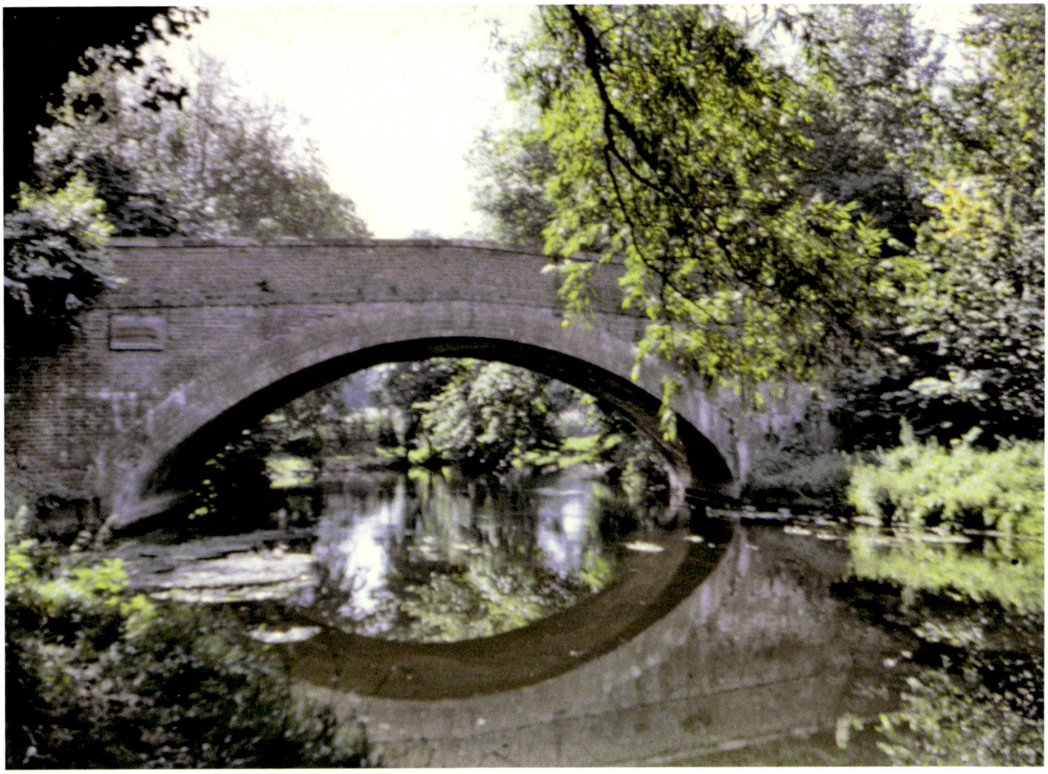

Clisby's bridge

The road from Cowley to Iver passes over the river Colne here, and a plate on the parapet states that the bridge was rebuilt in 1840 by Thomas Harold. On the Middlesex side of the bridge, by the road, stands a coal-tax post like the one shown. A tax was formerly charged on all coal brought into the London area – a scheme first introduced to assist rebuilding after the great fire of London of 1666. The Cowley post dates from 1861, when the area liable became the districts served by the Metropolitan Police. The project ceased in 1889.

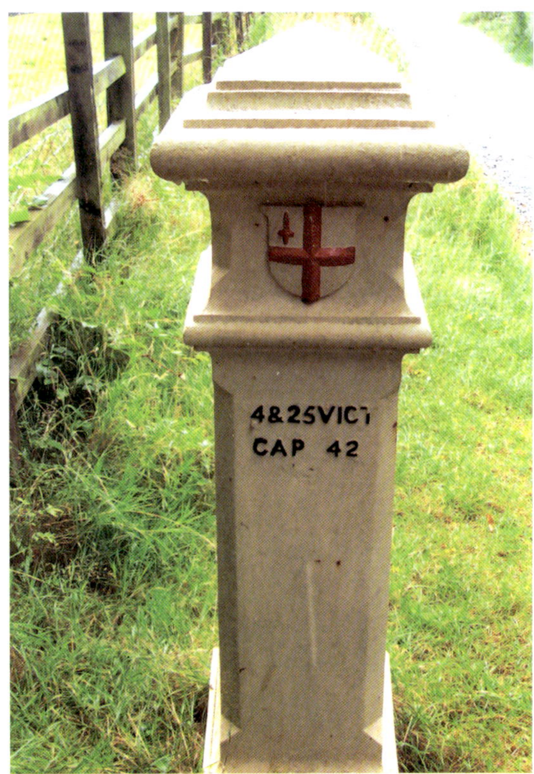

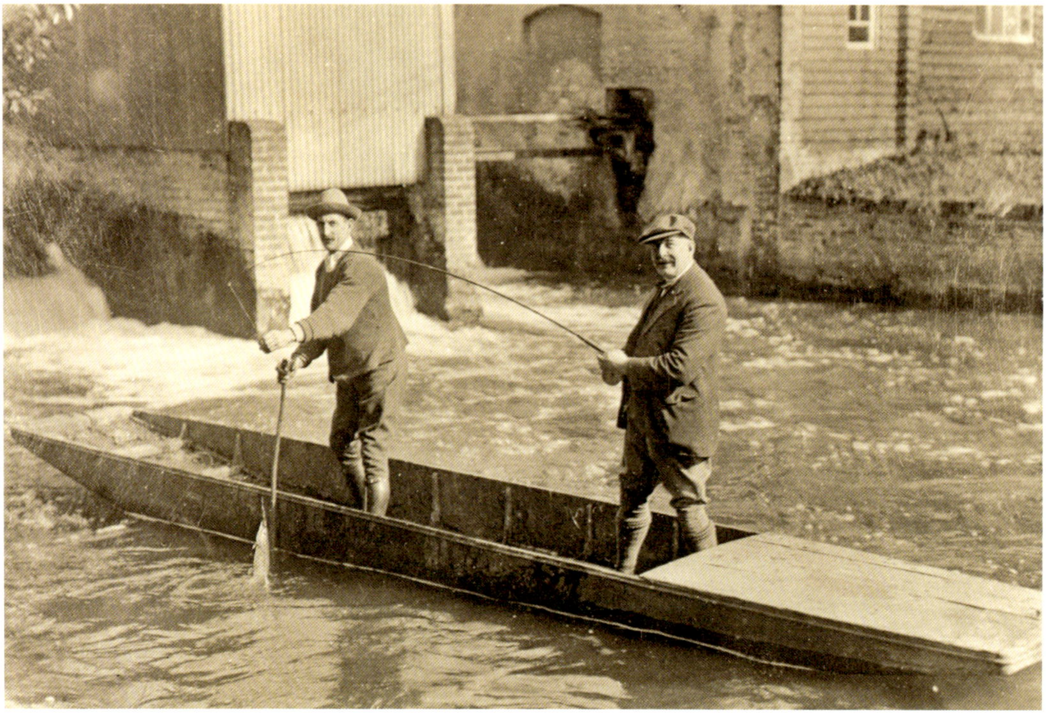

Fishing in the Colne

For centuries angling has been a popular activity, and remains so today. The local water bailiff, Mr Bunn, is seen assisting an Uxbridge shopkeeper, Mr Weston, fish for trout about 1910. In the background is Huntsmoor Weir, still in use today. The house by the weir, seen here on a snowy morning in 2009, is marked as Yiewsley Mill House in nineteenth century maps, but the mill itself burned down in 1873.

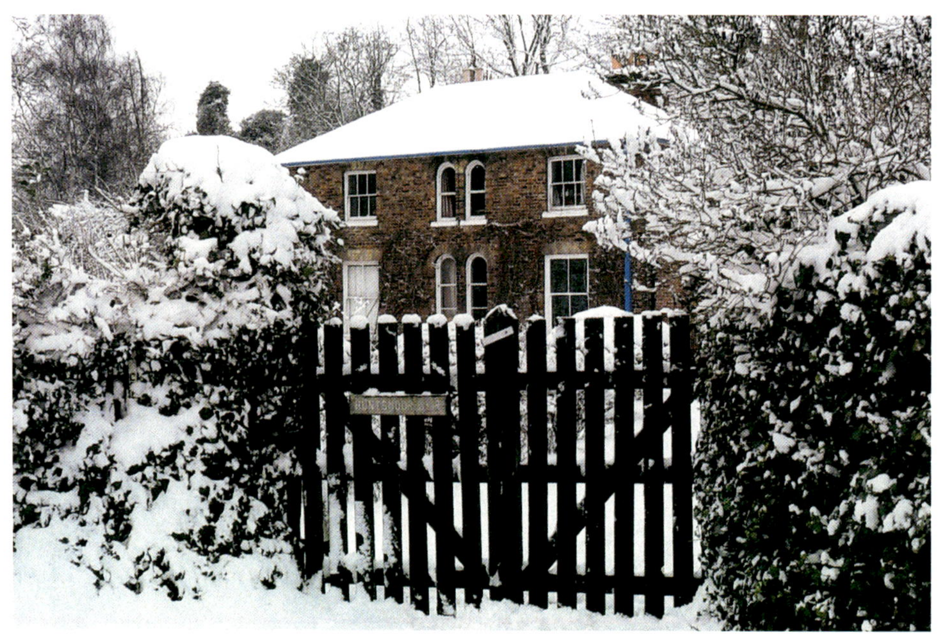

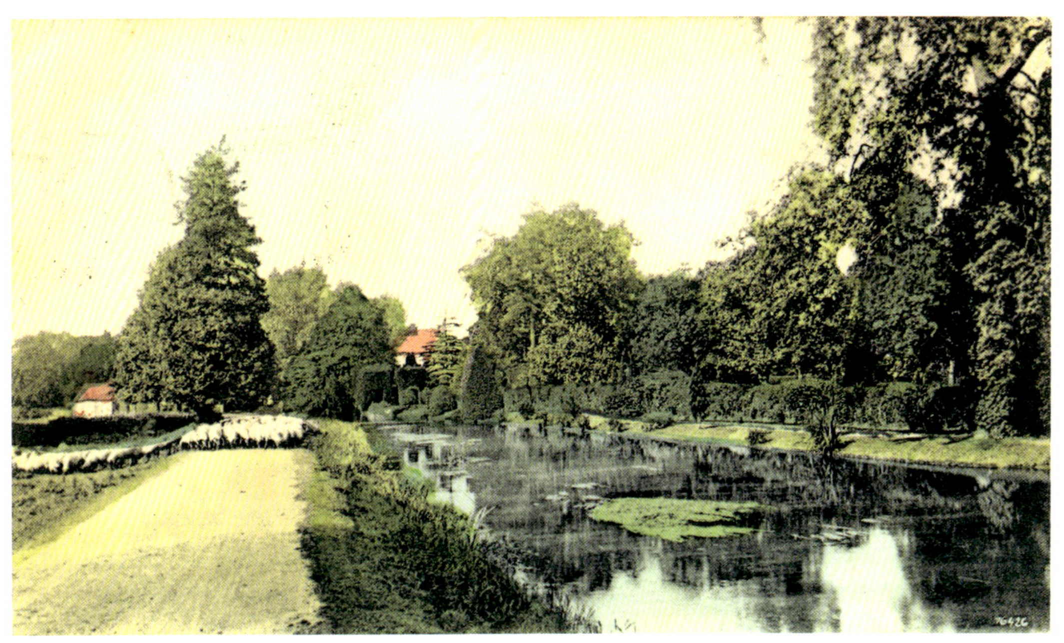

Old Mill Lane

Looking north in 1904 the Colne river is on the left, and on the right Fray's river. The latter is unusual because it is partly man-made. In the fifteenth century a man named John Fray diverted some of the Colne water north of Uxbridge into an existing tributary, thus increasing the flow of water and enabling flour mills to develop on it. The house at one of them, Benbow Mill, can just be seen in the distance. Nowadays there are more trees, but no sheep!

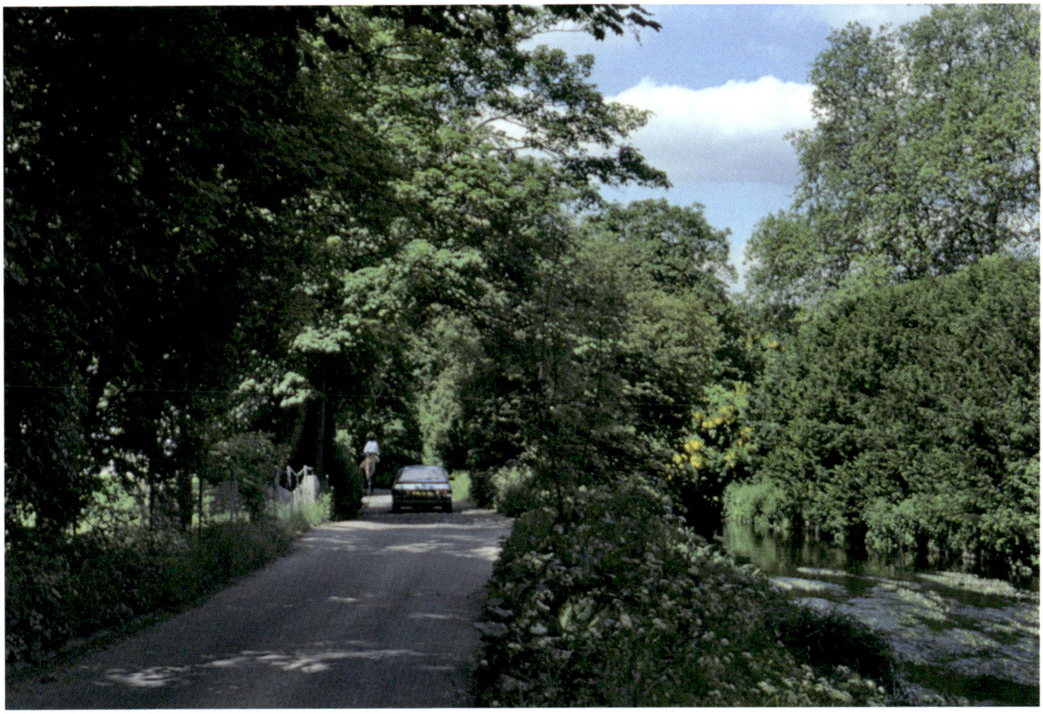

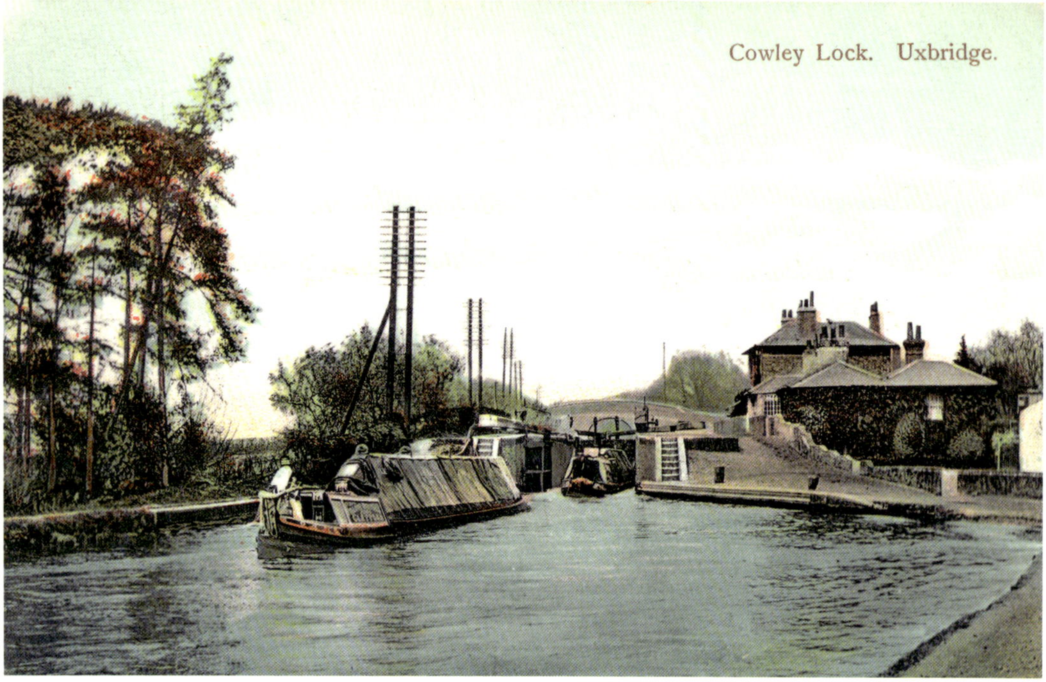

Cowley Lock. Uxbridge.

Cowley Lock

An Act of Parliament in 1793 permitted the construction of the Grand Junction Canal from the Thames at Brentford to Braunston in Northants., where it joined the Midlands canal system. The section as far north as Uxbridge was ready by 1798, but a lock at Cowley was needed to carry the new waterway over Fray's river. Some commercial development inevitably followed, and at Cowley a coconut fibre factory opened making ropes, mats and brushes.

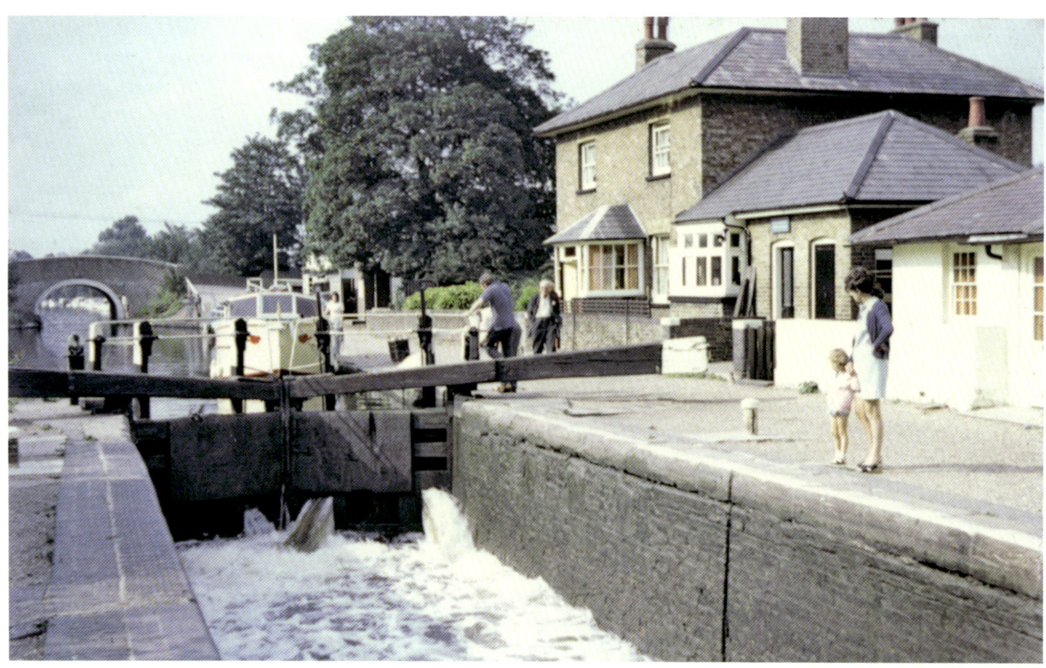

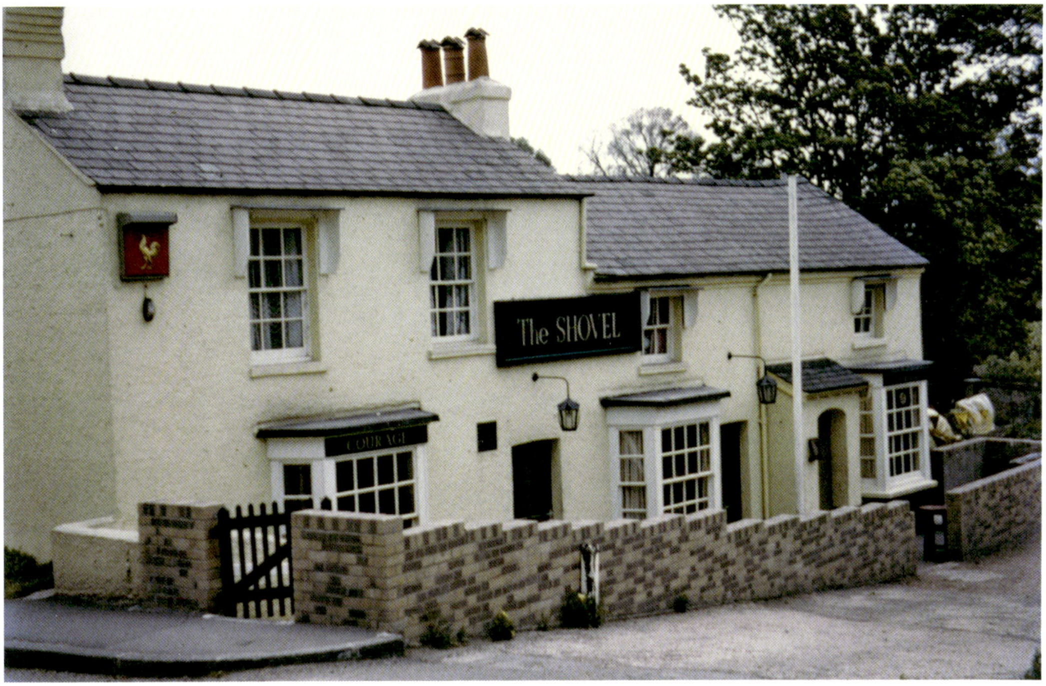

The Shovel Inn

The name is a reminder that the canal was cut by 'navvies', i.e. navigators, using picks and shovels. A massive labour force was used, many of them Irish, and the whole scheme through to Braunston was completed in 1805. The inn was renamed The Malt Shovel in 2001, and is now a licensed restaurant. The scene below, with the inn and the bridge, has been seen by millions, since it was a location in the film *Reach for the Sky,* starring Kenneth More as fighter ace Douglas Bader.

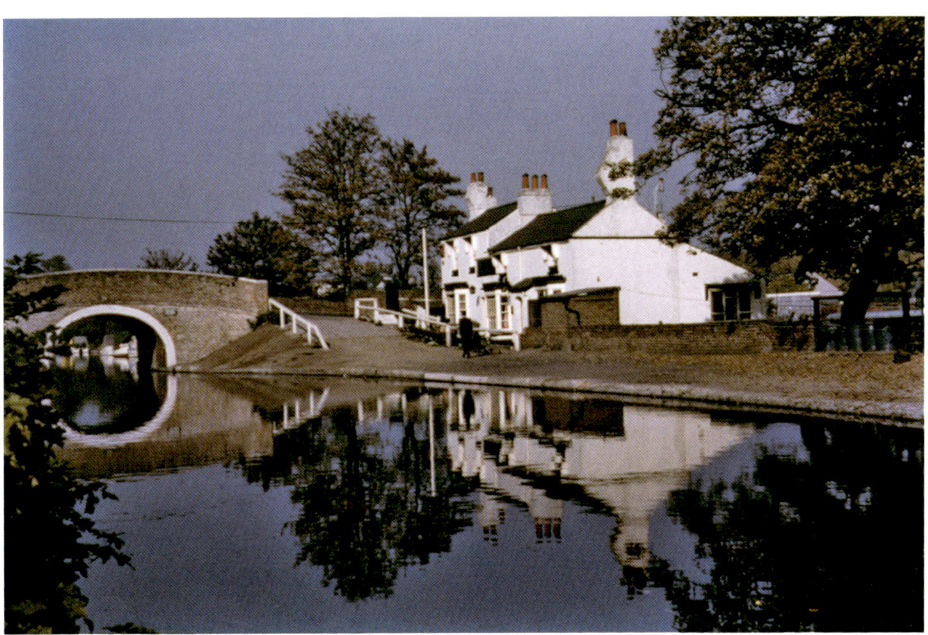

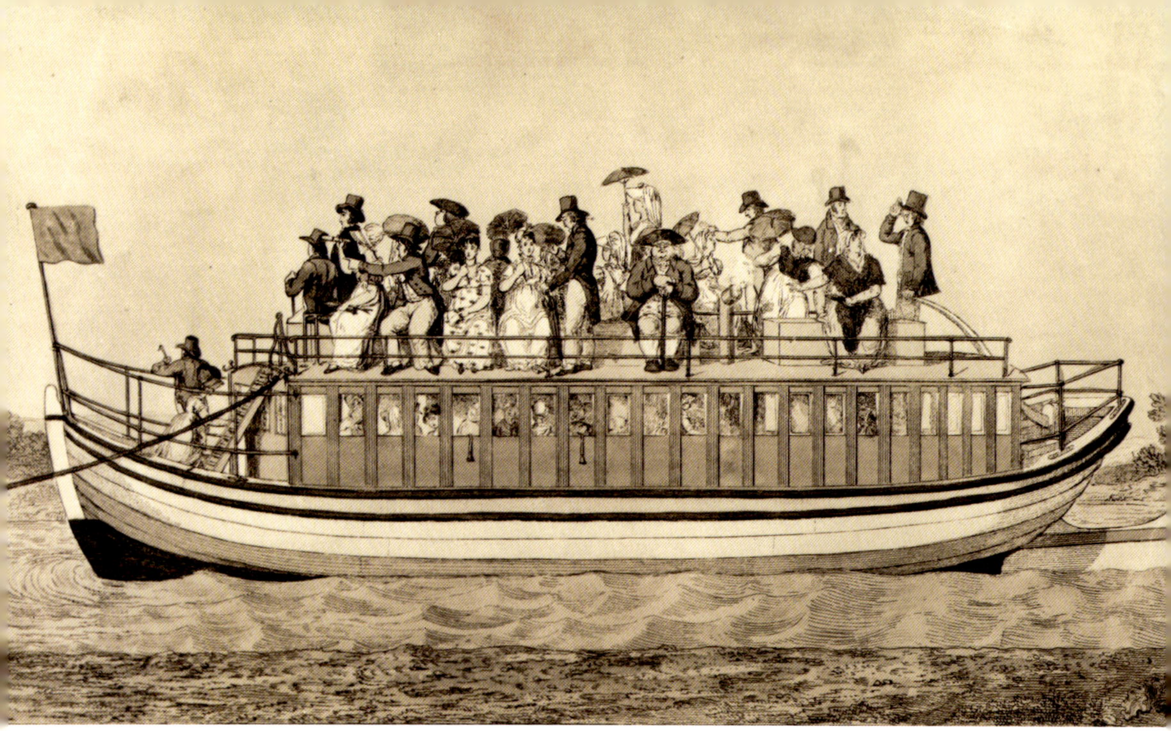

The Paddington Packet Boat

In 1801 a daily service commenced between Paddington and Uxbridge on the canal, and Londoners then had the opportunity of a leisurely trip to the pleasant countryside of West Middlesex. It is not clear how long this project lasted, but a dock was built for these vessels and other commercial traffic. The towpath bridge spanning the entrance to the dock is shown below.

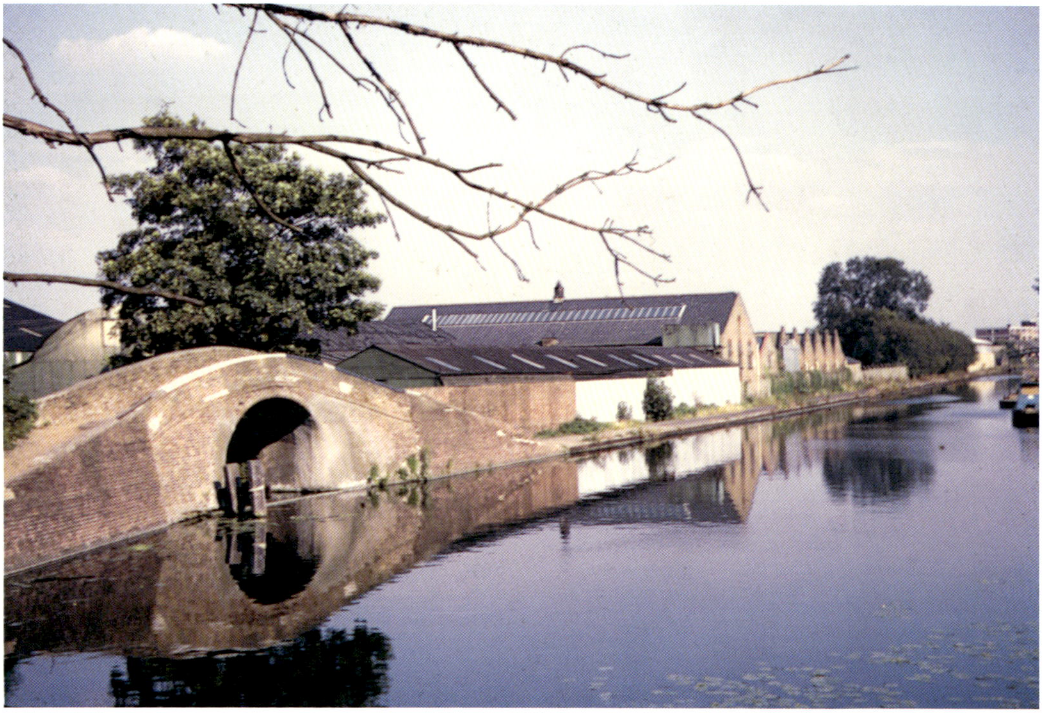

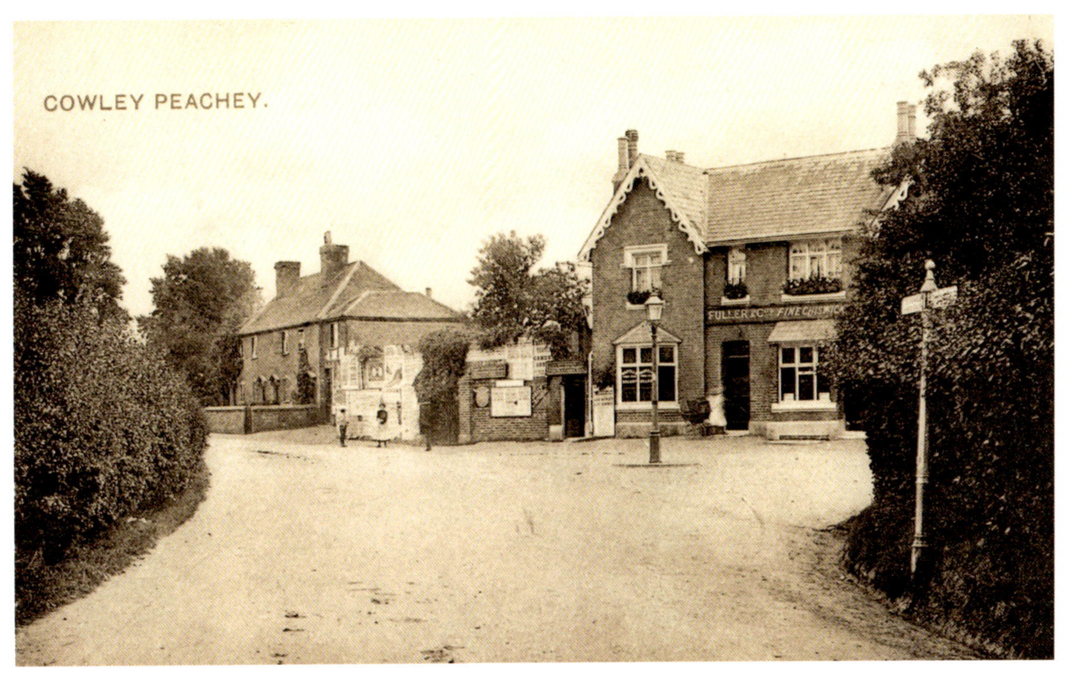

The Paddington Packet Boat

The early success of the packet boats led to the licensing of this public house in 1804, and here London trippers could seek refreshment before their return journey. This district was known as the Three Households in the eighteenth century, but has since been known as Cowley Peachey. (The Peachey family owned the manor of Cowley in the fourteenth and fifteenth centuries.) Below is the pub pictured in 1967. It now changes colour from time to time.

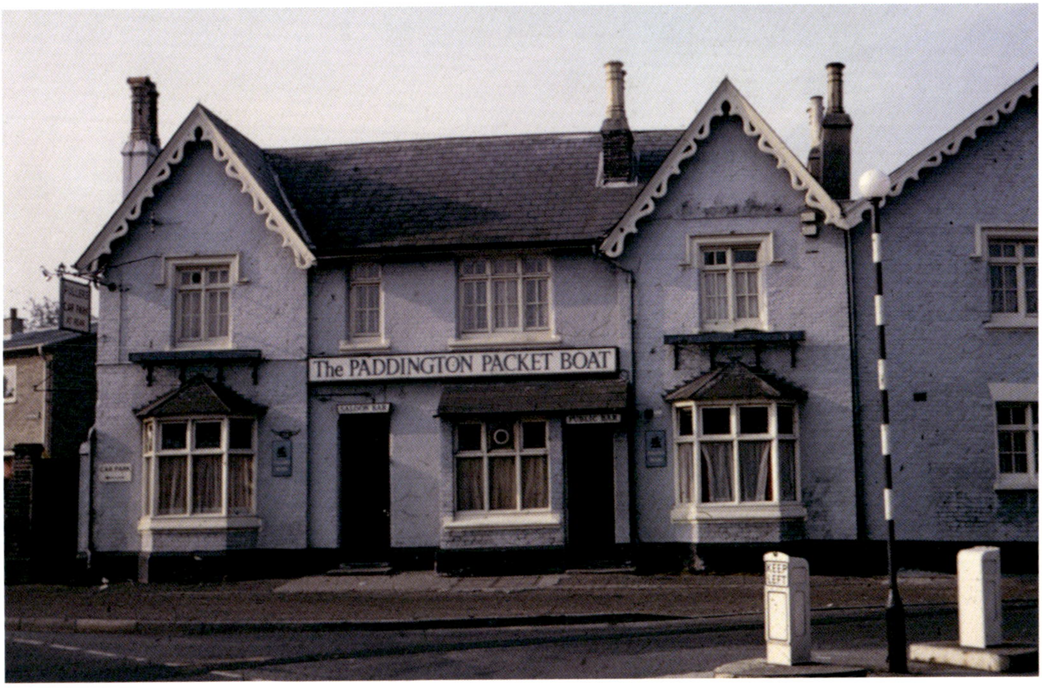

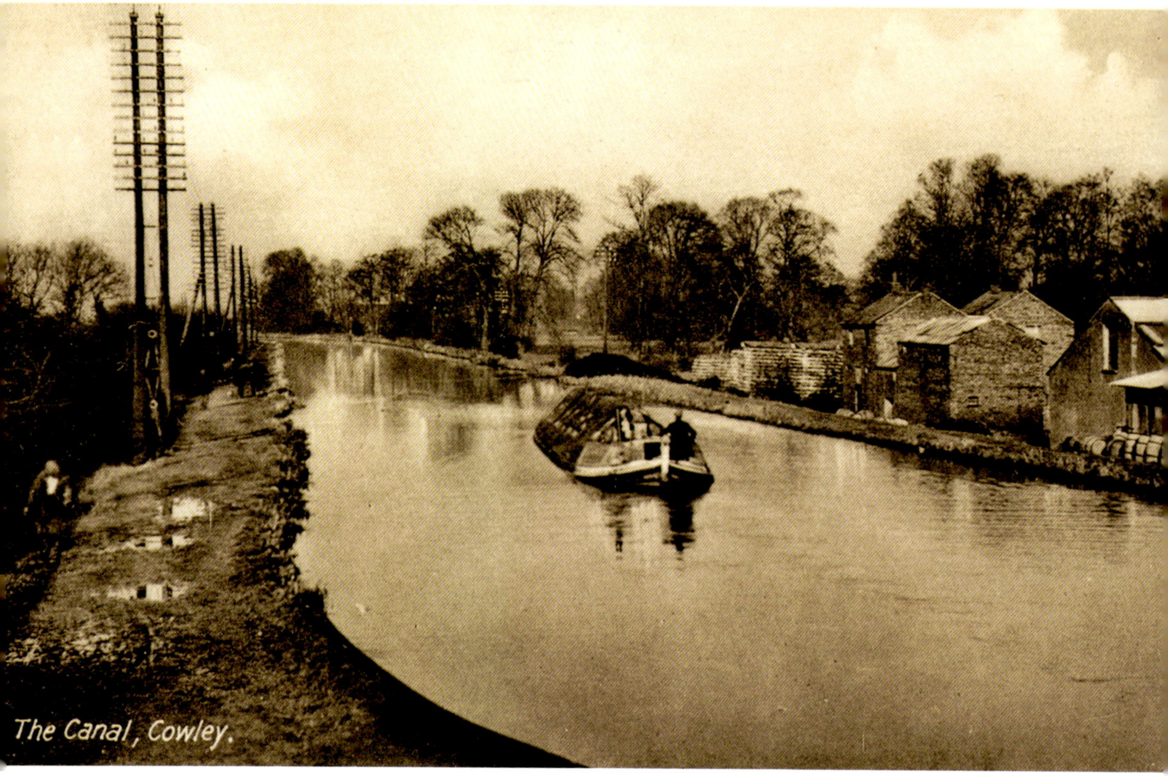

The Canal, Cowley.

Commerce and leisure

A narrowboat carrying goods at Cowley in the 1920s. Commercial traffic on the canal has now almost ceased, and the waterway is a centre of leisure activity. In 2002 the Cowley Peachey Marina opened off Packet Boat Lane, linked to the Slough branch of the canal. At a cost of £3.5 million, British Waterways London converted wasteland into a boating centre with moorings for 120 canal boats, a visitors' centre and a café.

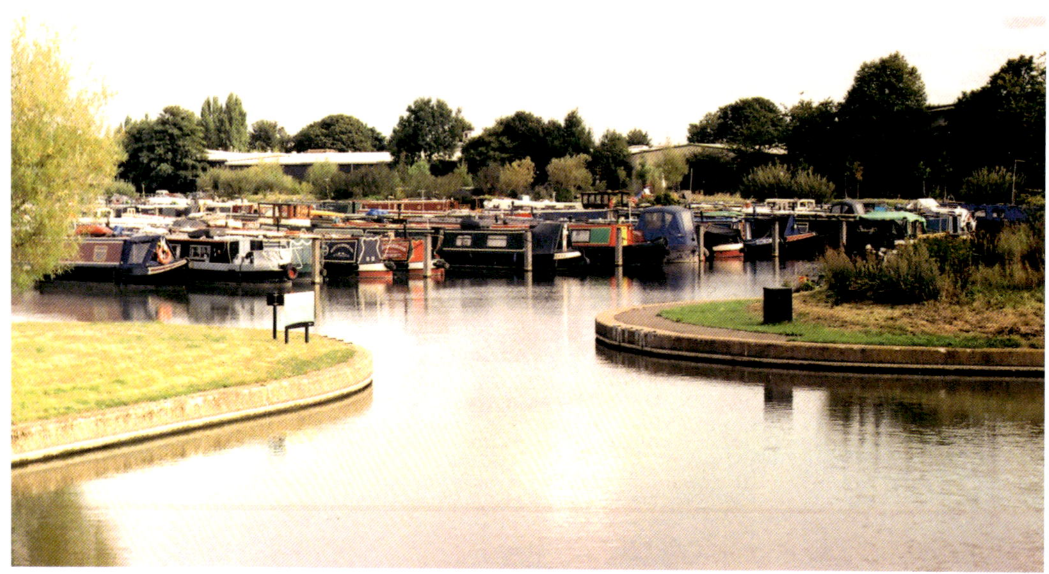

E. MOTH

GENERAL STORES & CAFE

roceries ... Confectionery ... Tobacco ... Patent Medicine

HIGH STREET, COWLEY Tel.: Uxbridge 93

WALL'S ICE CREAM

Breakfasts ... Dinners ... Teas ... Suppers

— A HOME FROM HOME —

CHAPTER 4

Trade & Industry

CONTRACTORS TO THE AIR MINISTRY, M.O.W., MIDDLESEX COUNTY COUNCIL, &c.

W. S. Try, Ltd.

Building Contractors.

Cowley, Uxbridge, Middx.

.I.O.B. (MANAGING)
CRETARY)
NGTON, F.I.O.B.

EFT/EMT

14th. January 195

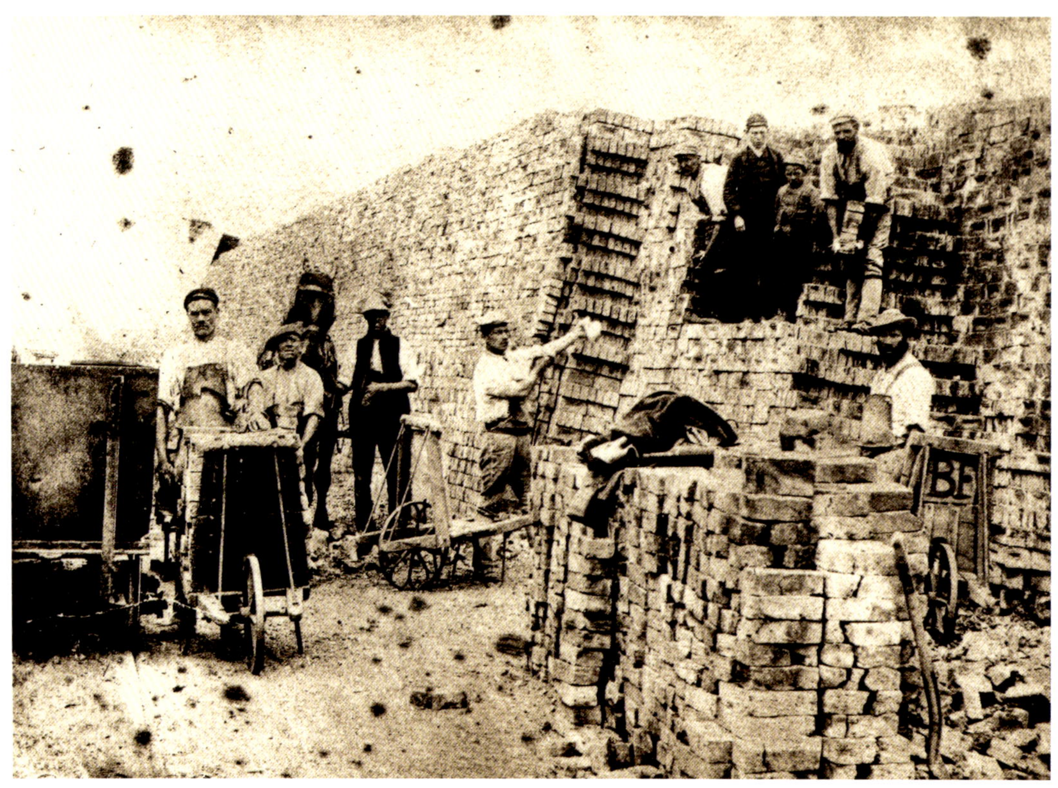

Local brickworks

The clay or brick-earth in the Cowley area is suitable for brickmaking, although there were larger deposits in Yiewsley and Stockley. The trade was boosted by the opening of the canal, which enabled the local bricks to be more easily transported to the London area. The trade goes back a long way, for below is part of the 1684 inventory of the property of John Hewes, who owned brickfields in Slough and Cowley. The amounts are in pounds, shillings and pence.

At his workeing place at Cowley in Middx a parcell of burned brickes consisting of aboute 8000	3	4	0
At his workeing place at Cowley a percell of bricks burning in the Clamne att the time of his death Consisting about three score thousand	18	0	0
At the same workeing place a percell of Rawe brickes consisting about thirty thousand	4	10	0
At the same workeing place a little parcell of sand	0	4	0
at the same workeing place a percell of fier wood	0	5	0
Two moulding tables for brickes and 2 bucketts	0	4	0
Debts sperate and Desperate	50	0	0

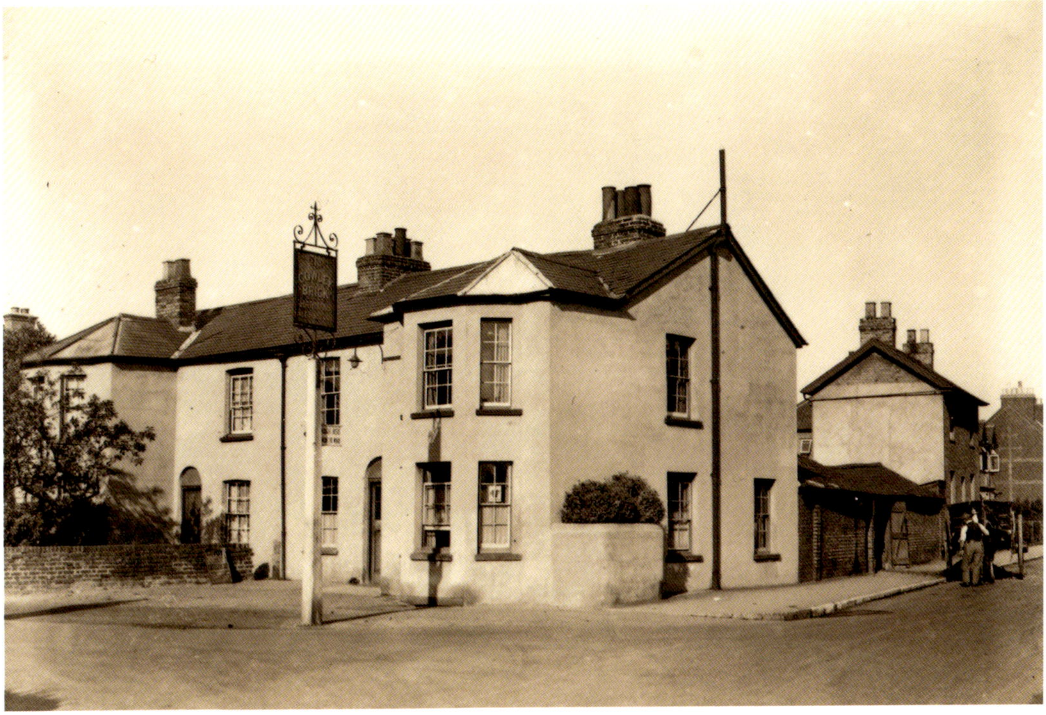

The Cowley Brick

In the late eighteenth century a new brickfield opened in Cowley Field, and a public house appeared nearby to offer refreshment to the workers. It was called The Cowley Brick, and is seen here in 1934. The firm was called the Whitehall Brick Co., and hence the name of Whitehall Road. Some bricks were imperfect – burned or mis-shapen, and these were sold off cheaply. One property where these burrs were used was Benbow Cottage, next to Benbow bridge. Surely Little Red Riding Hood's granny lived here!

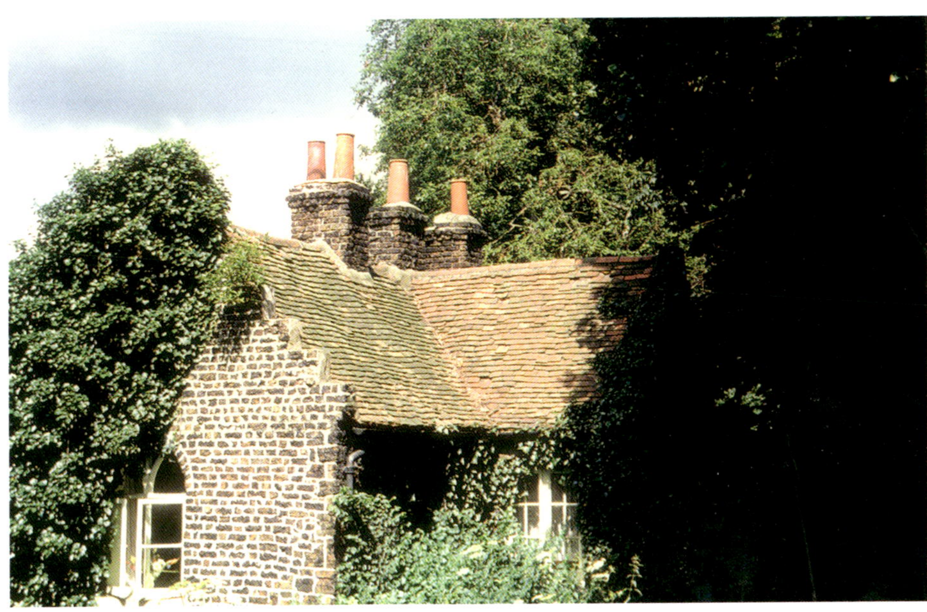

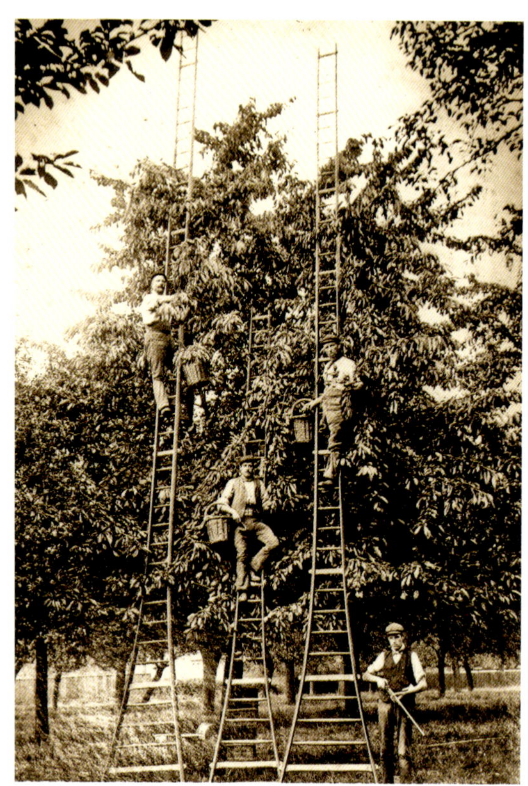

Cherry Ripe

Enormous ladders with splayed bases were used by these cherry-pickers in Cowley in 1914. A man with a shotgun scares the birds away. This small gang toured the local farms picking the fruit in season. In this country village the blacksmith was a vital member of the community, repairing farm machinery and shoeing horses. Here is Dick Wickham at his smithy next door to the Paddington Packet Boat.

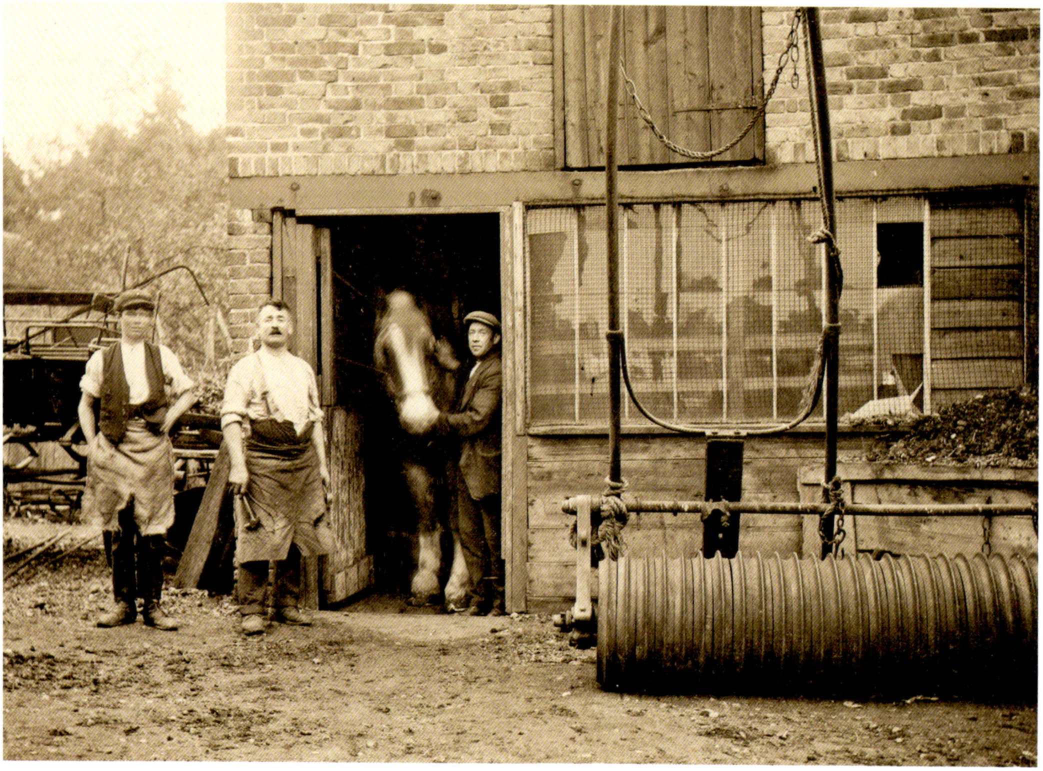

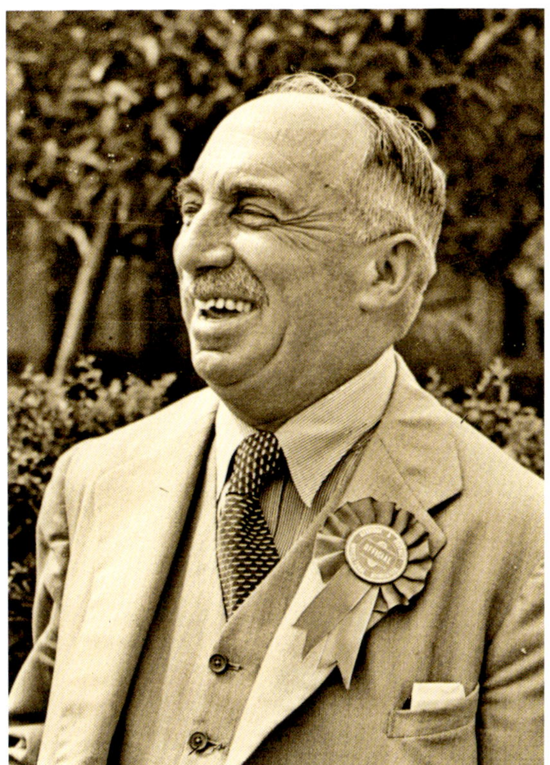

William Sidney Try

The influence of this man and his family on the history of Cowley has been considerable. Through his work as a builder, especially after he set up on his own at Old Vine Cottage in 1909, he changed the face of the district. He and his family supported the Cowley community in every possible way. He is pictured here officiating at Uxbridge Show in 1947. A view of his carpentry shop appears below.

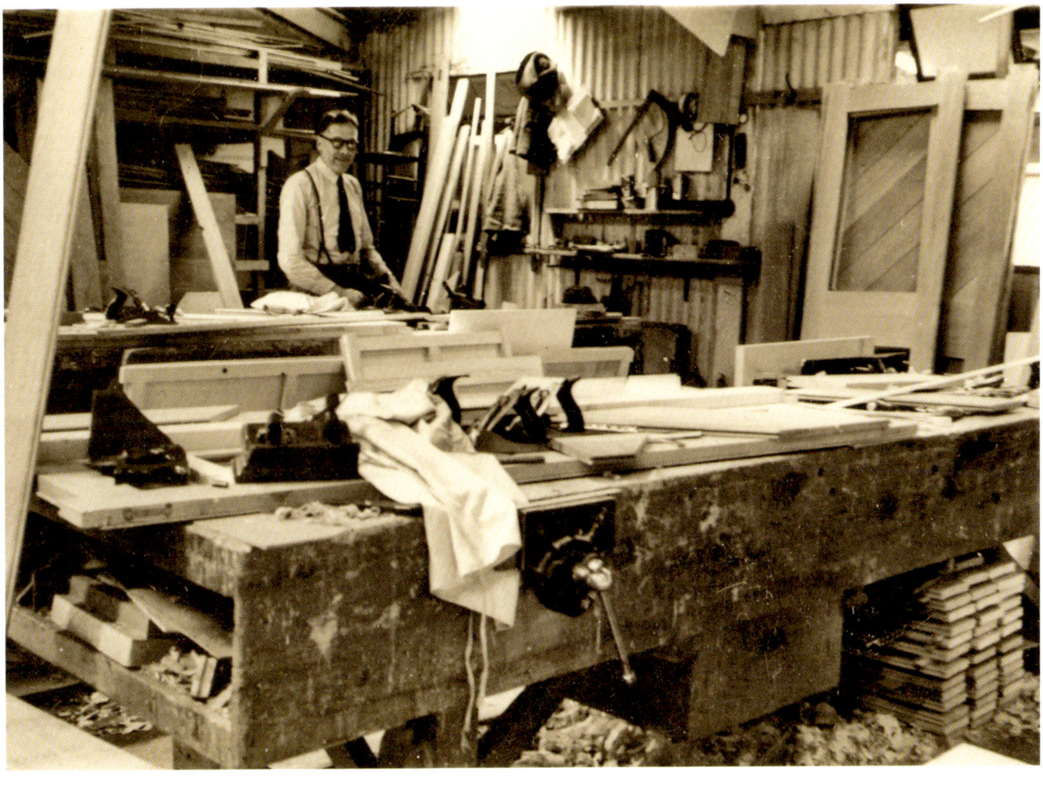

GOOD MORNING HEALTH MILK

KEEP FIT AND TRAIN on NON-PASTEURISED MILK

OBTAINABLE FROM

W. H. COX

MAYGOODS DAIRY

HIGH STREET

COWLEY

TELEPHONE UXBRIDGE 105

OVER 100 COWS KEPT

Two deliveries daily in this district

3

Cox's dairy

The business was set up by Herbert Cox at Manor Farm in the early twentieth century. After his death in 1933 his son, William Henry, took over, basing it on Maygoods Farm. He later took on Huntsmoor Farm as well, and at one time had 180 cows. Circumstances changed after World War II, and the dairy was sold to United Dairies in 1951. W. H. Cox is seen here in 1934 with his wife Alice, and their children Herbert, Marian and Doreen.

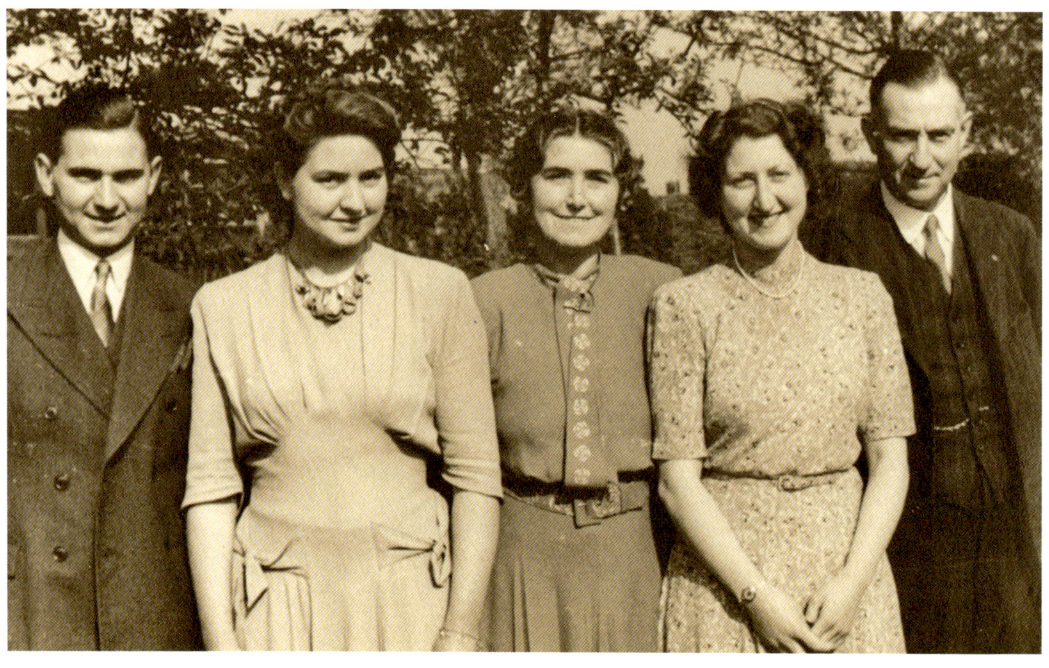

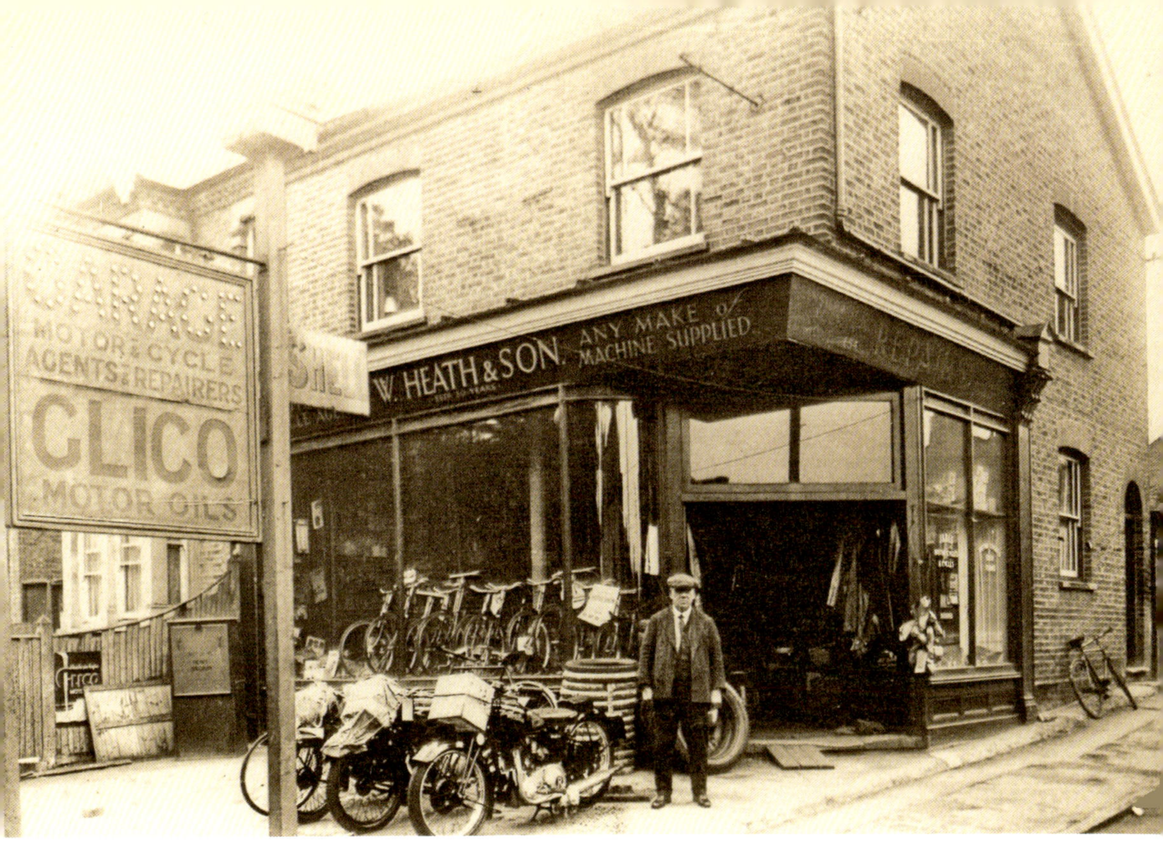

Cars and more bricks

William 'Billy' Heath set up business in Cowley Road in 1904 assembling bicycles, which were sold under the name 'The Cowley Gem'. He later sold motorcycles and cars, and ran a garage.

Uxbridge Flint Brick Company produced bricks by crushing flints quarried on their site, mixing them with slaked lime, adding colouring, and then putting them in hydraulic presses. The process was invented by a Swiss firm called Hunziker, and the Iver Lane factory began production in 1936.

HUNZIKER (GT. BRITAIN) LTD.

COWLEY BRIDGE WORKS

UXBRIDGE

Manufacturers of

UXBRIDGE FLINT BRICKS

(Available in the following grades)

ENGINEERING
WHITE & COLOURED
FACINGS
COMMONS

WE SPECIALIZE IN LIGHT PASTEL SHADES SUITABLE FOR INSIDE AND OUTSIDE FACING, ALSO WHITE BRICKS FOR LIGHT REFLECTION PURPOSES FOR WHICH OUR BRICKS ARE EMINENTLY SUITABLE, HAVING A LOW POROSITY AND A VERY HARD-WEARING SURFACE

Telephone:
UXBRIDGE 1313

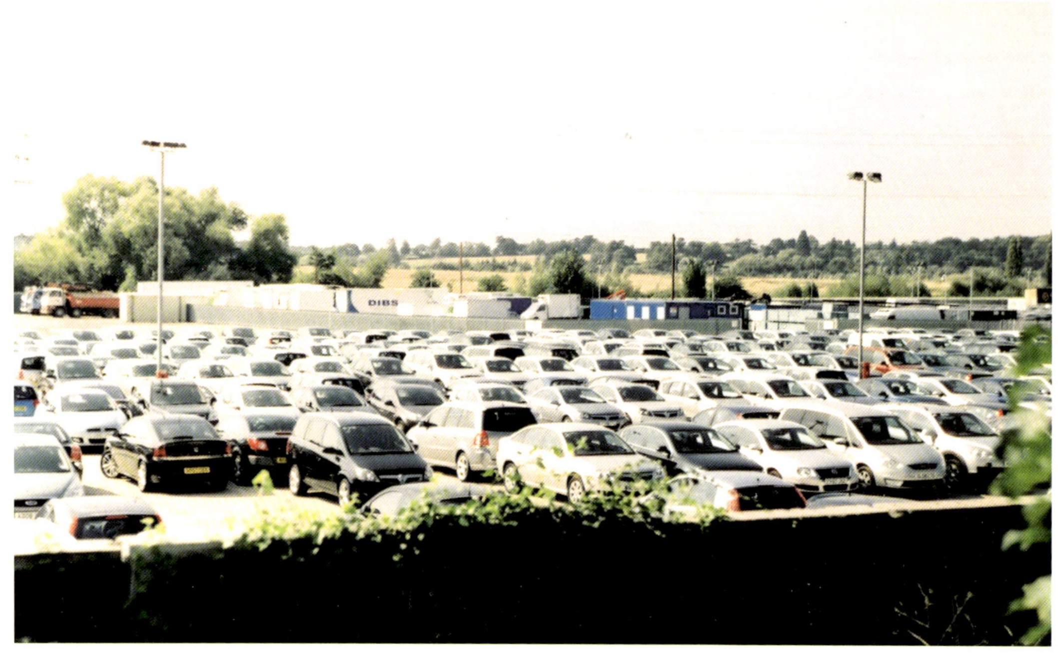

Brick Company

The brick company was taken over by Cape Building Products in 1956, and all brick-making ceased in 1974. Cape initially made boards and panels using asbestos – until the dangers were realised! They closed in 2002, since when the cleared site has become a vast car park. One building where these bricks were used was a Post Office Engineering Depot opened in 1938. It was closed and demolished in 1989, and the site is now a Peugeot dealership.

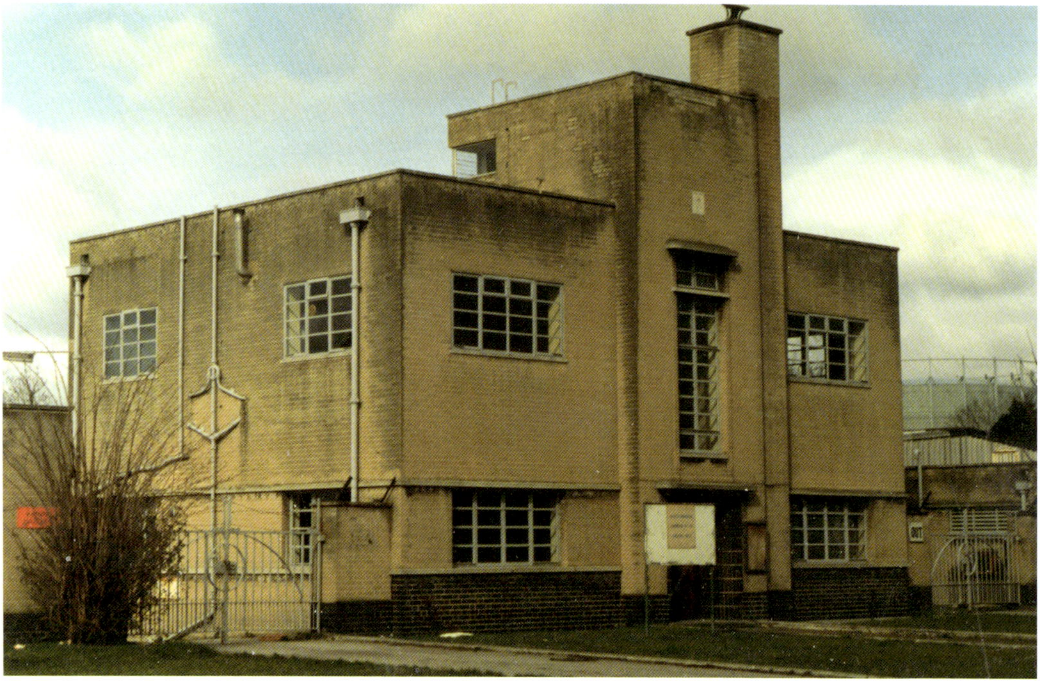

CHAPTER 5

Education

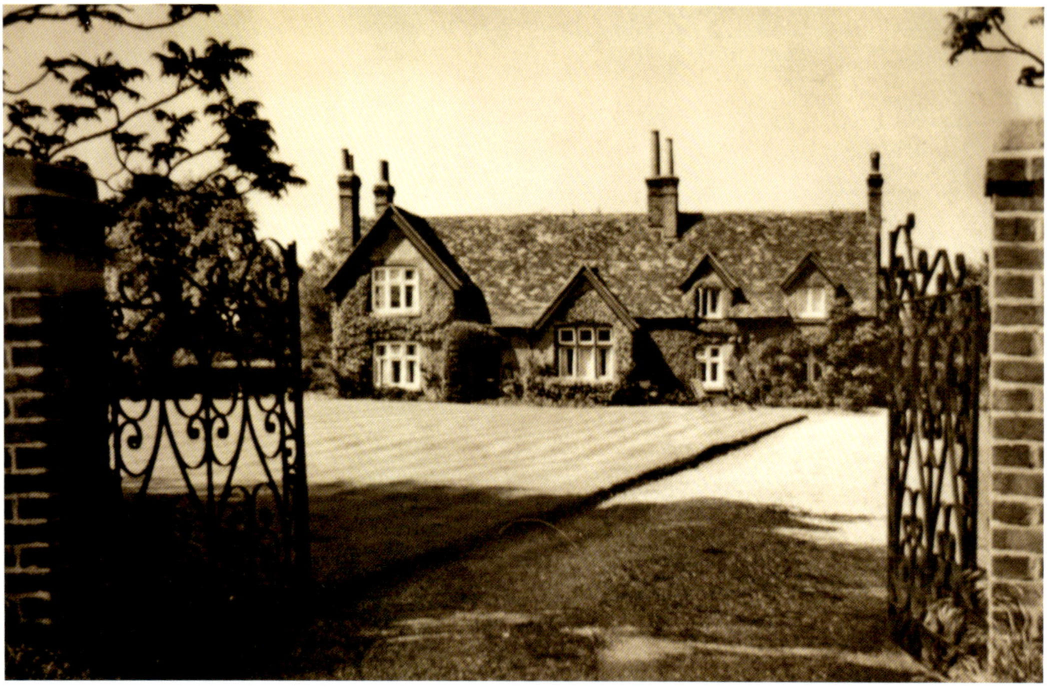

The Meads

A school opened in this building just east of the church in 1836, although it is thought that some form of education began soon after 1800, when Anthony Brown left £5 a year to educate small children. This church school, probably affiliated to the National Society, moved to another house in Church Road in 1877. The Meads then became a private residence, but was demolished about 1962, and replaced by this group of houses which retained the name.

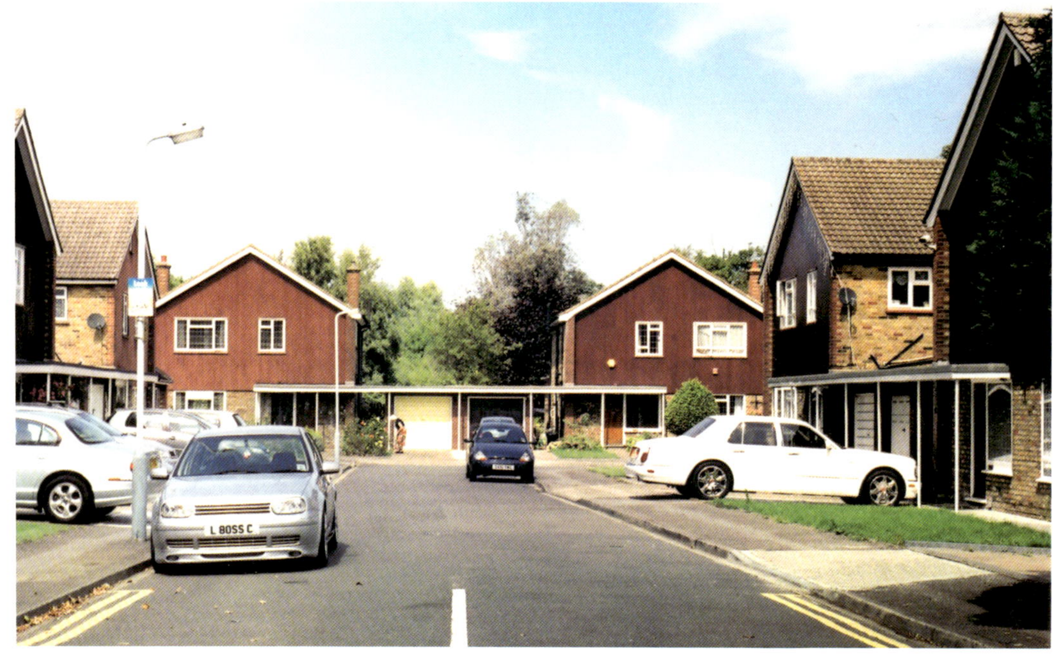

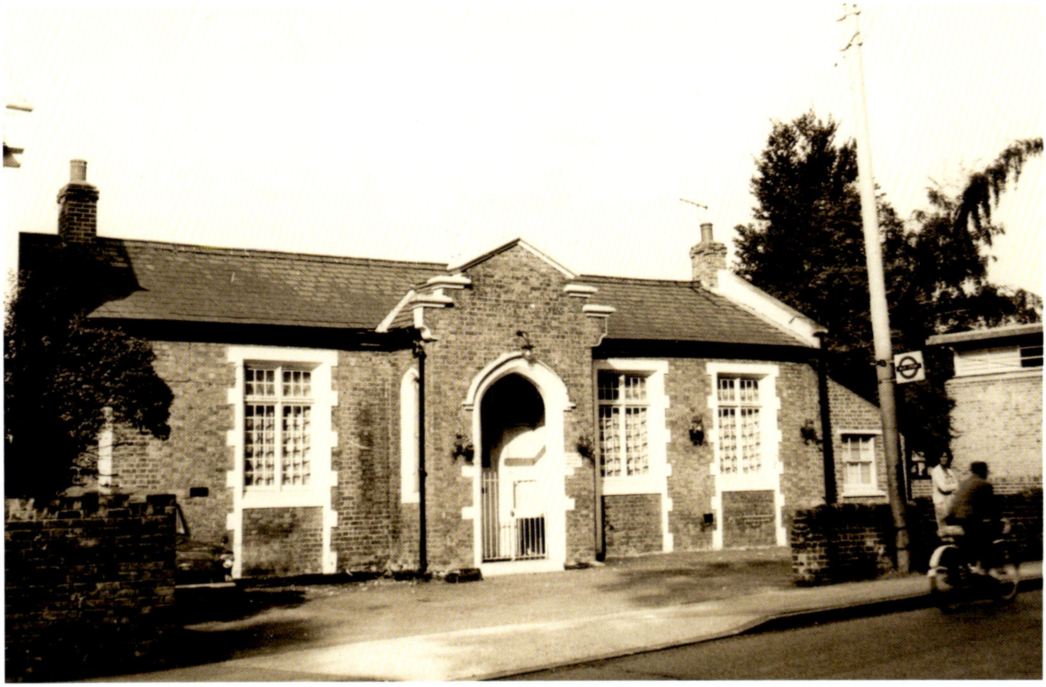

The Boys School

The Hillingdon and Cowley National School for Boys was opened in 1841 on Hillingdon Road, and was known by local people as 'the Turnpike Lane School' because it was next to that roadway. Cowley boys above infant age attended this school, which had 65 on the roll by 1865. The number was about 120 when the school closed in 1928. Amazingly, after several changes of use, the building survives. In 1990 extensions were added on either side to provide office accommodation.

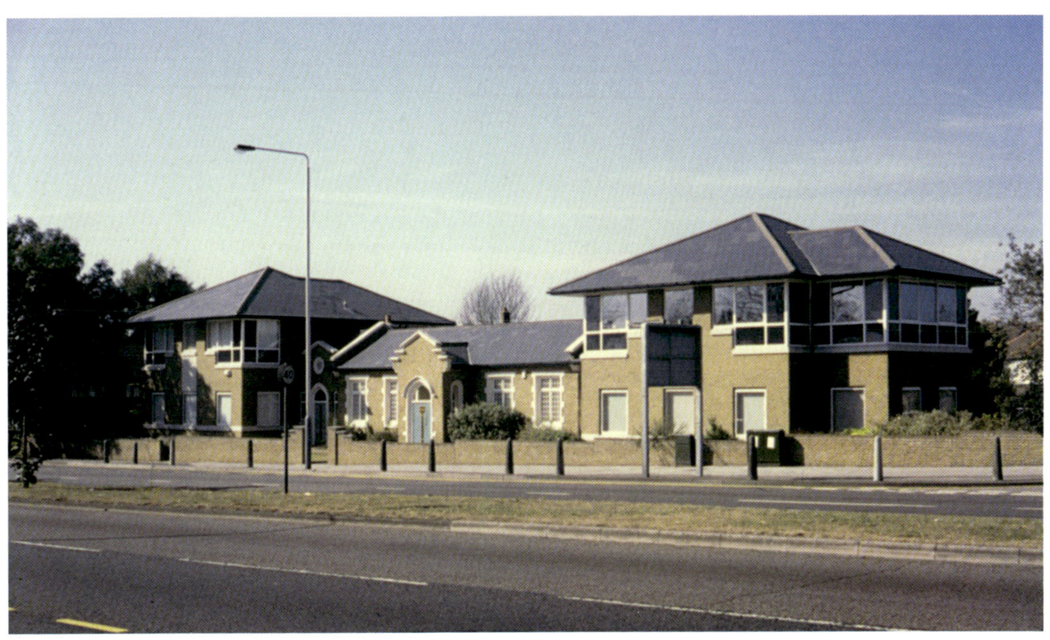

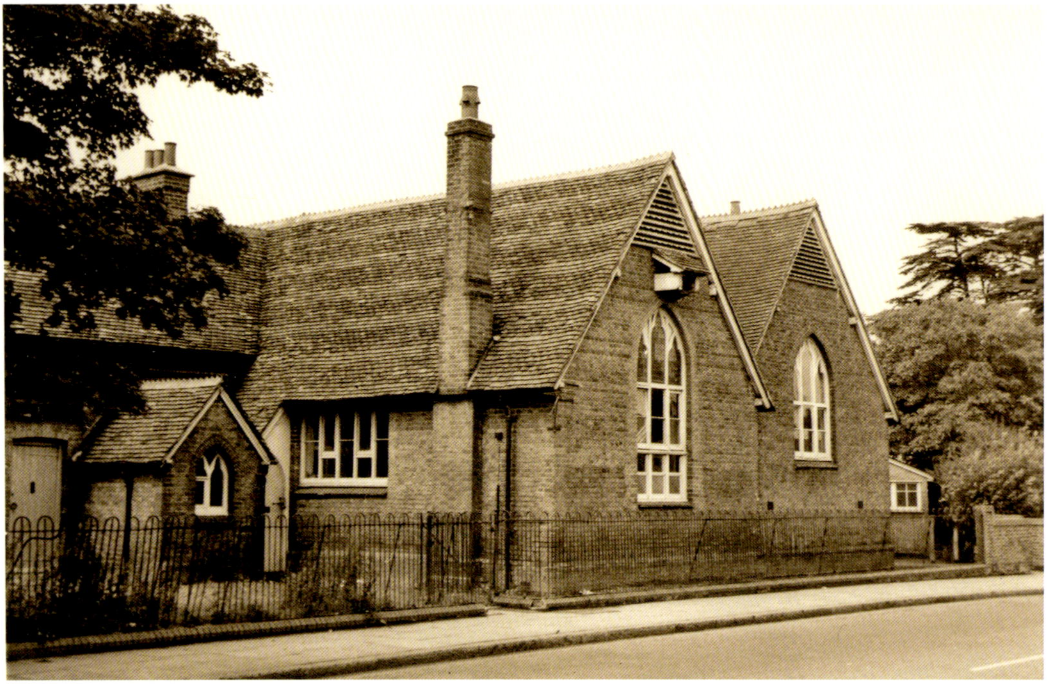

Cowley C of E School

This school opened in 1891 in the High Street at its junction with Iver Lane, at which time the schoolteacher lived in the house on the left-hand side of the photograph. Note the school bell on the gable, protected against the weather, the ringing of which encouraged the latecomers to accelerate. The group photograph shows the entire school in 1900 – a teacher and fifty children.

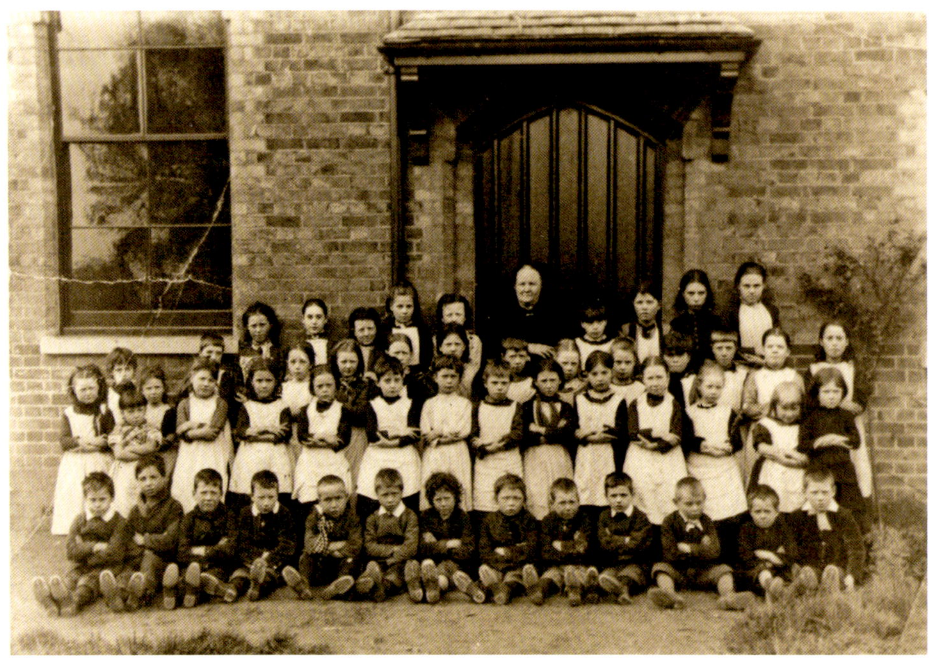

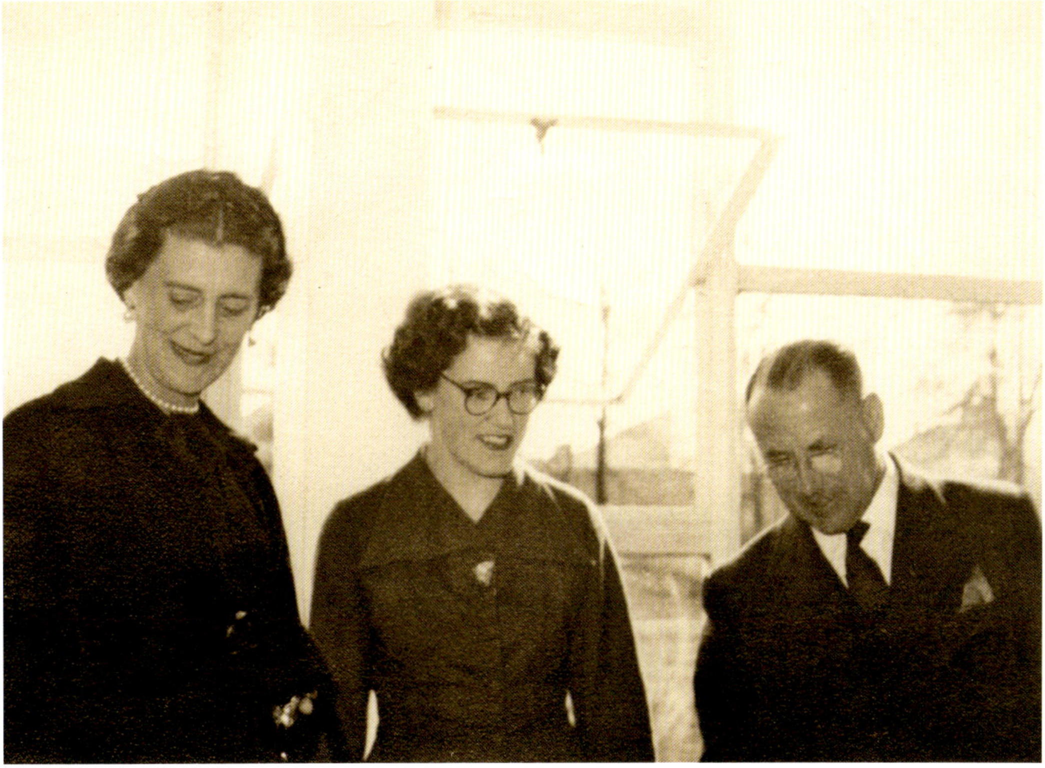

The new school

The opening of the Worcester Road School by Marina, Duchess of Kent in 1955. The increase in population had left the old school hopelessly overcrowded and outdated, so the Junior pupils were able to take over this new building. Also in the photograph is Harold Stoddart, head-teacher from 1935 to 1965. Below are the staff there in 1966, with the headmaster Mr Webb (back row on left) and his deputy, Mr Evans. Others on the picture are Mrs Holmes, Mrs Benstead and Mrs Sims.

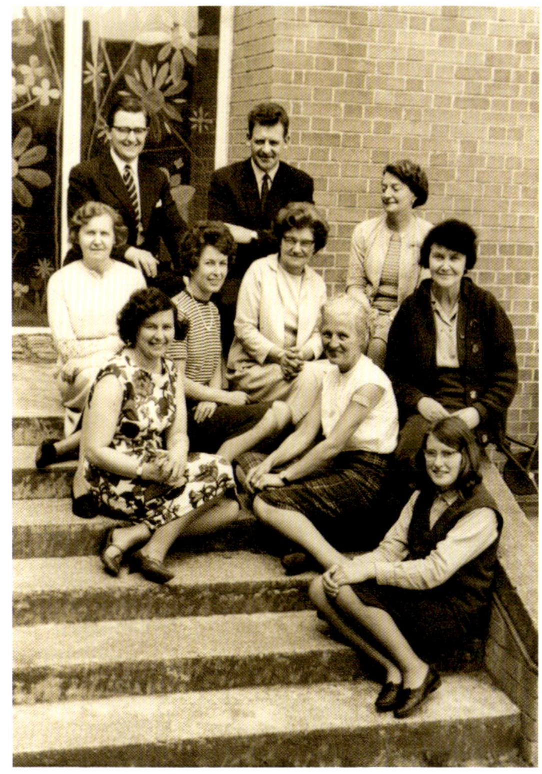

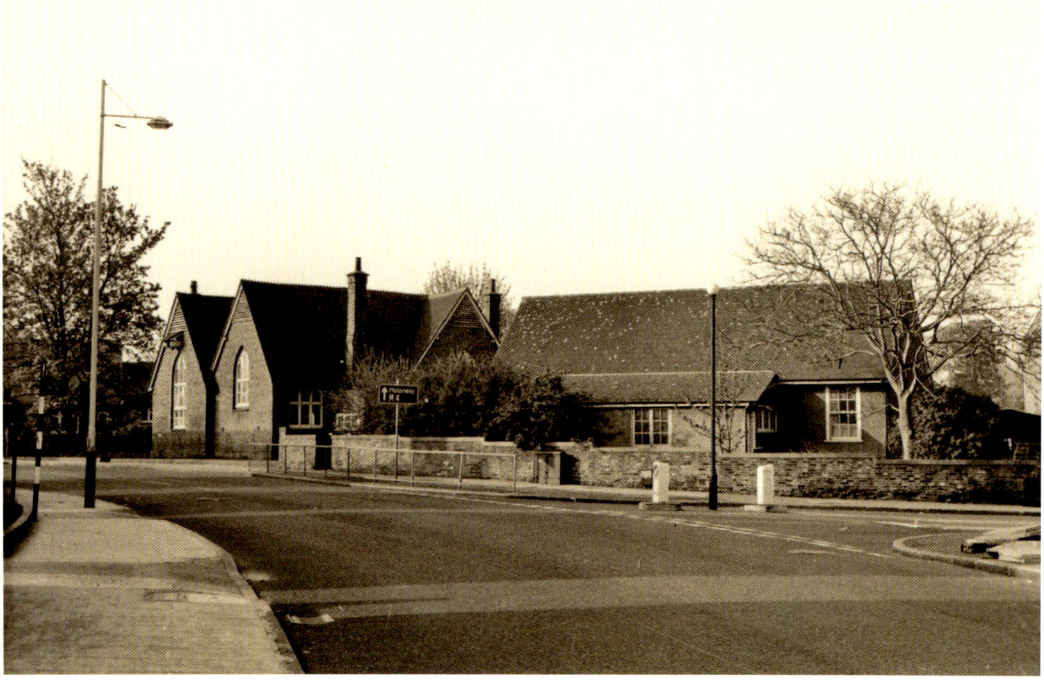

St Laurence Schools

The infants remained at the old building until 1967, by which time it was in a deplorable state. The heating was inadequate, the roof leaked, and two classes were being taught in the Church Hall. Below is a glimpse of the present school, with the main teaching block on the left, and the Nursery behind the trees.

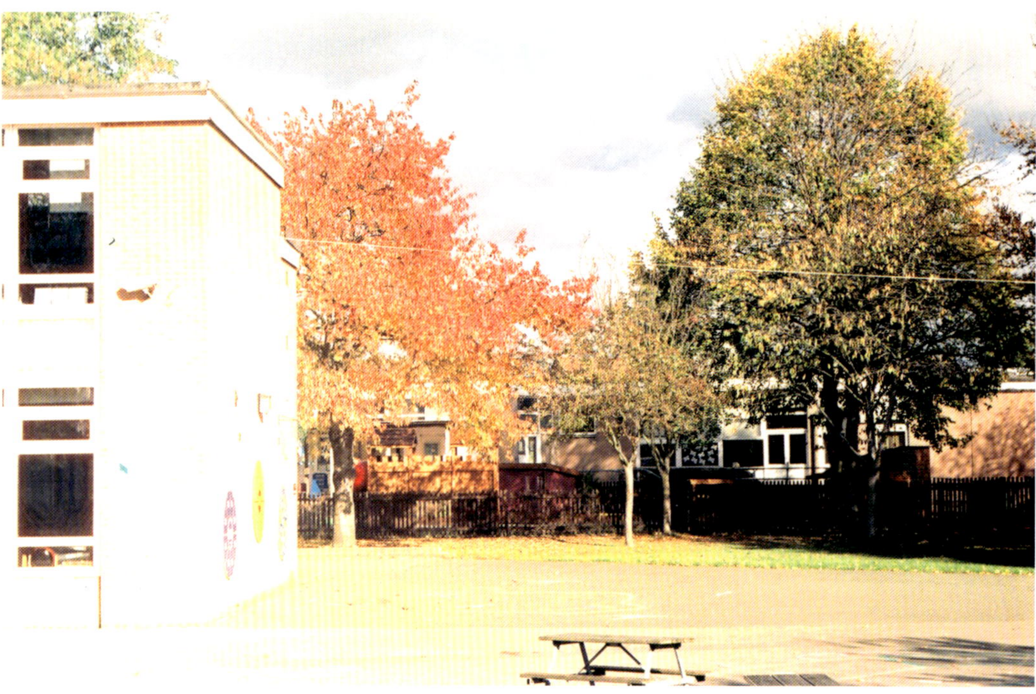

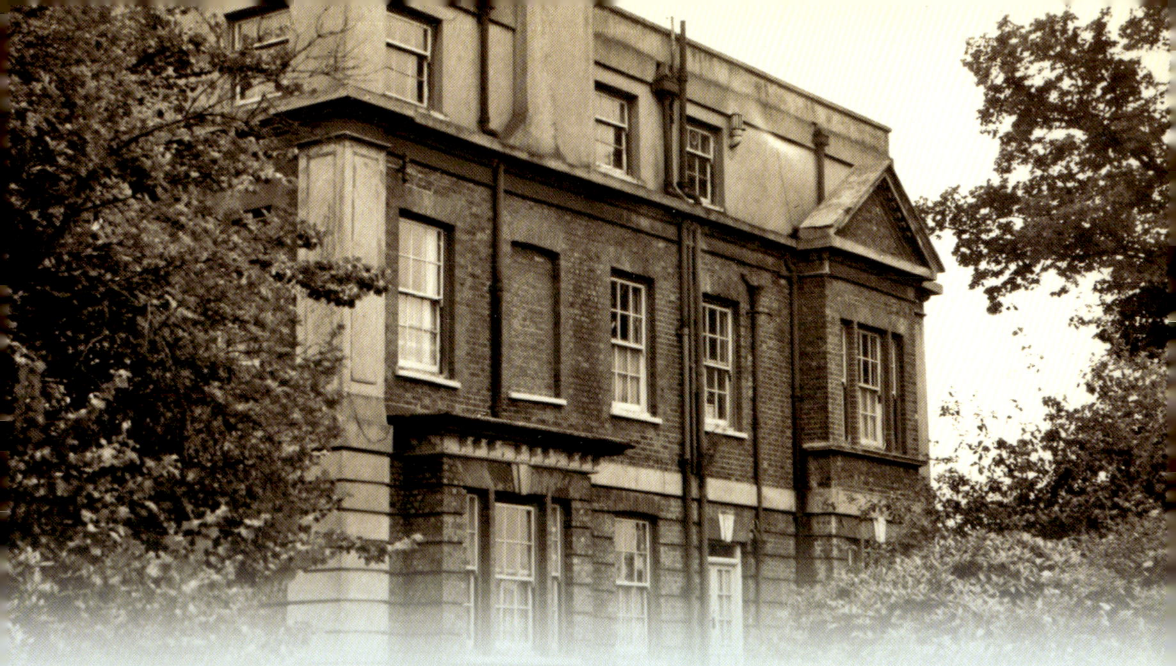

CHAPTER 6

Notable Buildings

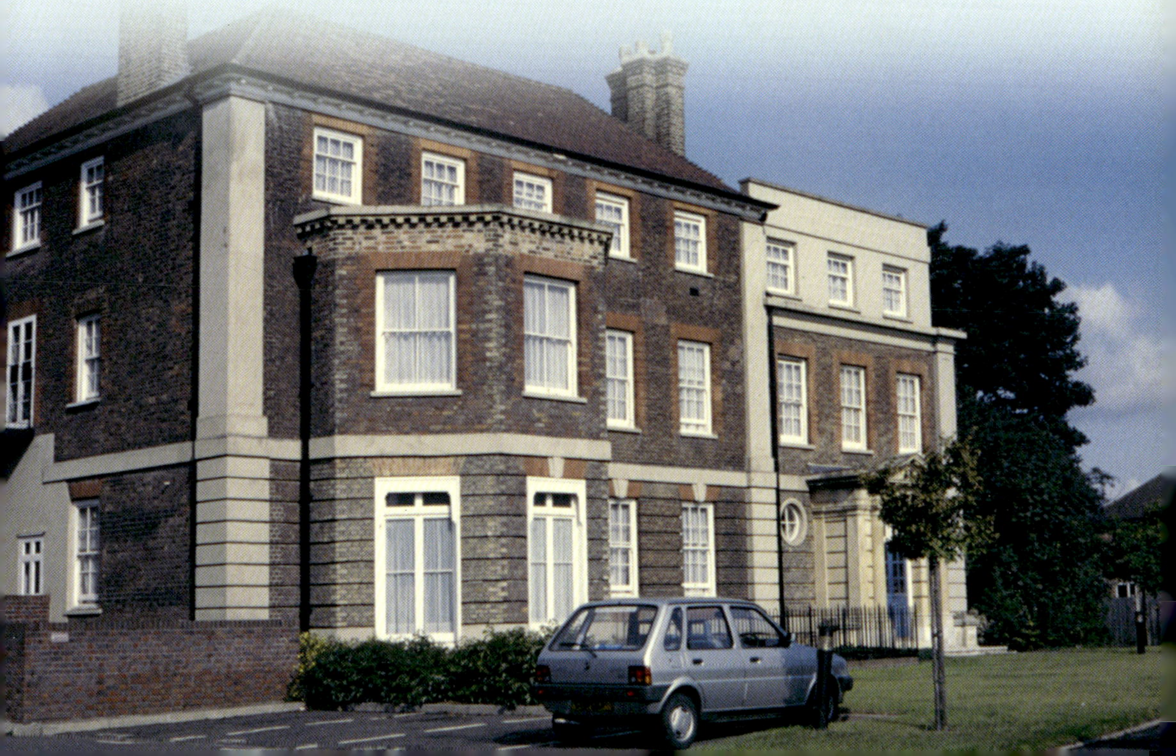

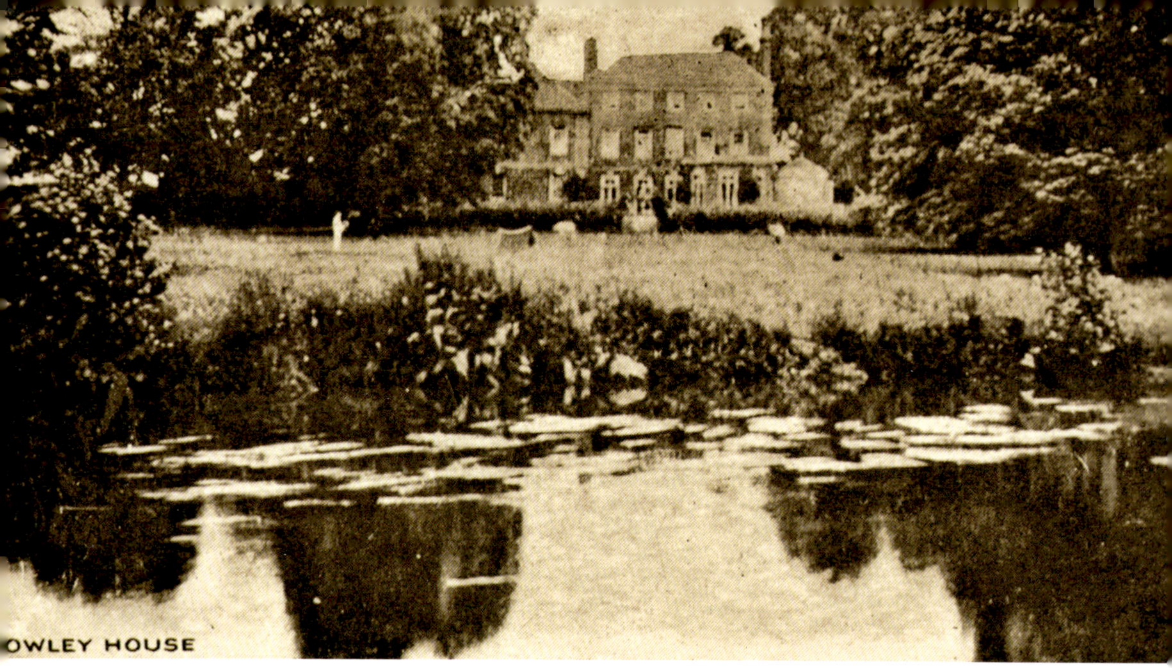

Cowley House

A rear view about 1920. The frontage is shown on the preceding page. Dating from 1738, the property was extensively altered in the early nineteenth century, and again after a serious fire in 1928. Until 1920, it belonged to the wealthy Crosier and Hilliard families, and remains the largest house in Cowley. It is now divided into apartments. The adjoining cottages, now called Cowley Lodge, were probably once the stables of the big house.

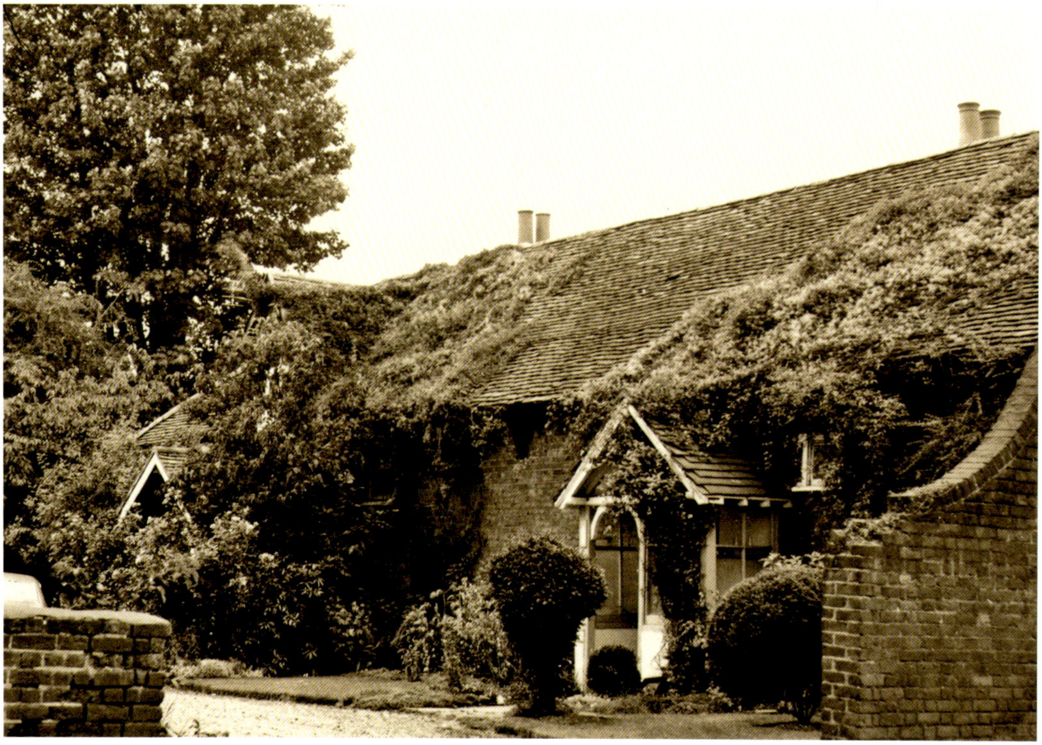

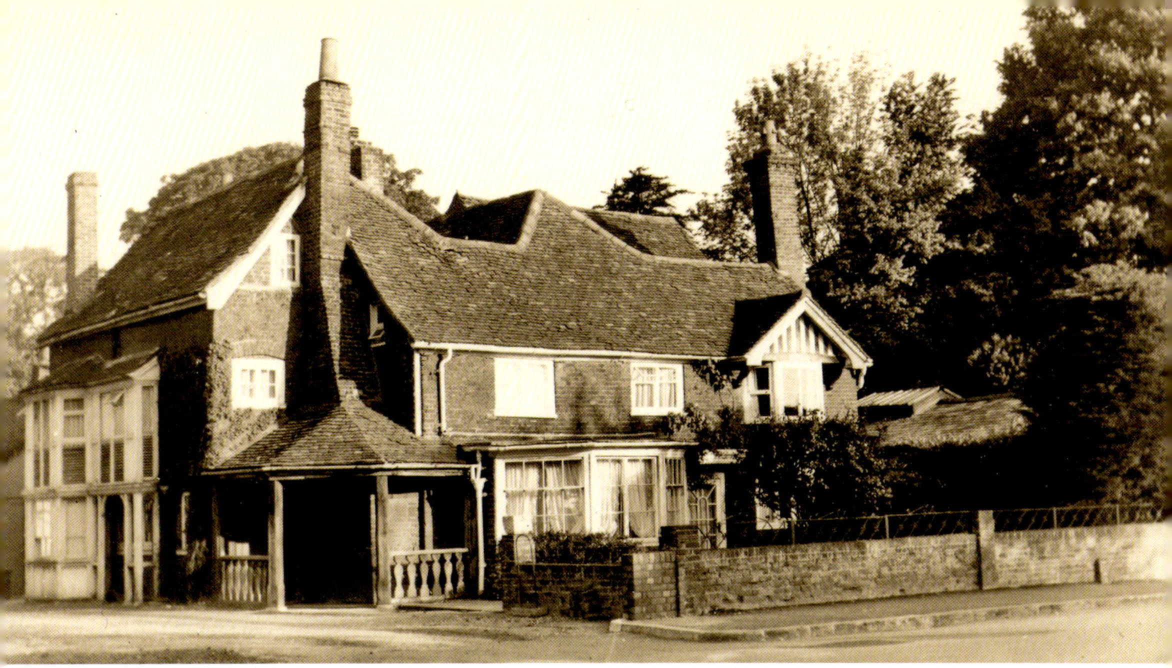

Old Vine Cottage

This charming property dates from the late 16th century, and once belonged to a notable family named Dagnall. In 1909 the builder W. S. Try moved here, and set up business, using the old smithy on the north side as a workshop. His family lived here for the next sixty years. The modern photograph shows a new extension replacing the blacksmith's shop, and the building is now used as offices.

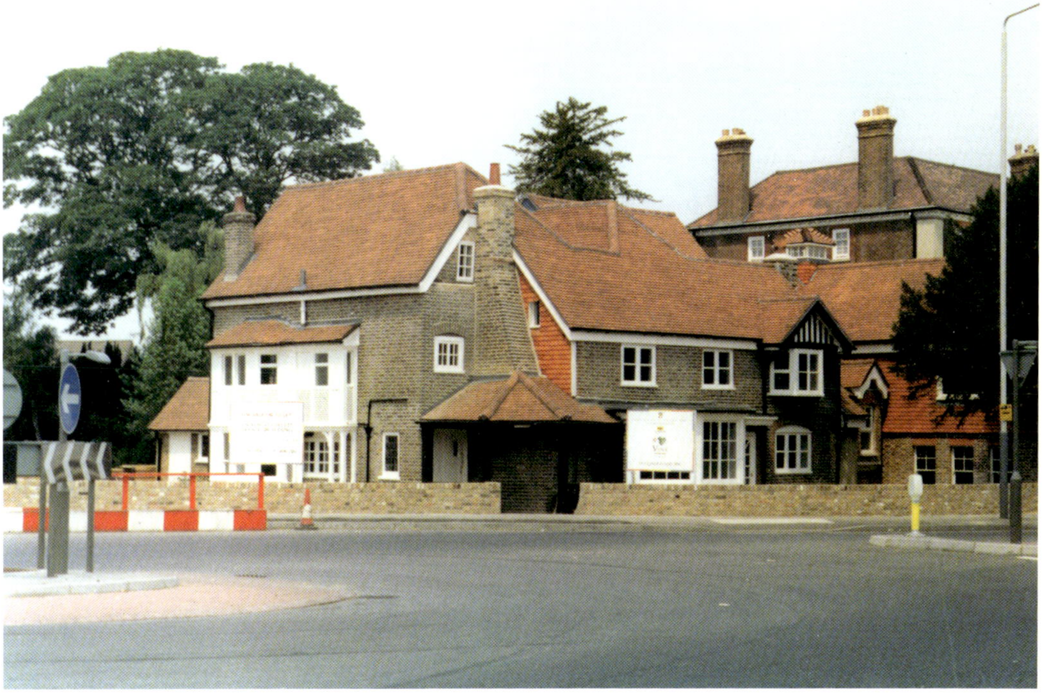

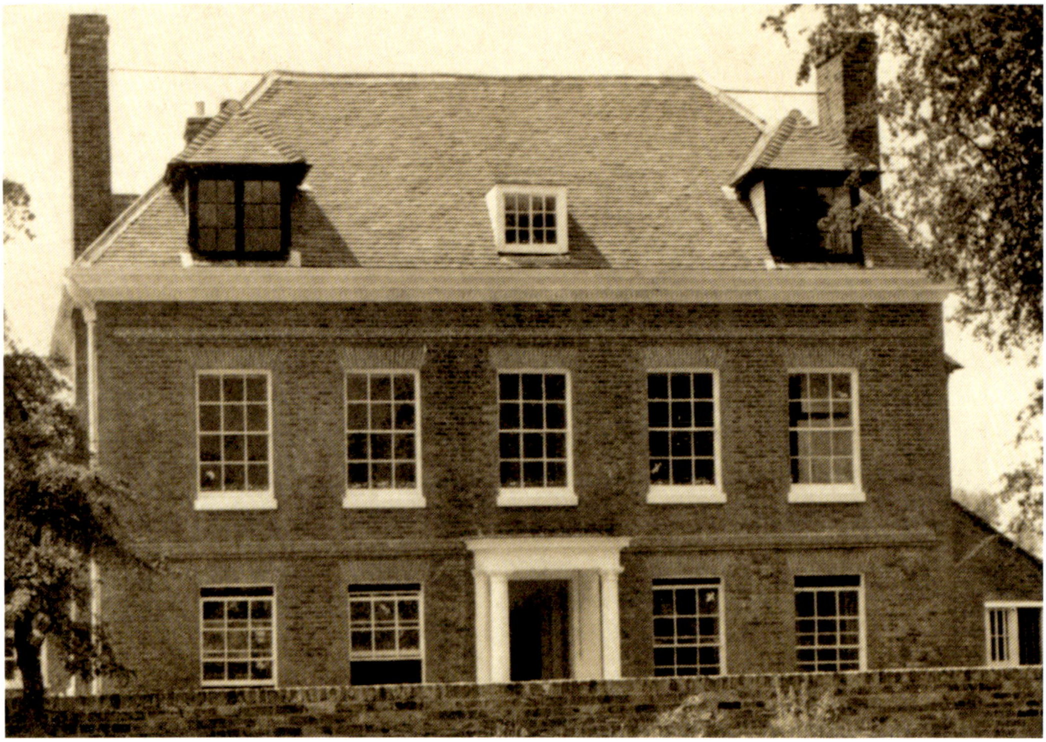

The Beeches and the Old House

Both these eighteenth century houses stand in the High Street. The Beeches, with its neat Roman Doric porch, was once a single residence. It was acquired by the Borough in 1966, and converted into flatlets in 1971. Interior modernisation took place in 2009. The Old House, a little further south, was once the home of Col. Peter Kay, managing director of the Lowe and Shawyer nurseries.

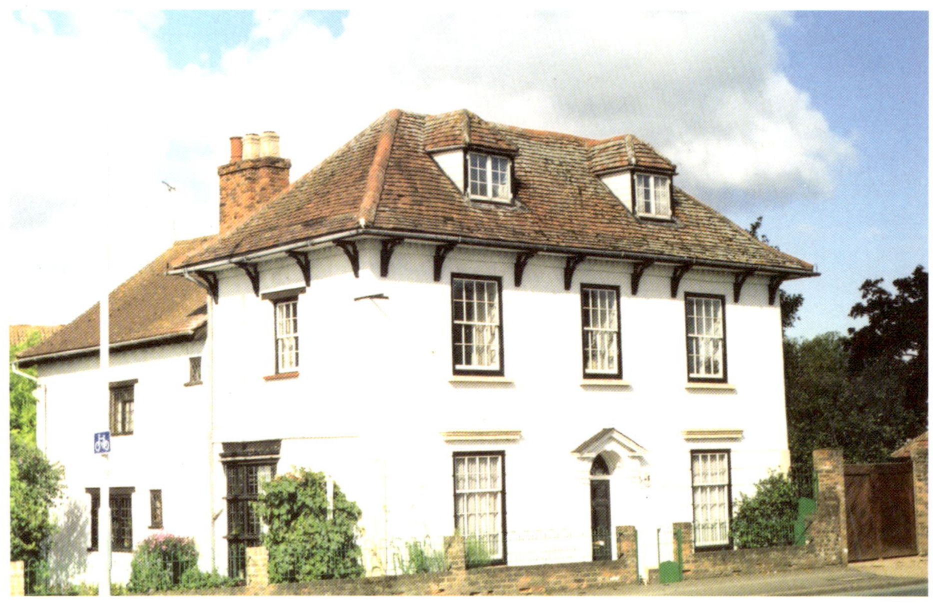

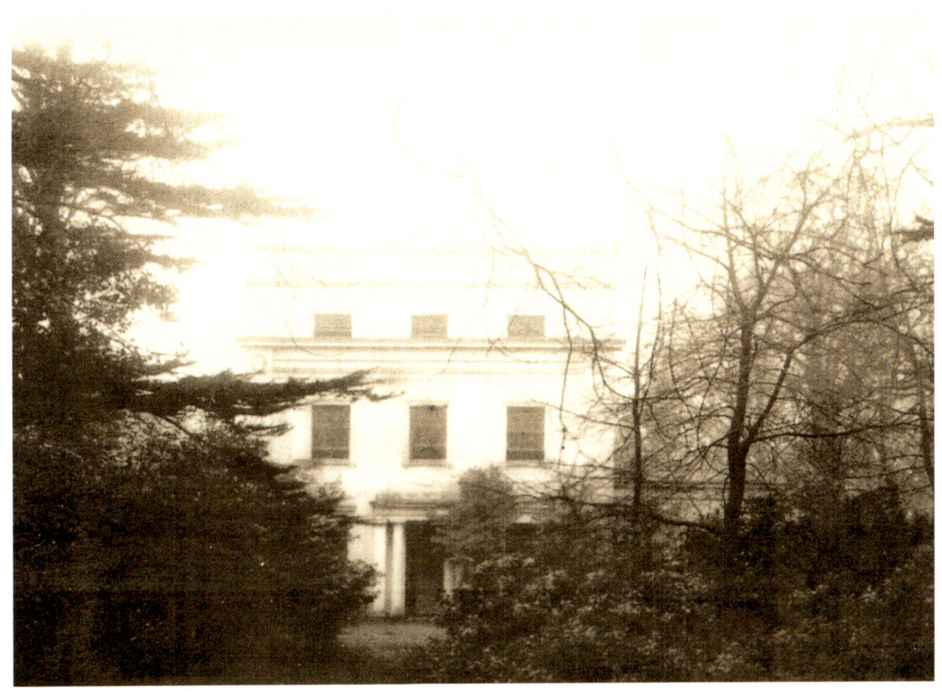

Cowley Hall

This rather poor photograph shows the Hall in 1930, just before it was demolished. In the early nineteenth century it was the home of Thomas Rose, a great friend of the artist J. M. W. Turner. Thornbury's biography of Turner states that the great man enjoyed coming to stay with Rose in order to go fishing. The estate was bought by Uxbridge Council in 1929, and converted into a Recreation Ground.

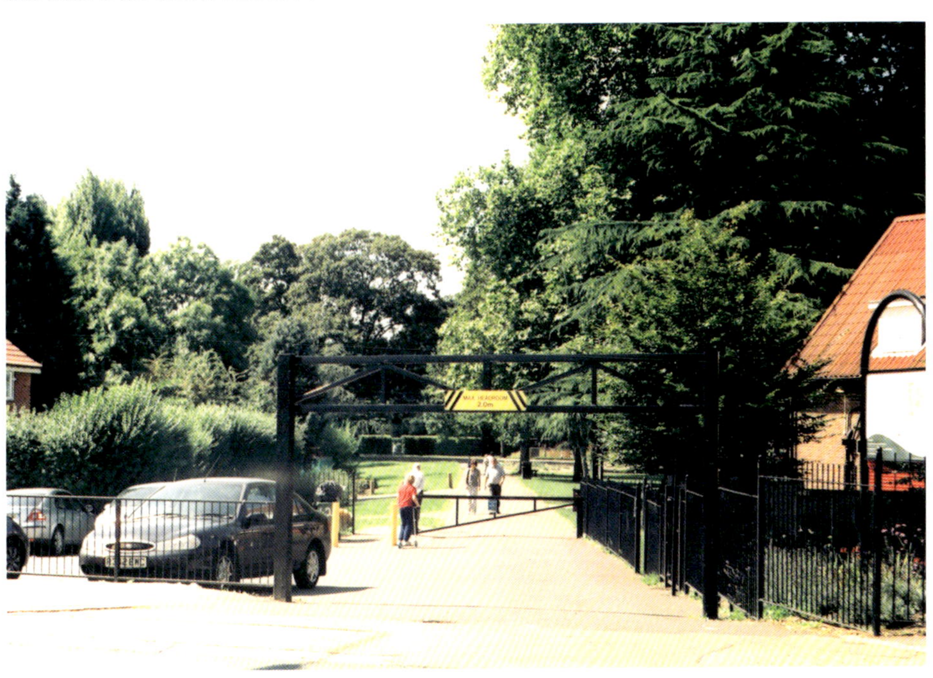

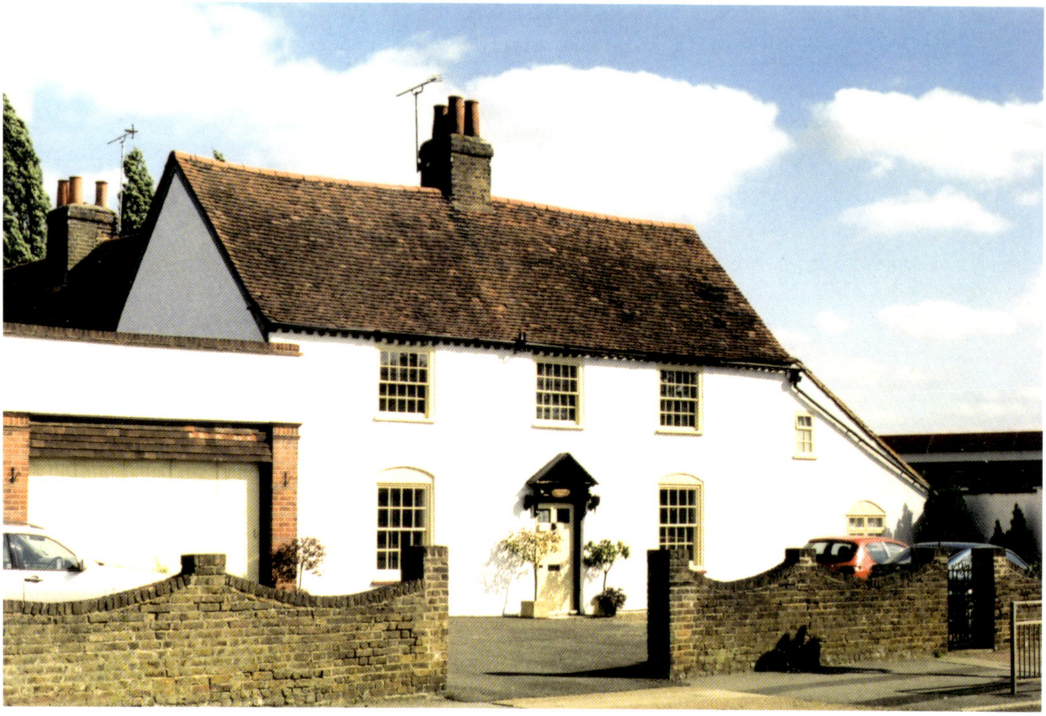

Maygoods Farmhouse and Cowley Grove

The farmhouse is said to date from the seventeenth century, but is almost certainly much older. In recent years it has become a guest house.

Cowley Grove stood near entrance to the road called Frayslea, and was demolished in 1965. It had certainly seen much alteration since it too was built in the seventeenth century.

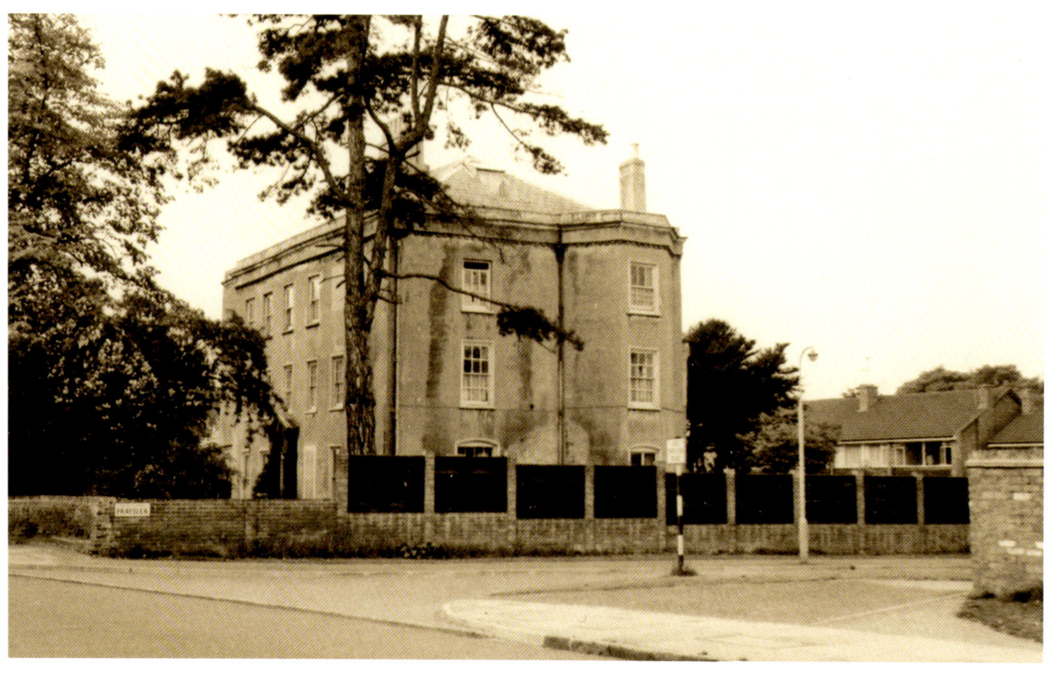

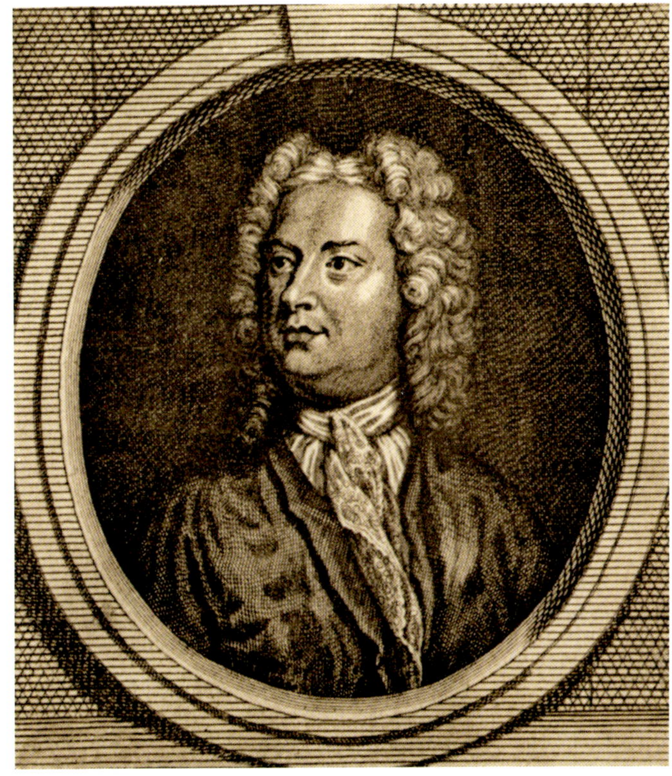

Barton Booth and John Rich
Both these men lived at Cowley Grove. Booth (1681-1733) was the most celebrated actor of his day. His success brought him fame and wealth, which enabled him to develop two new streets in Westminster – Barton Street and Cowley Street. They are still there today, near the Abbey. He was buried at Cowley church. The tomb of John Rich (1682? – 1761) is in Hillingdon churchyard. He was an actor and theatre manager, introduced pantomime into England, and built the first Covent Garden Theatre.

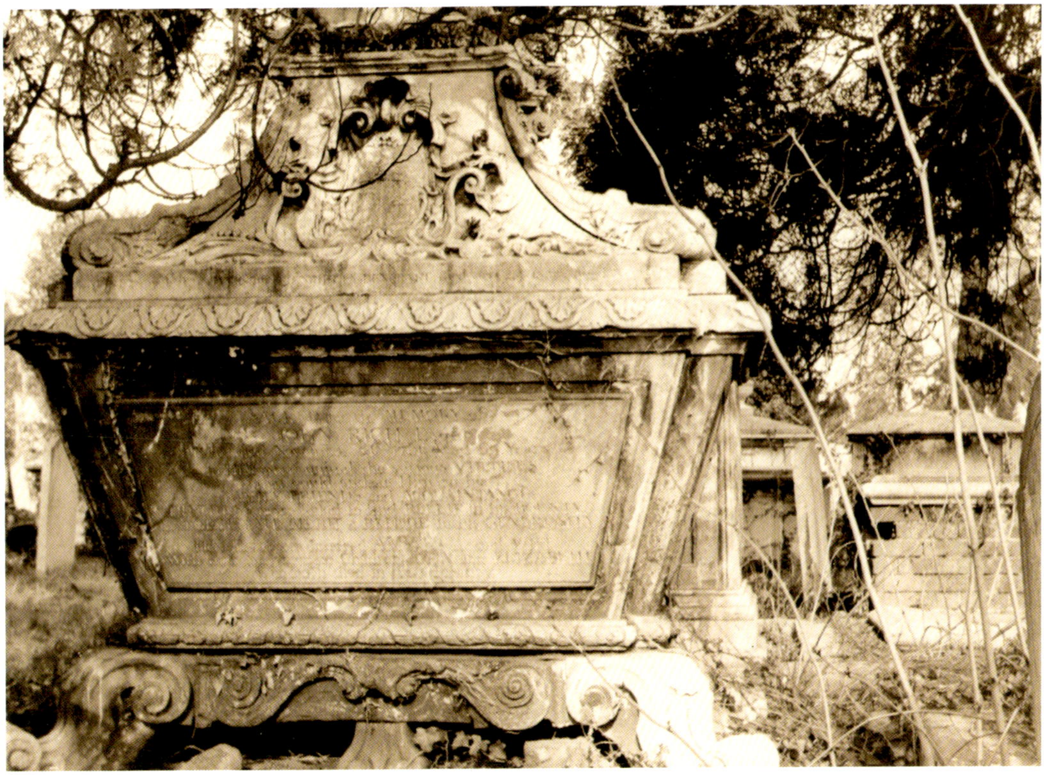

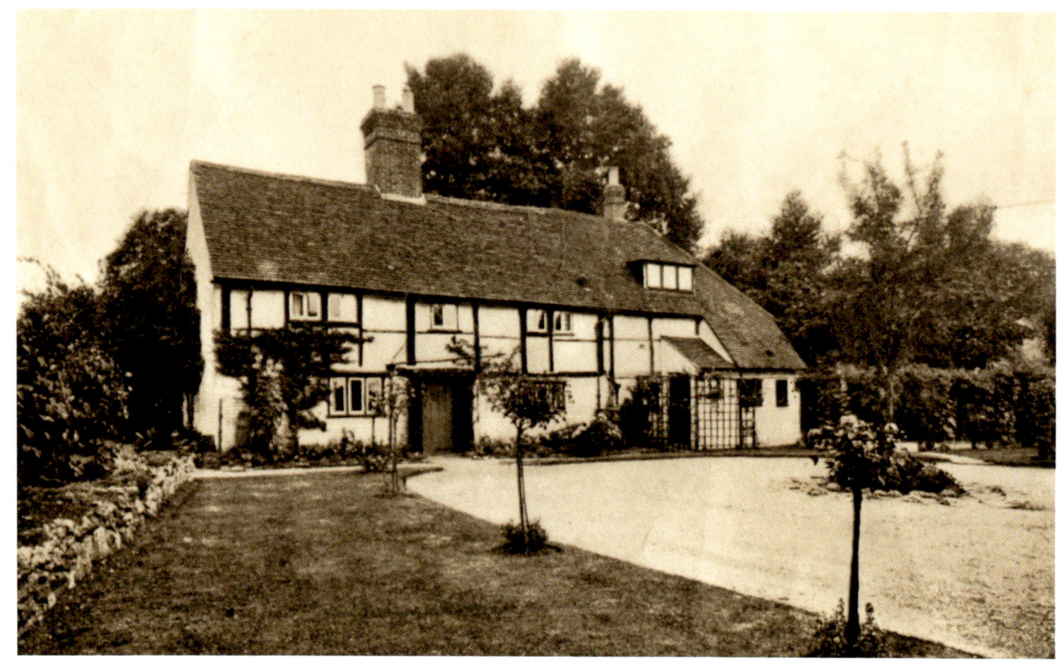

Barnacre and The Old Cottage

The seventeenth century Barnacre at Cowley Peachey is notable for its exterior timber framework. Nearby on the west side of the main road is The Old Cottage, the oldest house in Cowley. Originally a hall house, (i.e. one large room), a large chimney was eventually installed enabling the property to be split into several rooms. The two houses on this page must be two of the 'Three Houses' named on the 1754 map. The third, Cowley Peachey House in Packet Boat Lane, has completely disappeared.

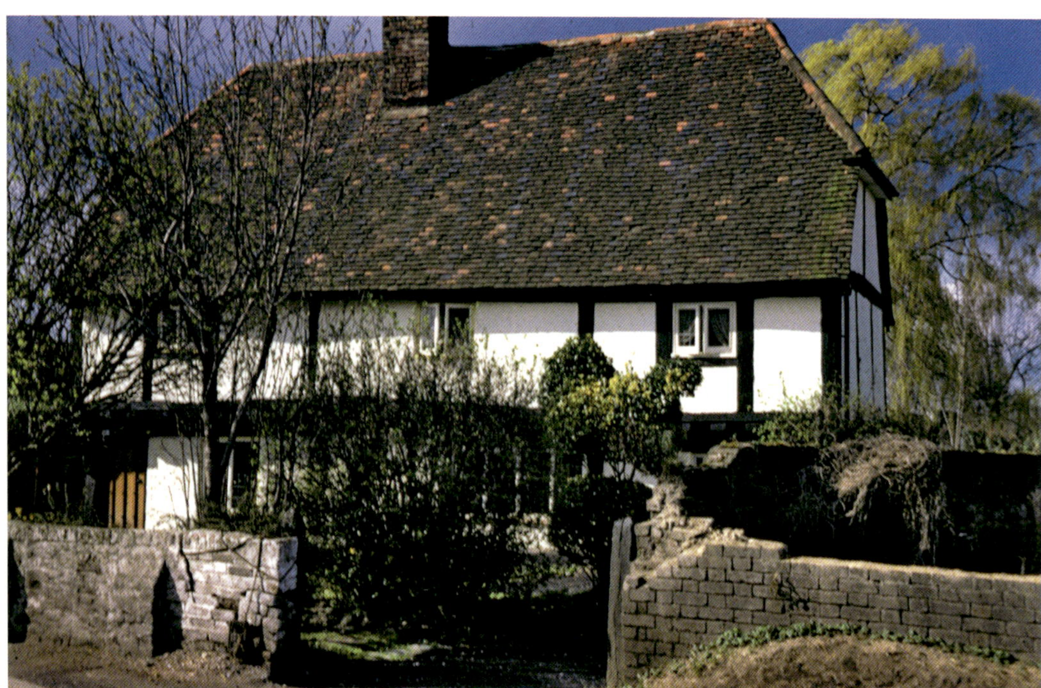

GREAT WESTERN RAILWAY.

rcular No. 1529.

OFFICE OF SUPERINTENDENT OF THE LINE,
PADDINGTON STATION,
September 23rd, 190

Opening of a New Station at Cowley

. 141/78777.)

On Sunday, October 1st, 1904, a new Station named "**Cowley,**
uated between Uxbridge and West Drayton, will be opened for traffic, the distan
ing 1 mile from Uxbridge and 1½ miles from West Drayton.

Insert the following particulars in your Station Hand-book :—

Station commodation.	Crane Power	Station.	County.	Railway.	Position.

CHAPTER 7
The Railway

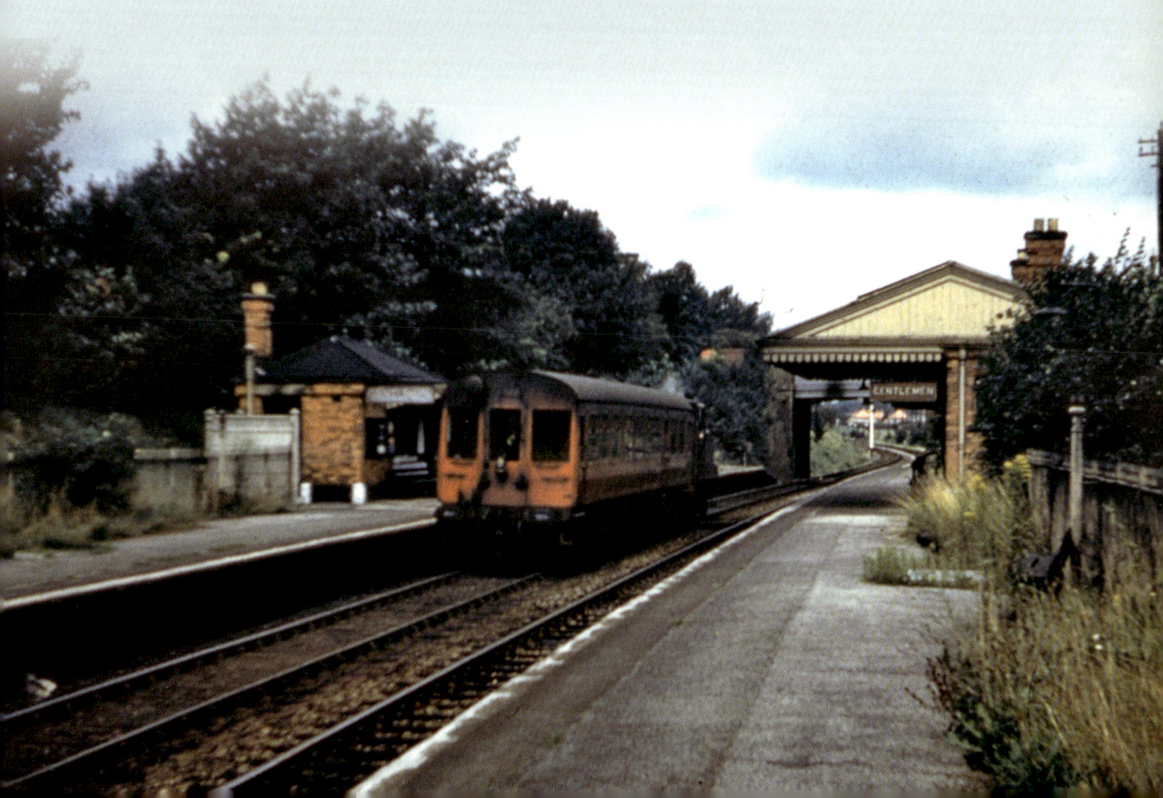

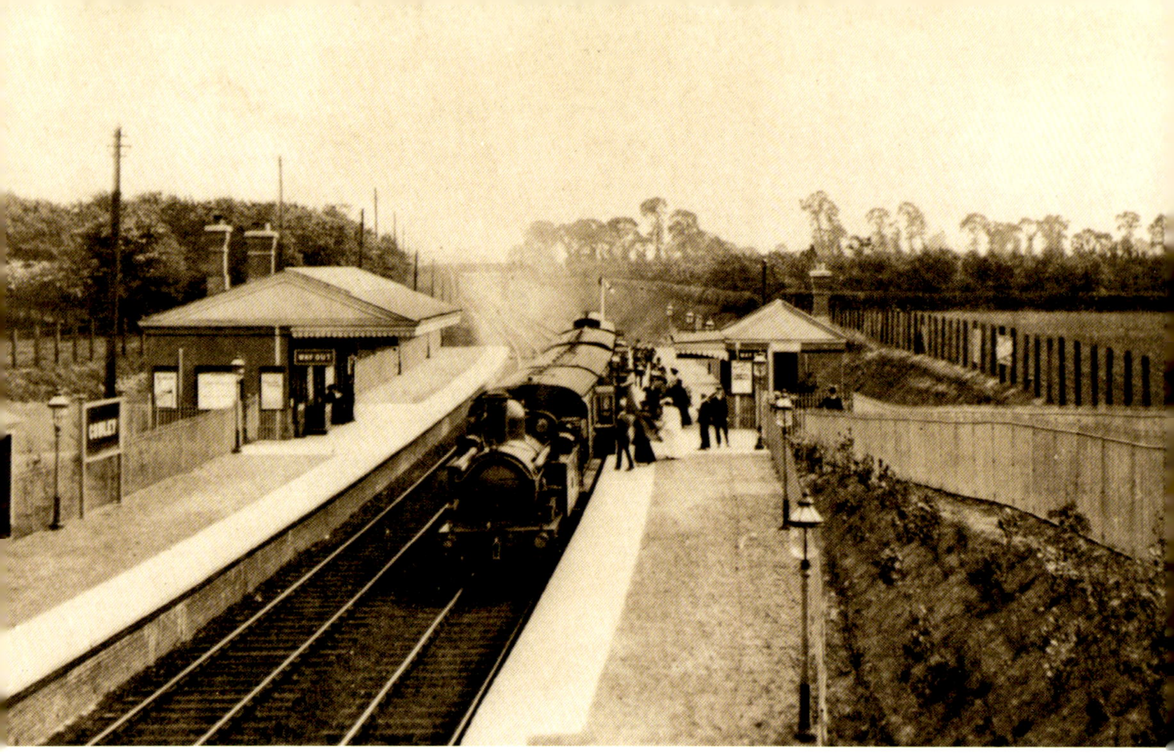

Cowley station in 1905

The GWR branch line from West Drayton to Uxbridge was opened in 1856, but it wasn't until October 1904 that a station at Cowley came into use. The top photograph was taken from the station bridge in Fox Lane, which was re-named Station Road in 1907, and shows a train pausing on its way to Uxbridge. The lower picture shows a train arriving from Uxbridge.

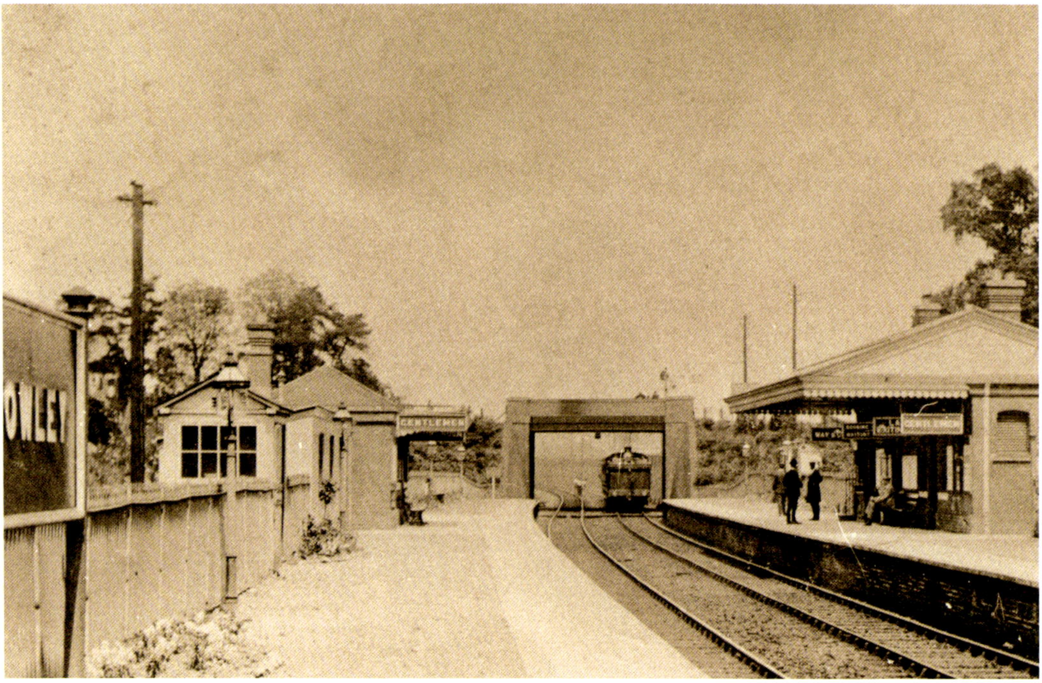

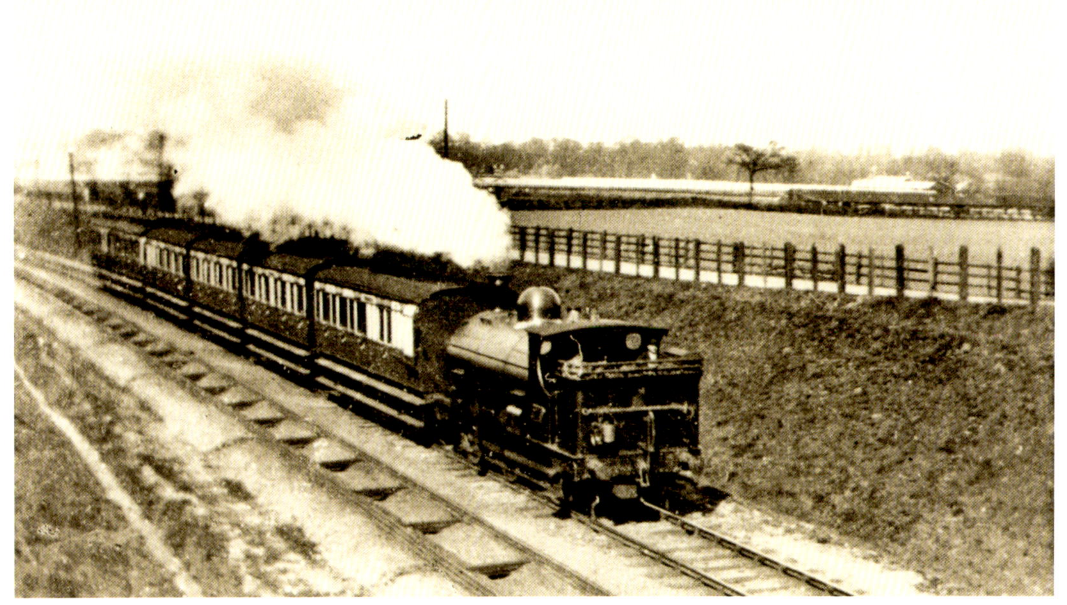

North of the station

Two scenes in the cutting, north of the station bridge. One shows a GWR saddle-tank locomotive pulling a train in 1912. Note the original permanent way on the left, and the open fields in the background. The lower picture was taken in 1960, with houses in Cleveland Road on the left. This section of the cutting, now part of Brunel University, has never been filled in. A scheme to turn it into a railway museum is on hold, but a section of Brunel's broad gauge track has been laid there.

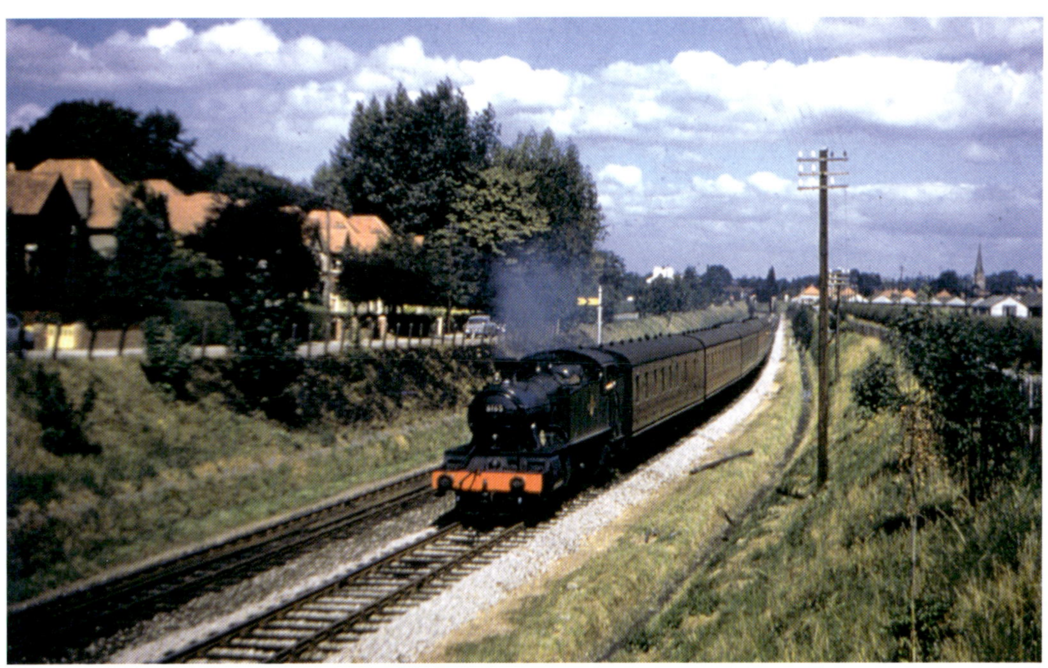

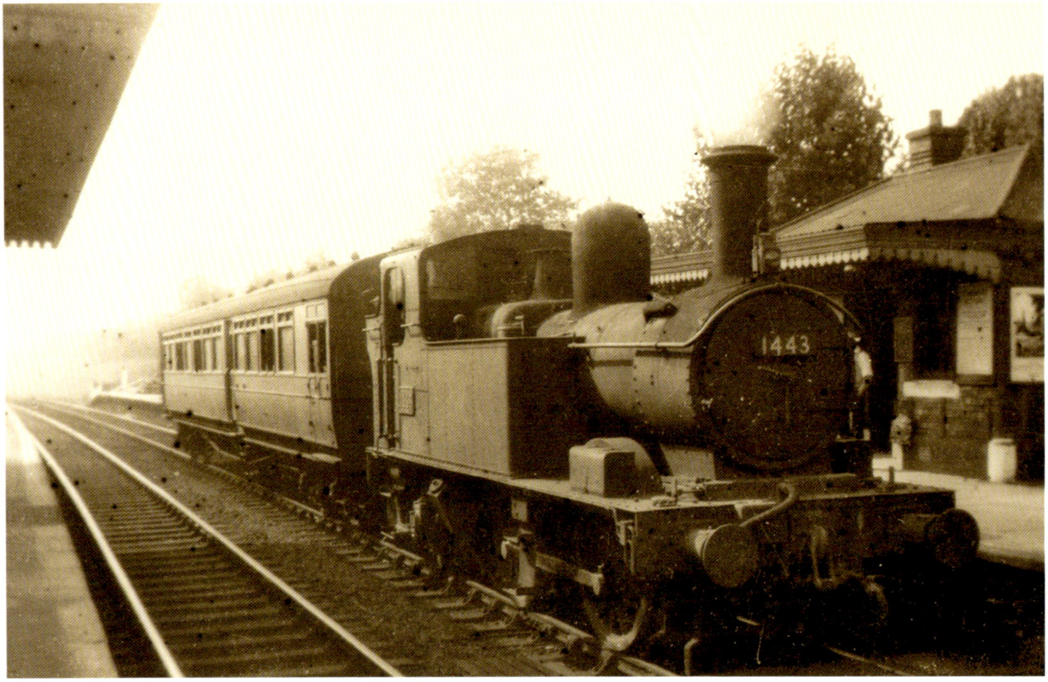

Steam Engines

A 'push-and-pull' train at Cowley station in the 1950s. The majority of the service on the branch line was operated in this way, from a bay platform at West Drayton. (A similar unit ran from there on the Staines branch.) The lower photograph was taken from Cleveland Road.

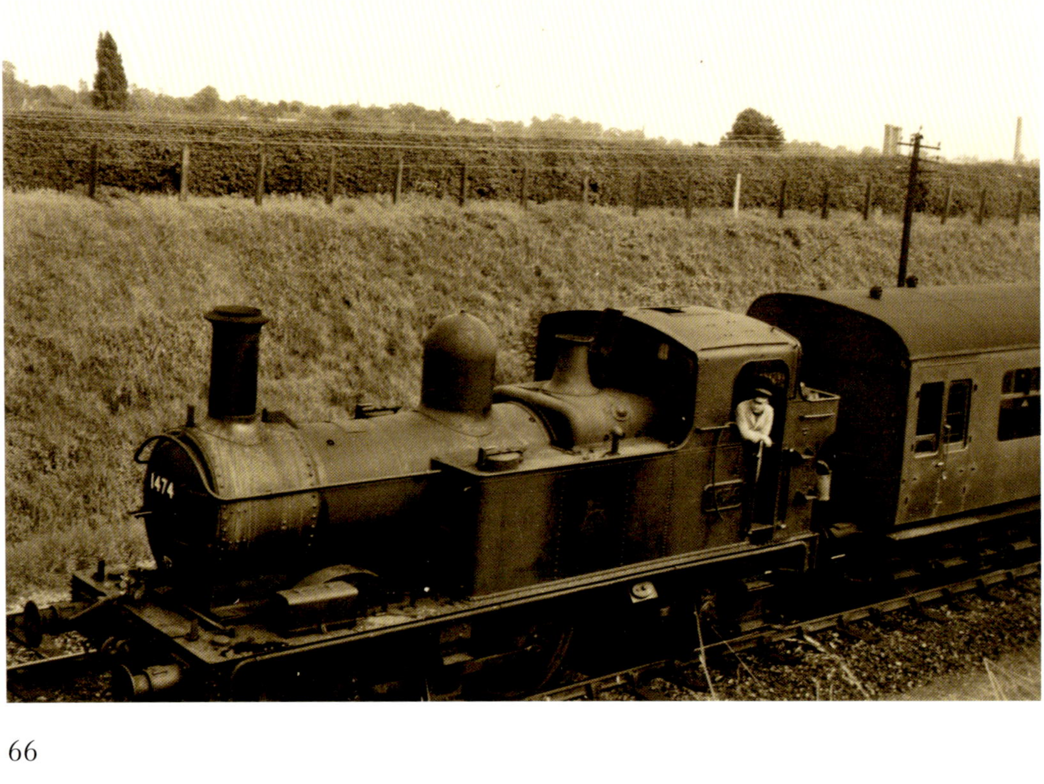

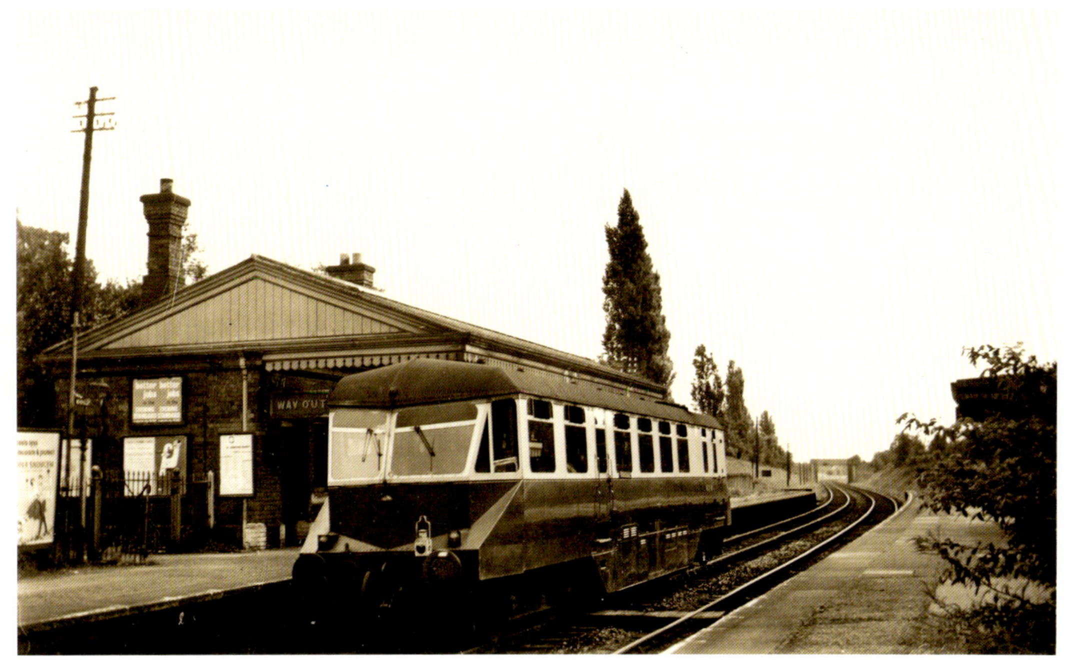

Railcar

In the later years of the line it was sometimes served by diesel railcars. The type shown dates from the 1930s, and was built at Southall by a company called AEC; this one is in the original GWR livery. A later type of diesel unit is shown below. The photograph was taken from the Greenway bridge, with the Cowley Brick public house in the top left-hand corner.

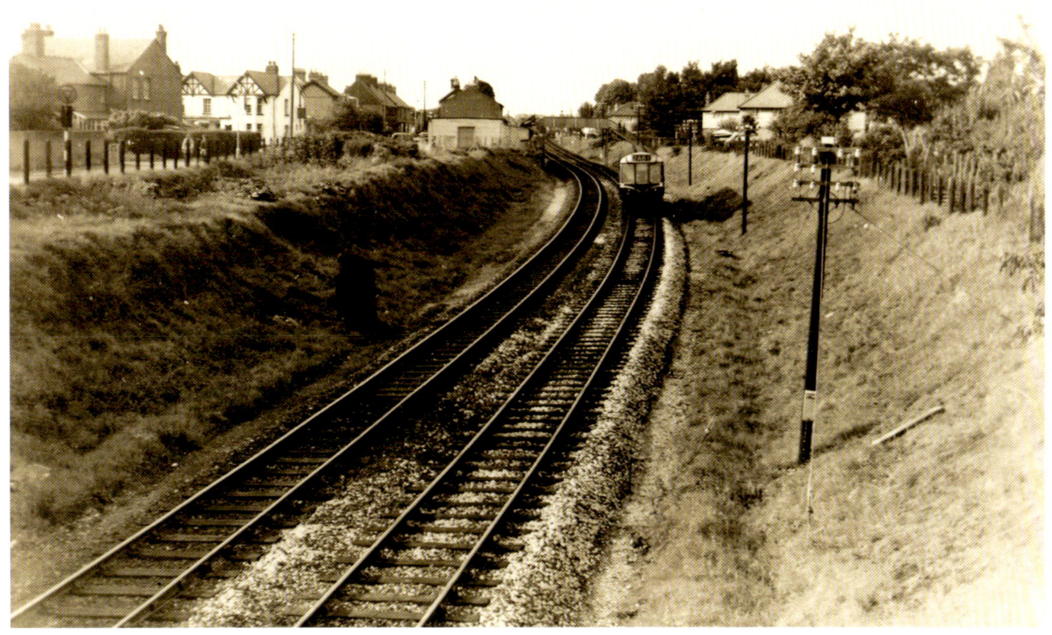

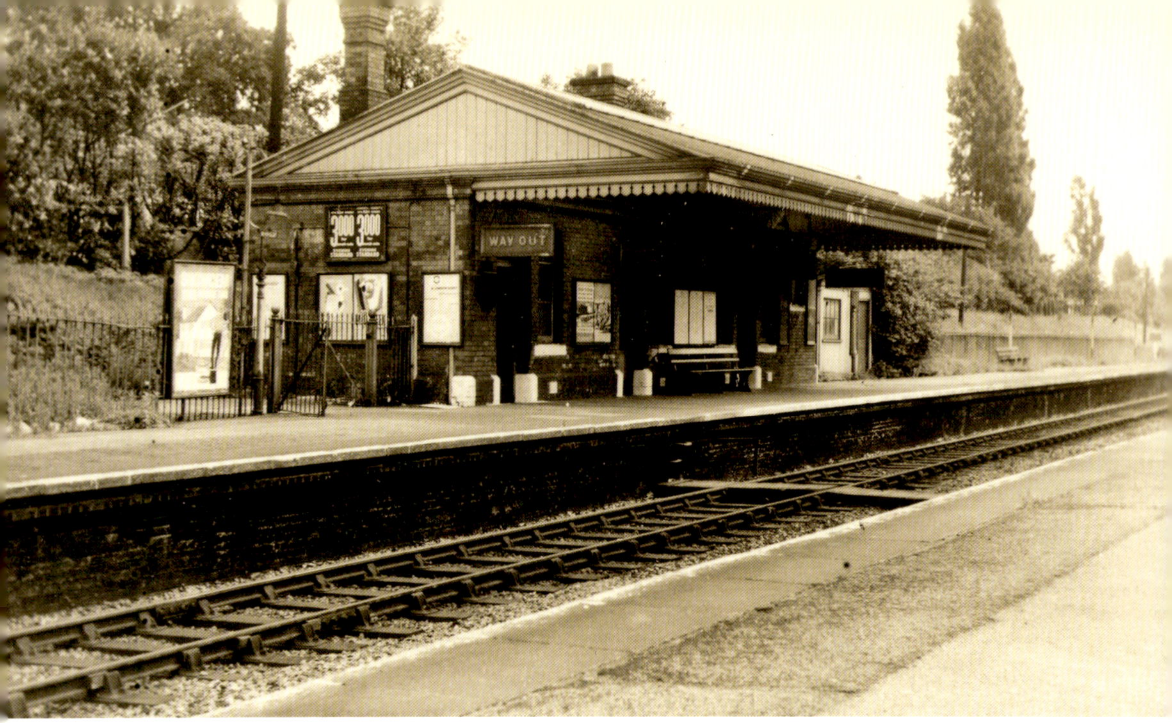

The platforms

The London platform at Cowley was slightly larger and grander than the other one. After all, passengers on this 'up' side would be expected to travel further than those only going to Uxbridge. When the line was first opened in 1904, the fare from Cowley to Uxbridge was just one penny, and the Company therefore installed a slot machine for the benefit of passengers. These photographs were taken in August 1962, when there was already talk of closing the line.

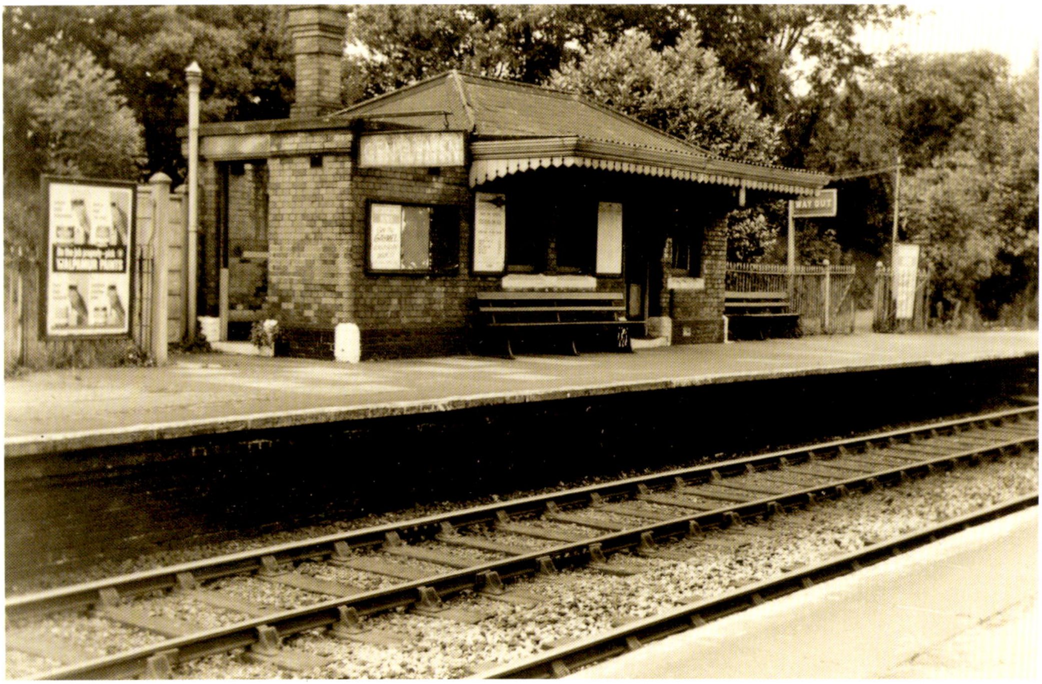

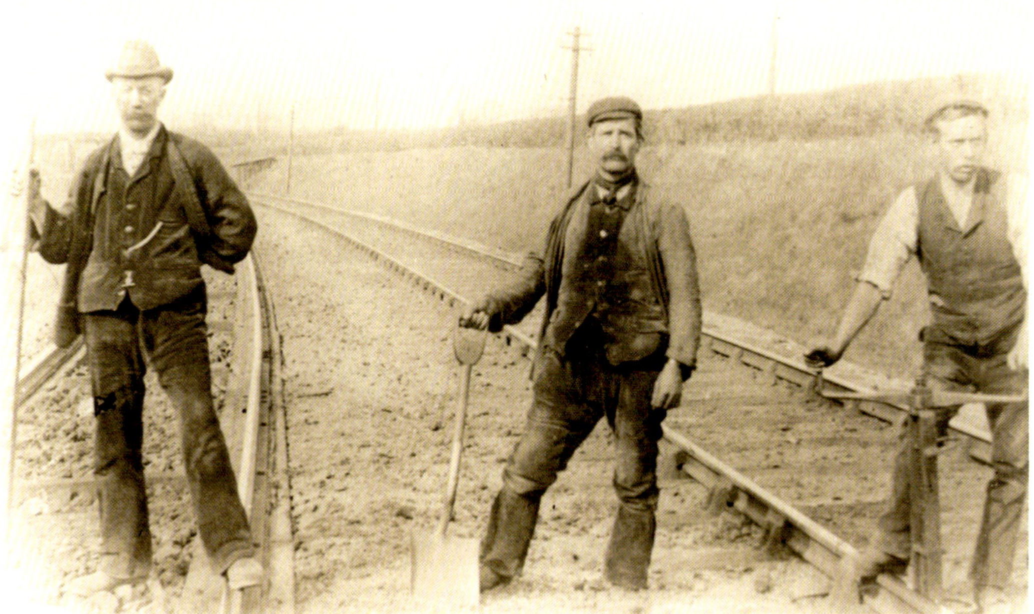

Track Maintenance

These three workmen in the cutting alongside Cleveland Road are checking the alignment and gauge of the rails. On the left is the old-style track, with sleepers under the rails, and occasional lateral braces. In March 1964 a modern tamping machine is seen performing the same task at roughly the same place.

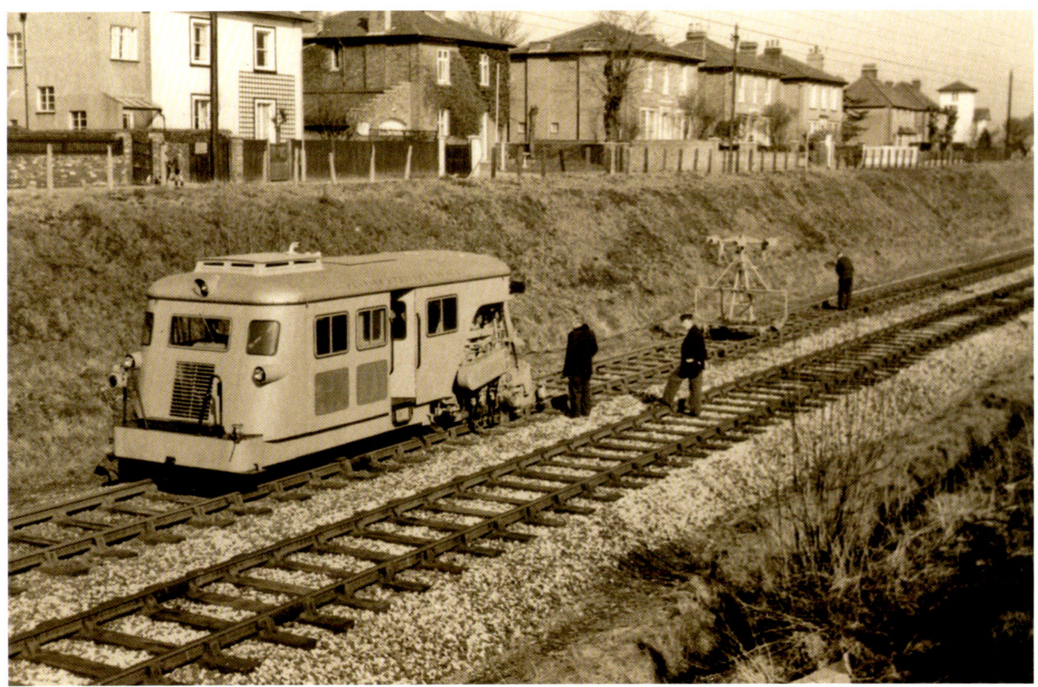

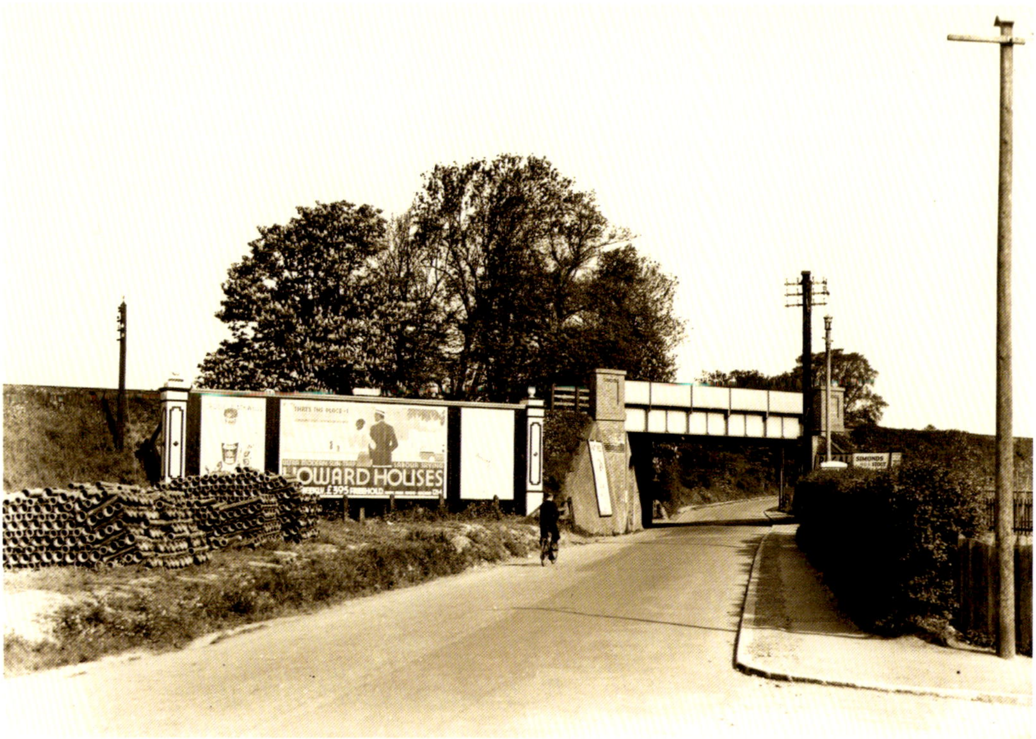

Closure of the Line

The branch line passed over the High Road at Cowley Peachey, where the low bridge prevented double-decker buses running through to Yiewsley. The bridge was eventually raised a few inches in March 1962, but it was hardly worth doing, for the decision had already been made to close the branch line. Like many others it was losing money.

The last train left Cowley in September 1962, and the line closed completely in 1964. The lower picture shows the station just after it shut.

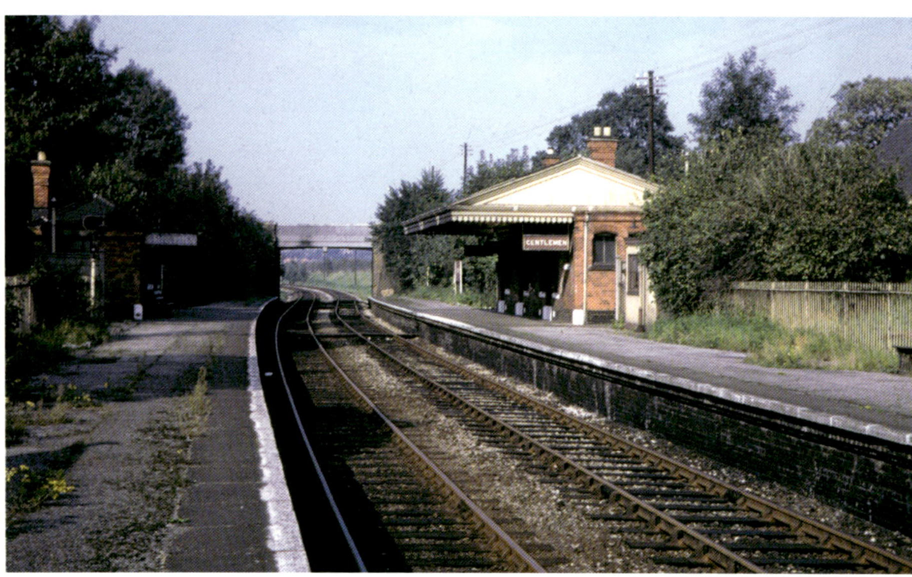

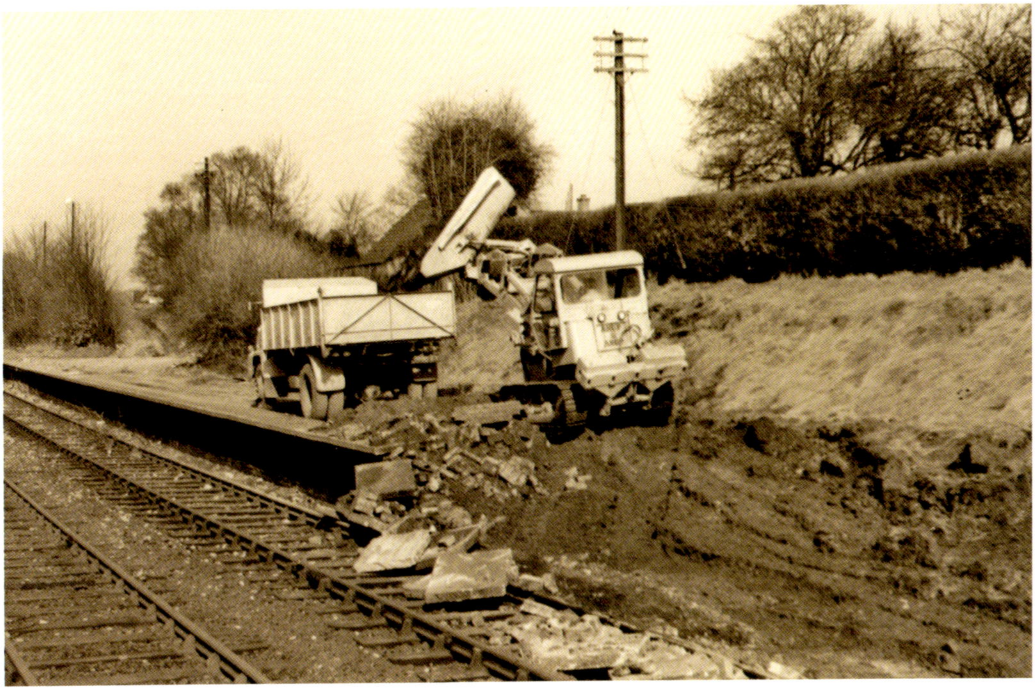

The railway disappears

The demolition of the station in March 1965. The so-called 'Beeching Axe' had fallen, and hardly a trace of the station survived. Below we see the track being cleared away in May 1965. Just one year after this the first students arrived at the nearby Brunel University - potentially thousands of passengers. It was too late. The railway had gone.

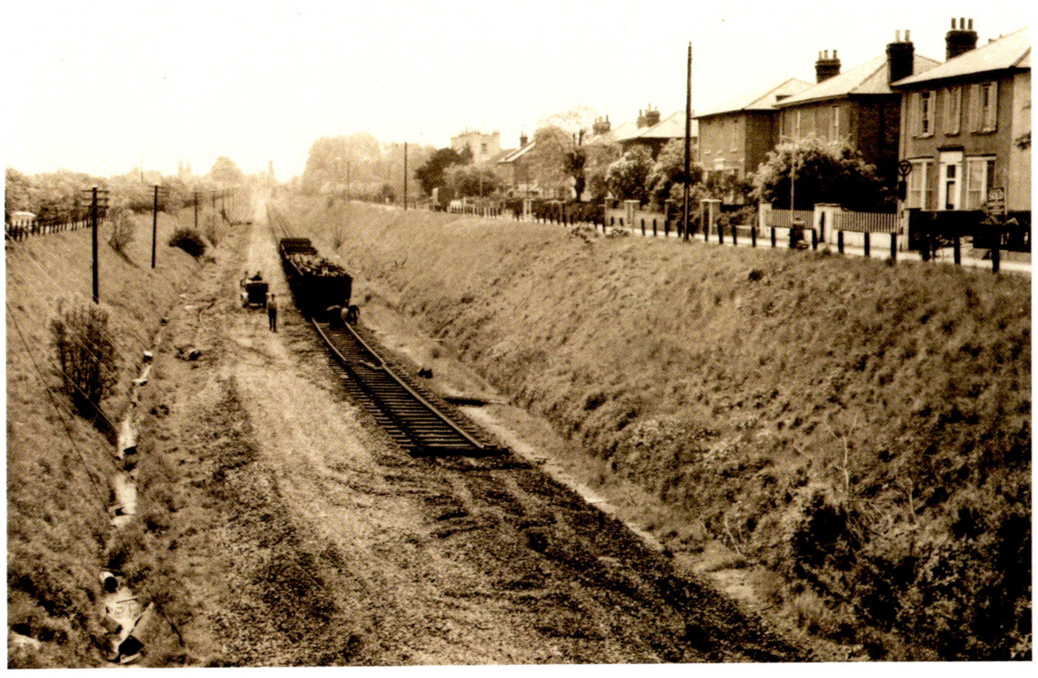

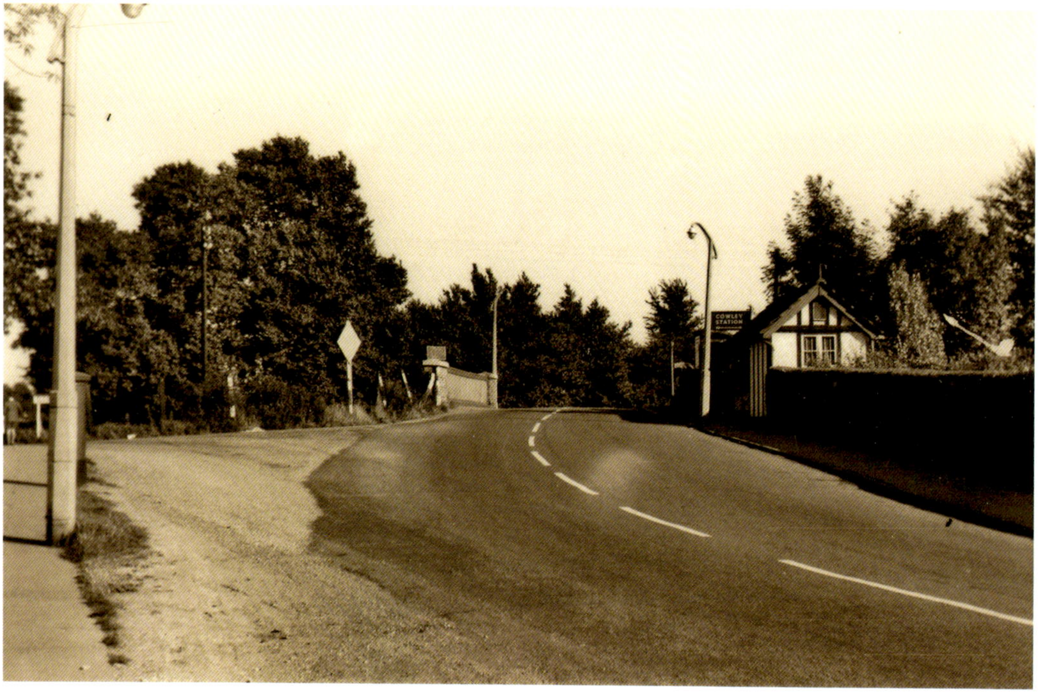

Station bridge

The bridge in 1962. On the right is the kiosk where for years Mr and Mrs Newbury sold cigarettes and sweets to the passengers. Since the closure of the line the little kiosk has gone, and newcomers to the district probably think that the bump in the road is a traffic-calming measure.

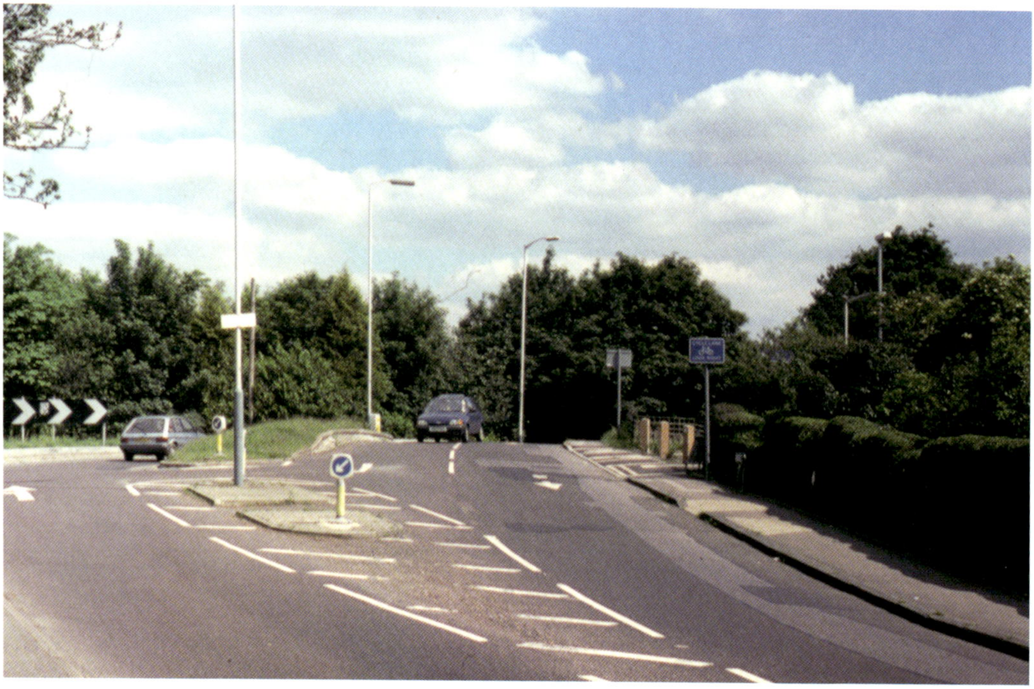

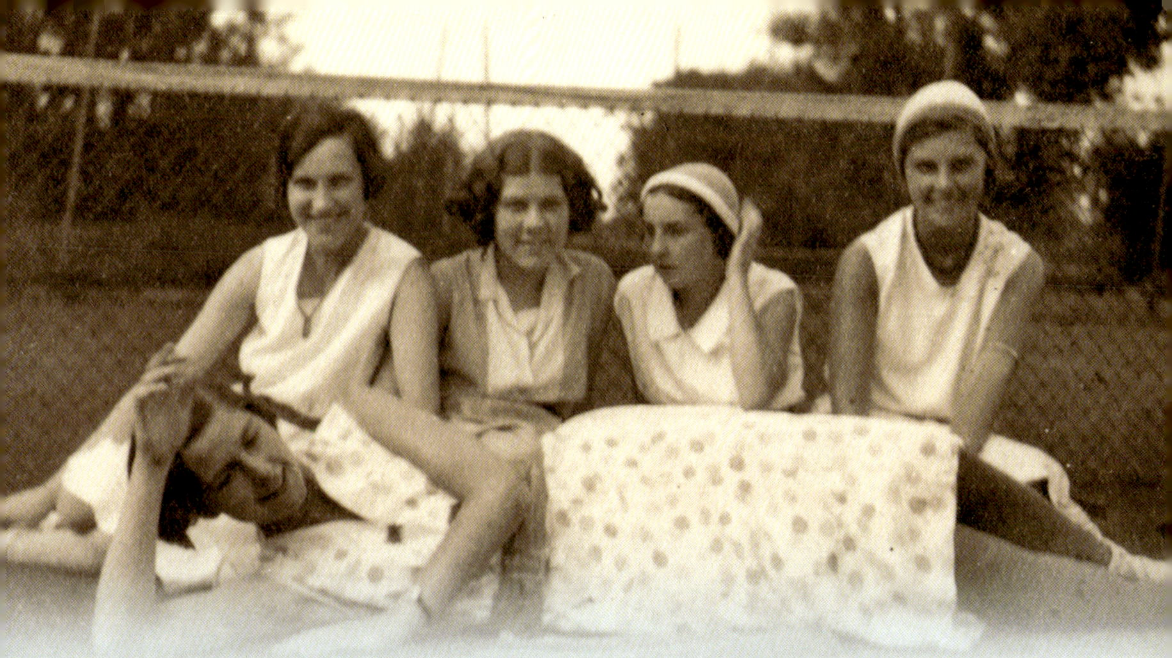

CHAPTER 8

Sport and Leisure

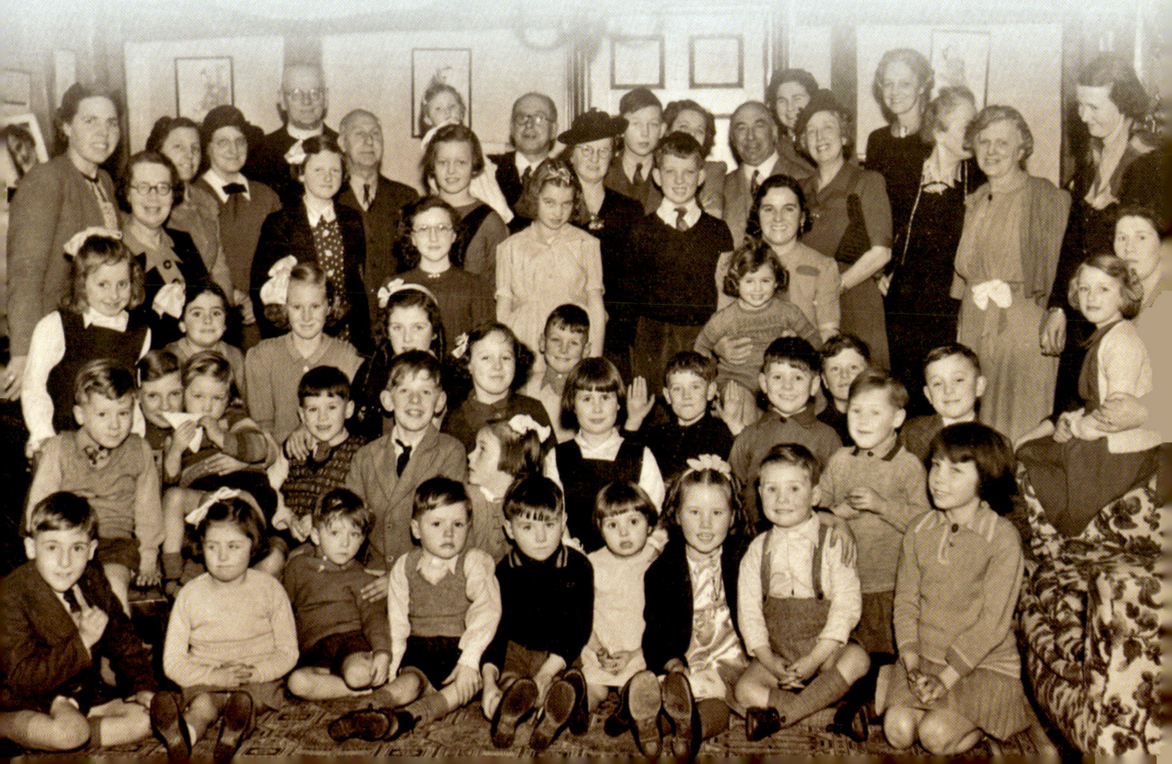

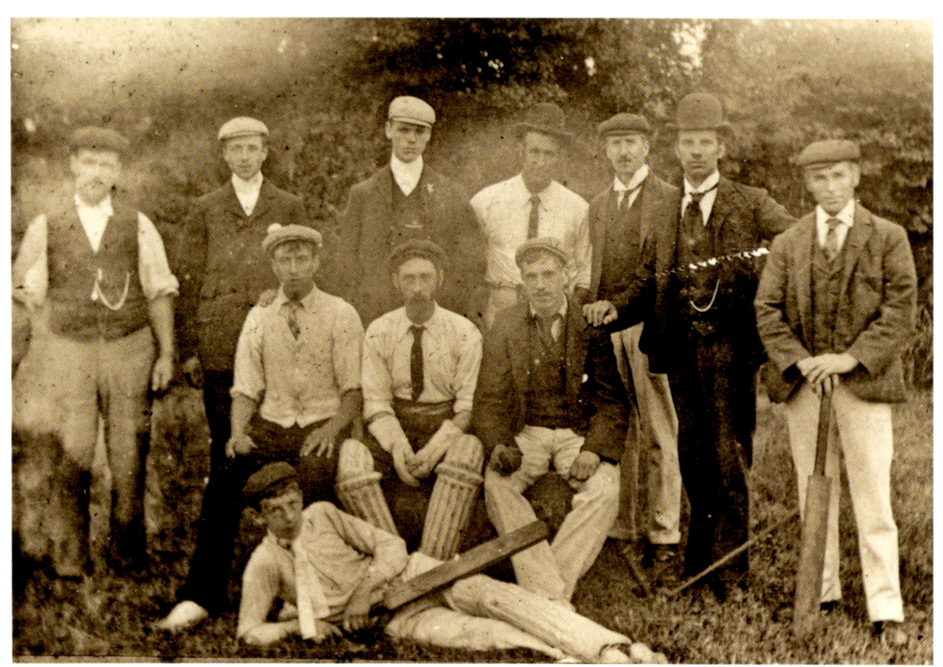

Cricket and football

The Lowe and Shawyer cricket team in the early twentieth century. As the workforce at the nursery increased, so did the potential number of players. By the 1930s the club had moved to a ground off Park Road on the Hillingdon House Farm estate. Below are members of the Cowley Football Club in 1908, proudly displaying the cup they had won as winners of the Uxbridge Junior League. Mr W. S. Try is seated on the extreme left.

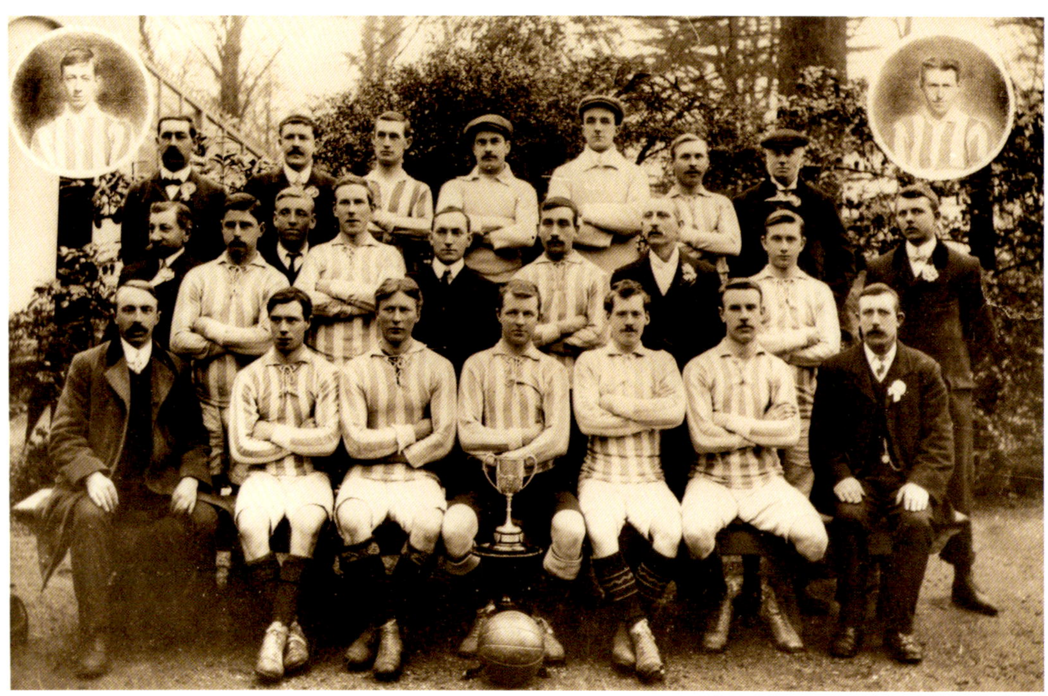

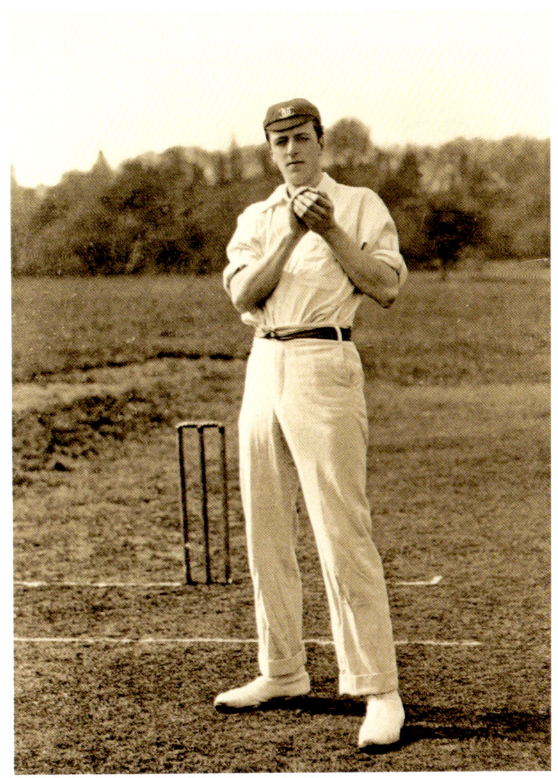

Bernard Bosanquet
The Middlesex and England cricketer Bernard Bosanquet (1877-1936) lived with his parents at Cowley Cottage in the early twentieth century. His great claim to fame was the 'invention' of the googly – an off-break bowled with a leg-break action. He worked this out with a tennis ball on his dining room table – possibly in Cowley. (Photo courtesy MCC Library). Cowley Cottage was later occupied by Air Vice Marshal Sir Cecil Bouchier (1895-1979), who prepared the Allied air plan for D-Day. The house was demolished about 1960.

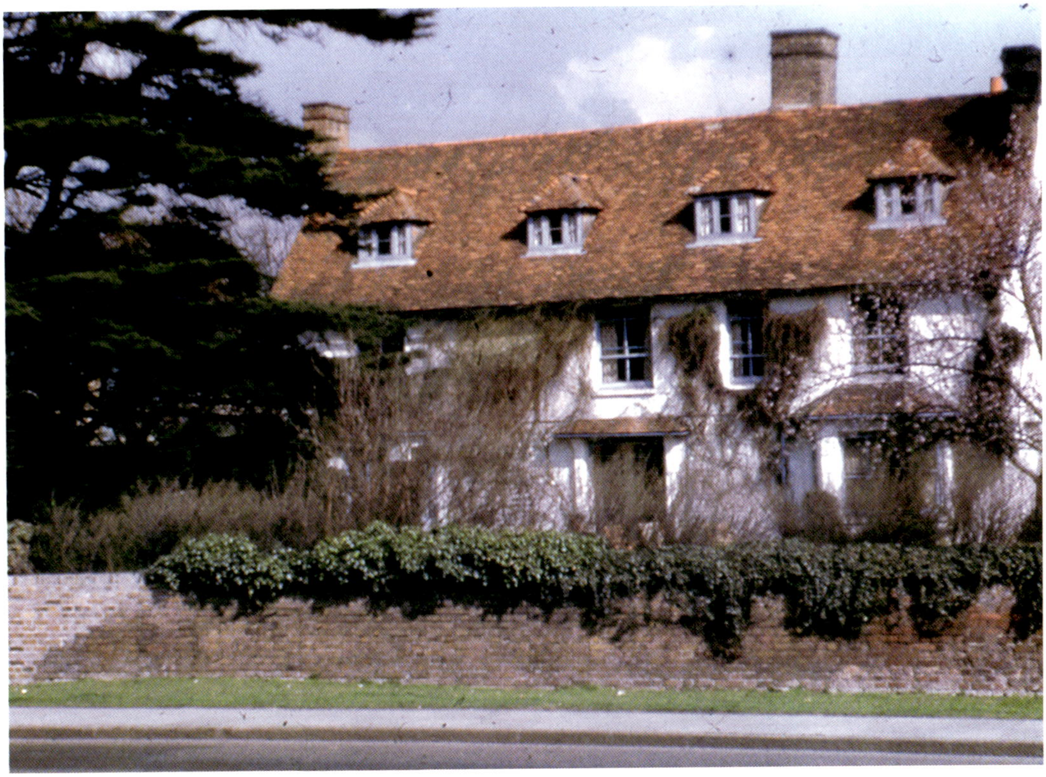

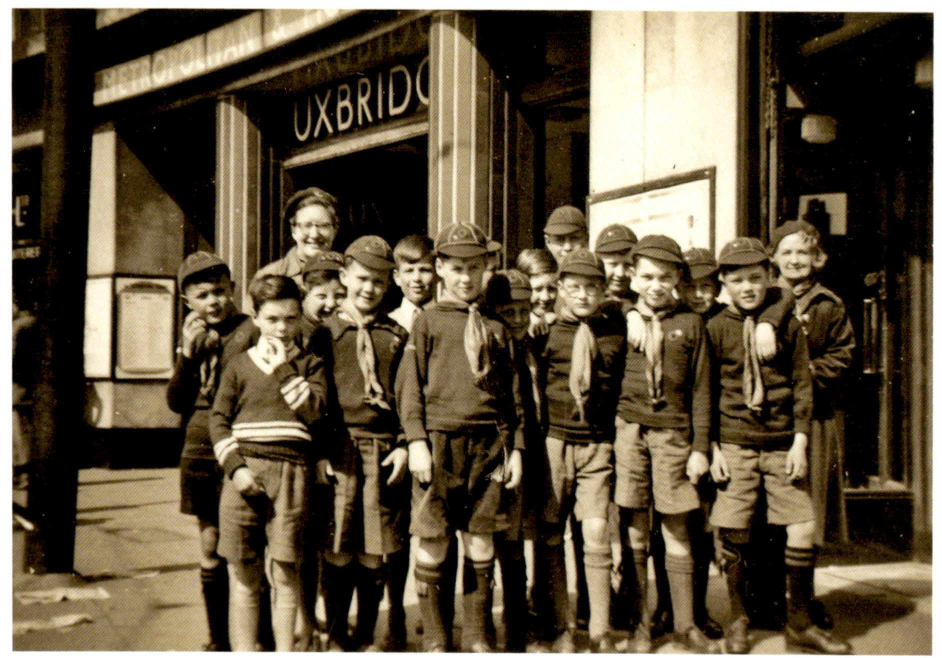

Young people

The post-war years were a peak period for community life. A cub pack was formed in Cowley in 1938, and continued for some time after the war. Here these junior Scouts are outside Uxbridge underground station in 1950 with their leader, Beryl Wilkins. A Youth Club also flourished at this time, and performed an annual pantomime in the parish hall. Their 1950 show was *Mother Goose*, produced by Peter Nutchey, and starring Shirley Nickolay, Beryl Goodchild and Donald Wells.

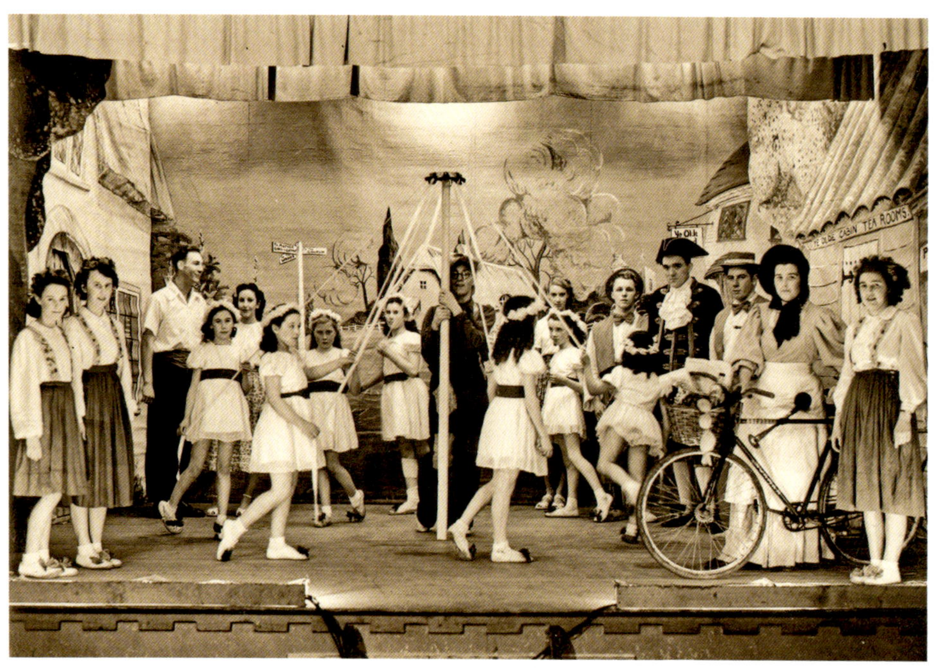

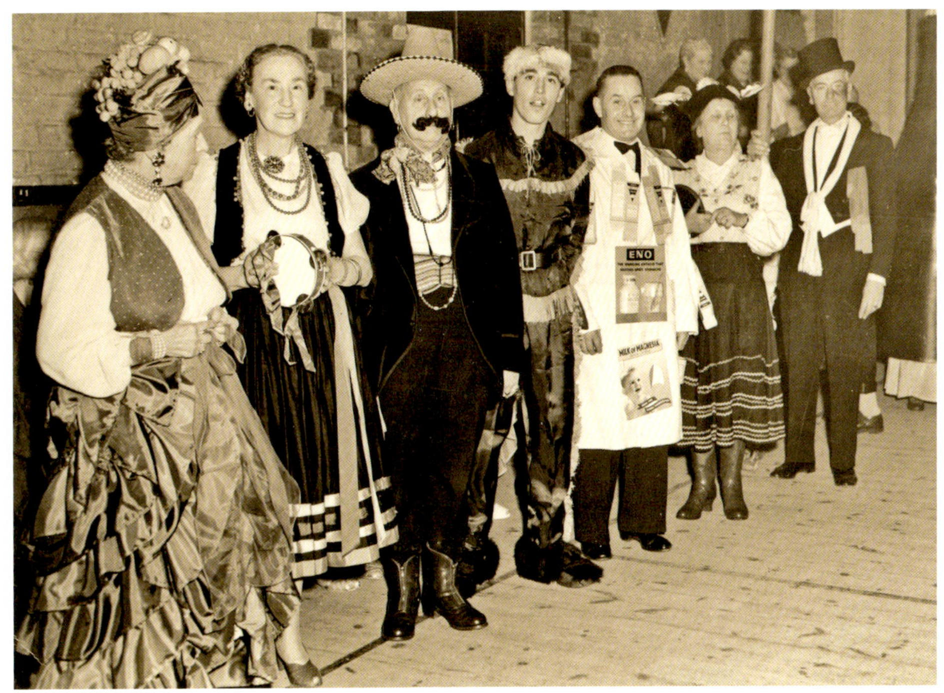

Dance and drama

An Olde Tyme Dance Club was very popular at this period, and here members are pictured at a fancy dress evening. Third from left is Cllr W. E. Black, a prominent member and sometime chairman of Uxbridge Council. *Six Wives of Calais* was the title of a play produced by the Women's Institute in November 1948. Back row (l to r): Mrs Conway, Mrs Johnston, Mrs Bird, Mrs Steele. Front: Mrs Vaisey, Mrs Pritchard, Mrs Davies, Mrs Bainton.

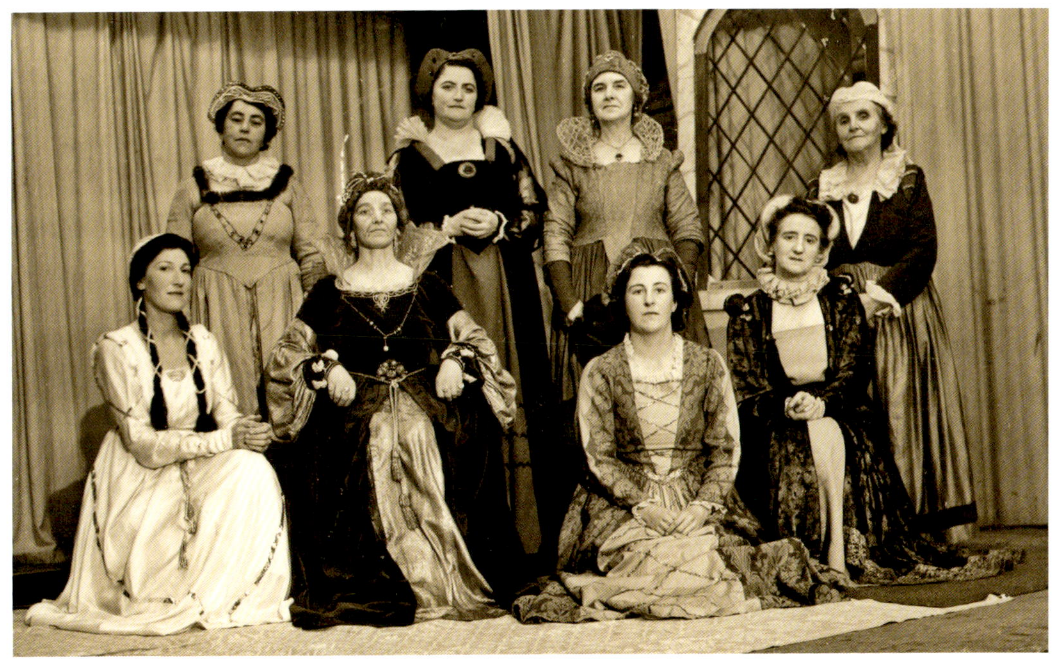

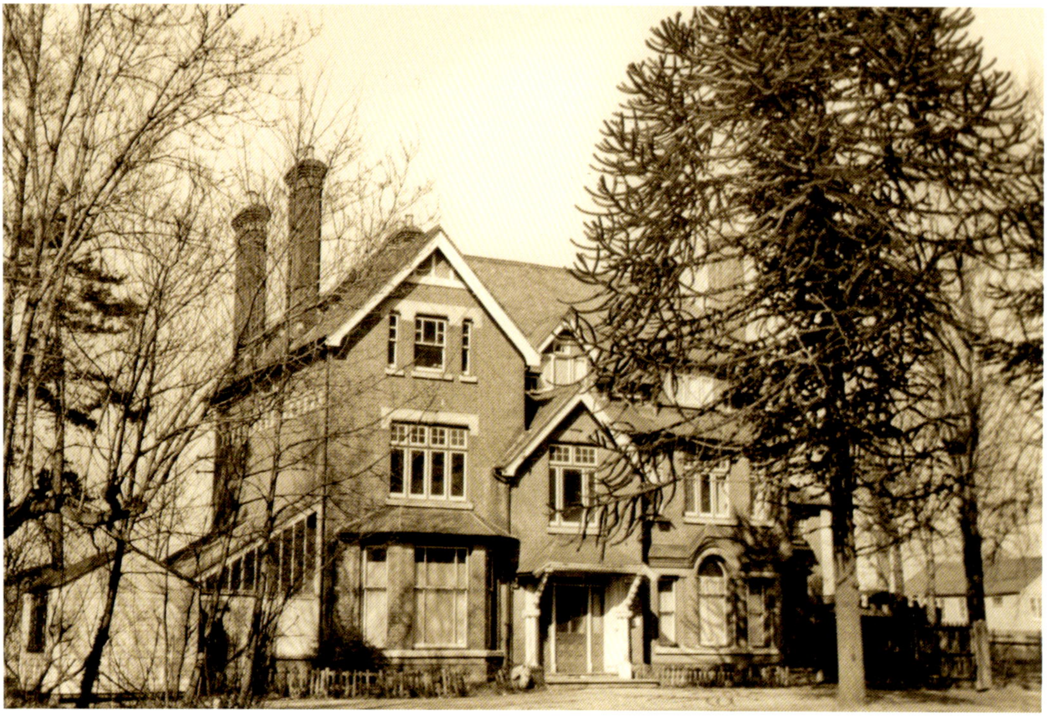

Uxbridge Football Club

In 1948 a Victorian house in Cleveland Road called 'Honeycroft' was purchased for Uxbridge F.C. Founded in 1871, the club had never had a permanent home before. The house now became their headquarters, and a pitch was laid out on the former garden behind. The owners, the Cleveland Investment Company, eventually asked the Club to leave, and in 1972 they were fortunate to find a vacant ground at Yiewsley. They are still there today. 'Honeycroft' was replaced by the Ratcliffe Close housing development.

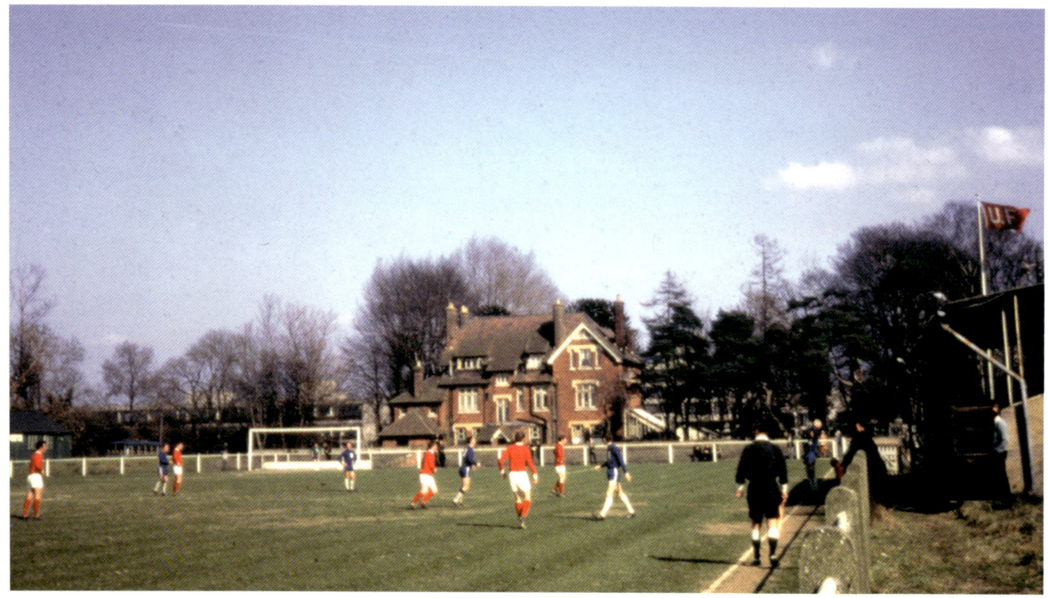

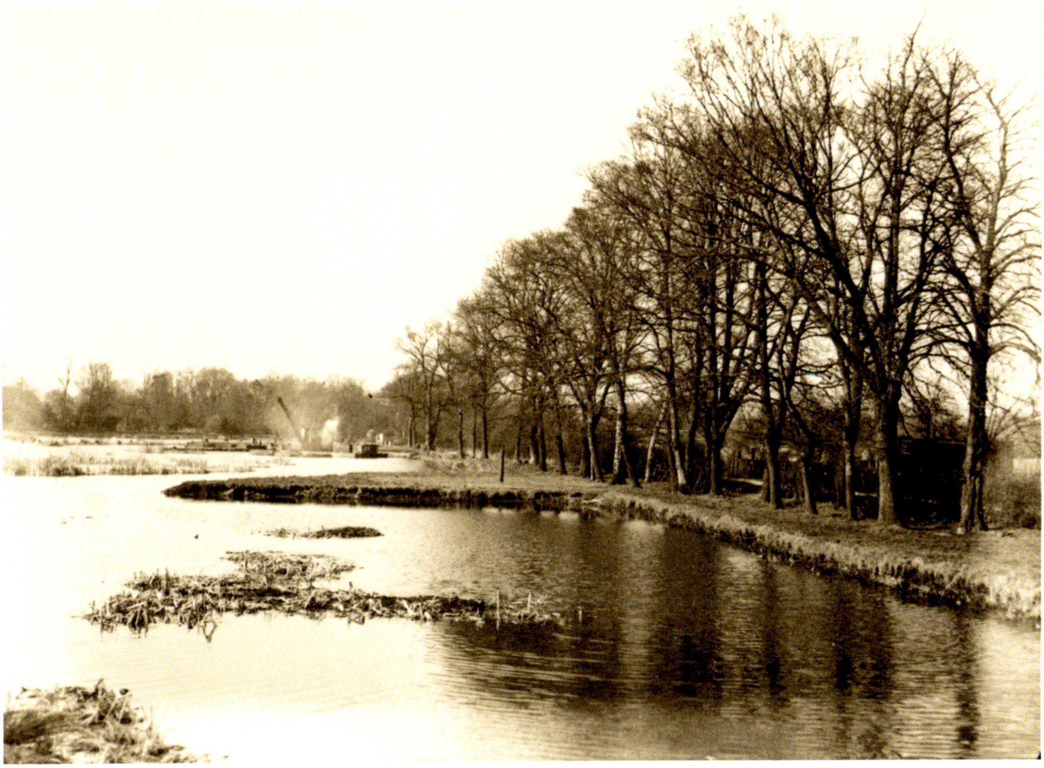

Little Britain

The lake at Cowley Peachey was formed by the extraction of brick-earth and gravel, and the photograph, taken in April 1934, shows work in progress in the distance. The name derives from the fact that the lake is roughly shaped like a map of Britain. Today the lake is a pleasant area for anglers, bird-watchers and ramblers.

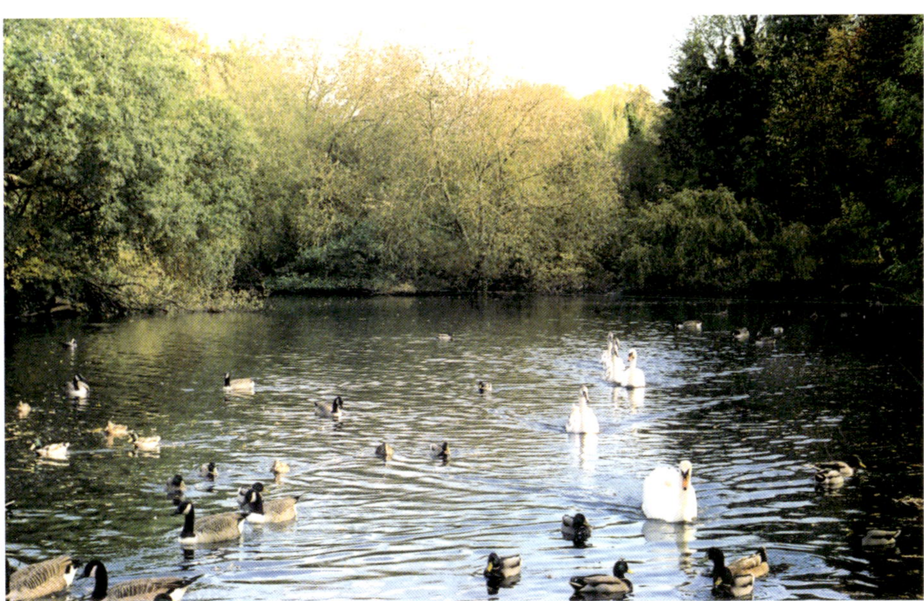

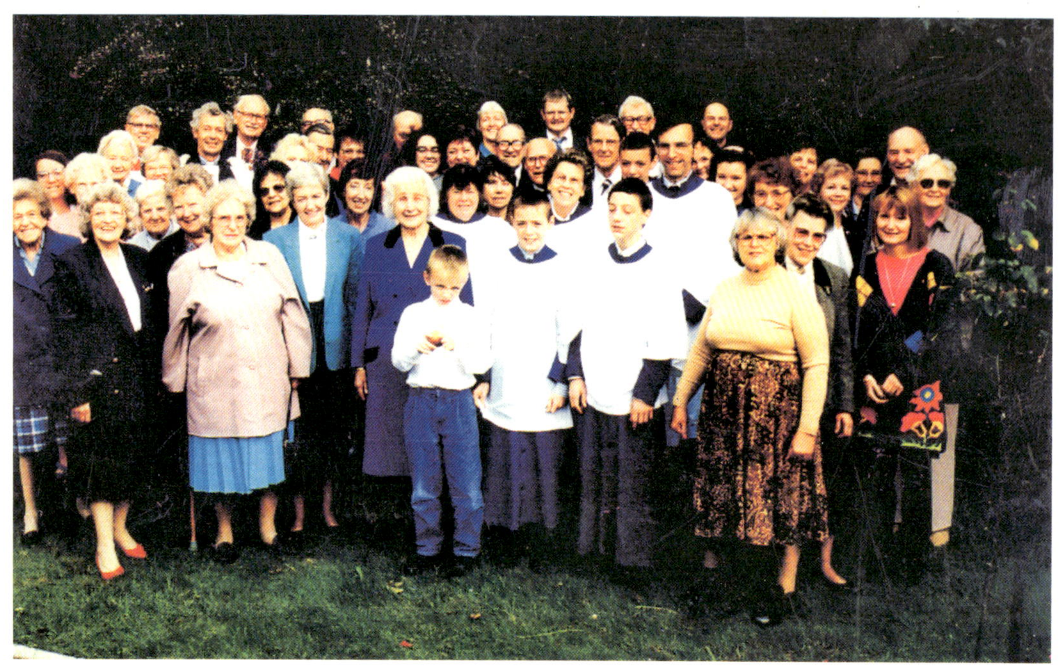

Sacred and secular

Members of the church congregation in 1992. In recent years church members have been running a very successful mid-week meeting called 'The young at heart'.

Cowley Women's Institute, formed in April 1919, is the second oldest branch in the county. Members are seen celebrating their ninetieth birthday in the picture below.

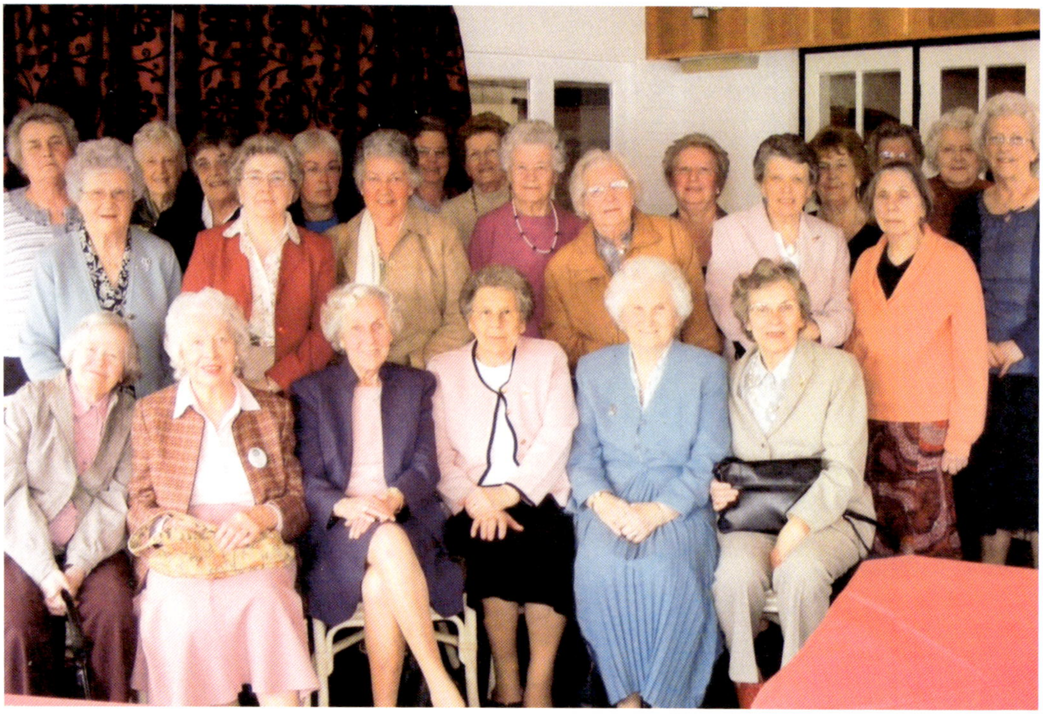

610 Light Anti-Aircraft Regt. R.A. (T.A.)

Tel. : Uxbridge 2575/6.

Buses 222, 224 and 458 from Uxbridge pass the door.

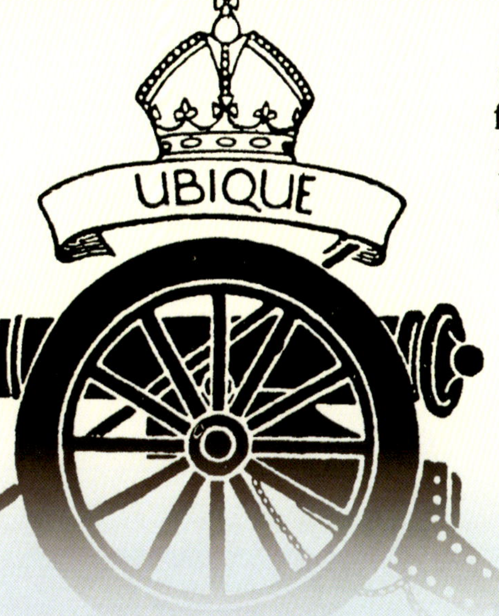

Nearest Rly. Stn. : G.W.R. Cowley—from Paddington. L.P.T.B. Uxbridge (Met. and Piccadilly).

CHAPTER 9
World War II

A Garden Party, P.T. & Dancing Display

to be held at

The Old Vine Cottage, Cowley

on Wednesday, 27th June, 1945, at 7.30 p.m.

(if wet, in The Church Room)

Refreshments. *R.S.V.P.*

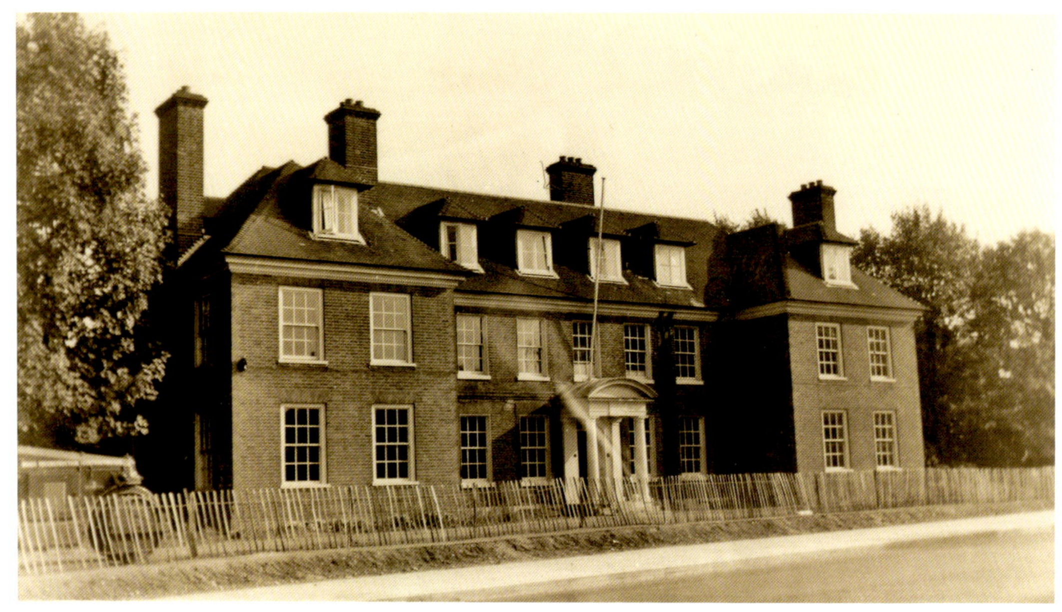

Defence

Cowley Place in the High Street, was taken over, just before the war, as a recruitment and training centre for the Territorial Army. It was an Anti-Aircraft unit, which means that some of the men were deployed on Chandlers Hill at Iver Heath, where the main AA gun unit was based during the war. Cowley Place was cleared away in 1966, and replaced by an Air Ministry housing estate. As invasion threatened in 1940, concrete pill-boxes were hastily installed at strategic places. One of these, now very overgrown, can still be seen on the Slough arm of the local canal.

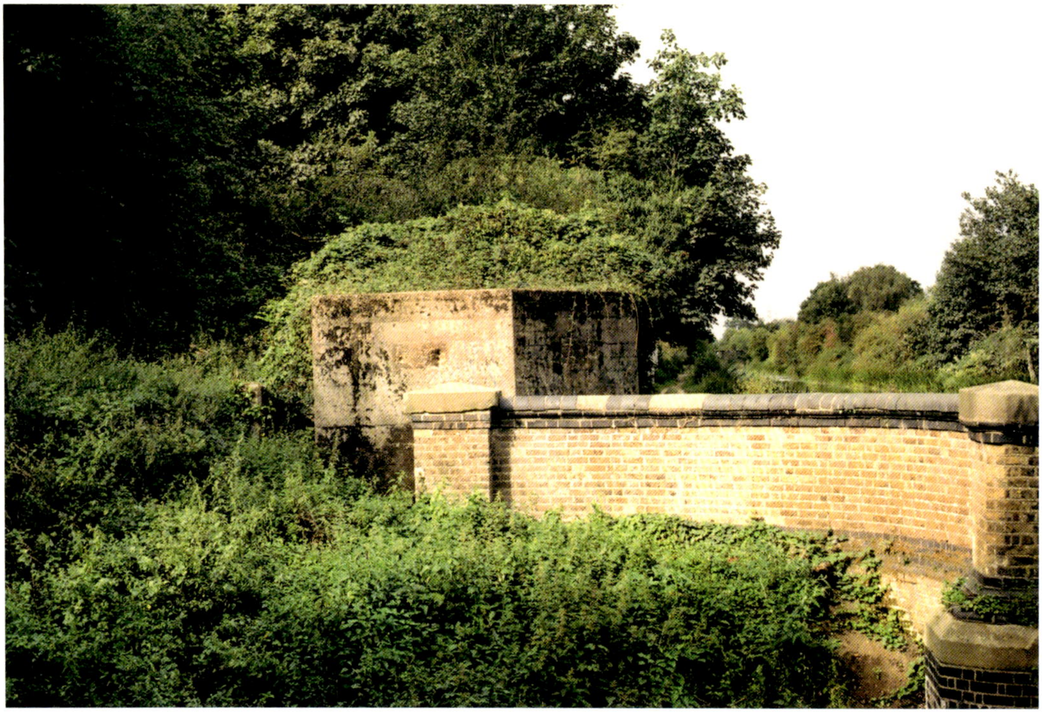

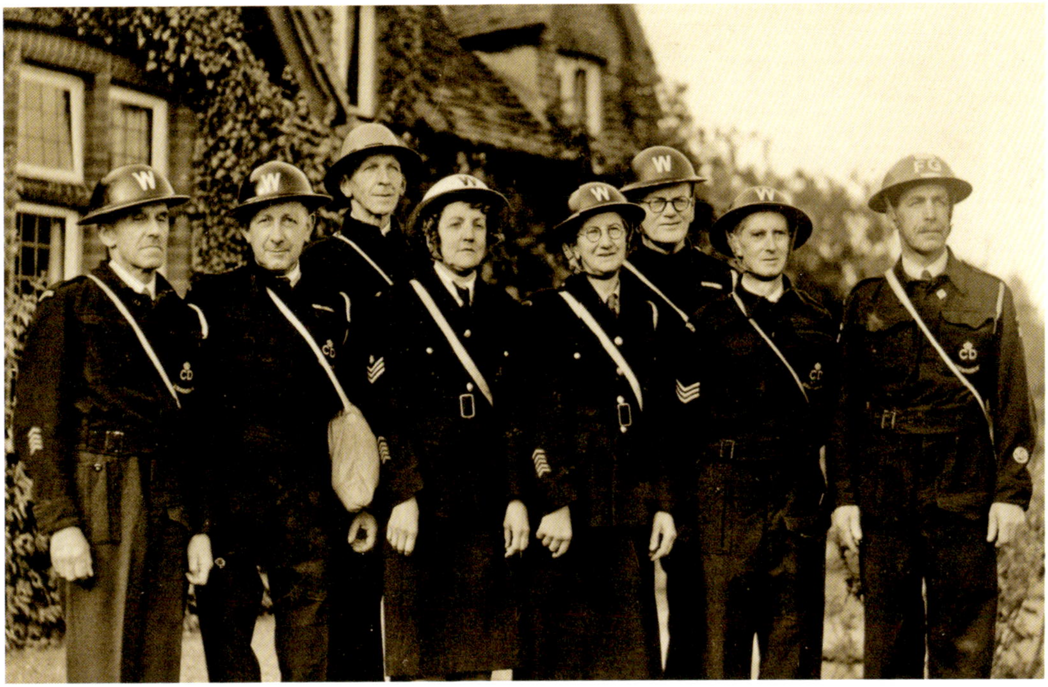

Air Raid Precautions

Air raid wardens were recruited even before war was declared, and this group are: Mr Gore, Mr Brown, Mr Yates, Mrs Cowland, Miss Barbey, Revd Boylette Stewart, Mr Melville and Mr Mosley. Many of W. S. Try's men were in the ARP, and are shown here in the garden of Old Vine Cottage. Mr Try is on the left. Some were sent to London to work on repairing bomb-damaged properties.

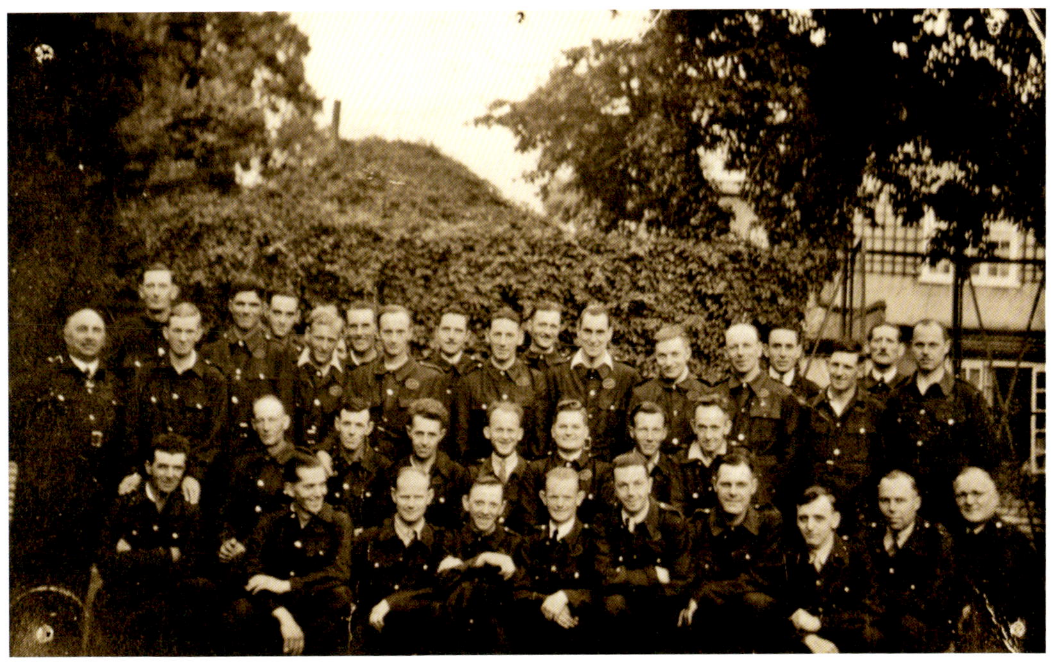

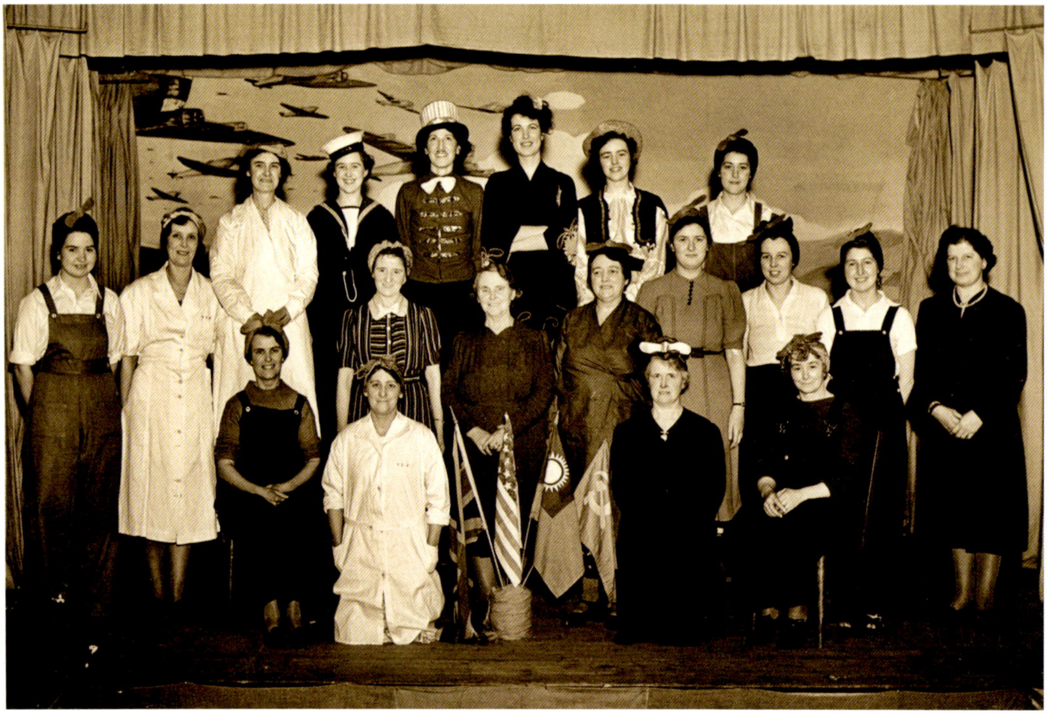

Wartime conditions

The Women's Institute regularly put on shows in wartime. In March 1943 three hundred people packed into the church hall to see a show during 'Wings for Victory' week – a National Savings campaign. Workers at the Lowe and Shawyer nursery went over to food production. By 1942 well over a thousand tons of tomatoes were being grown, together with onions, sugar beet and lettuces.

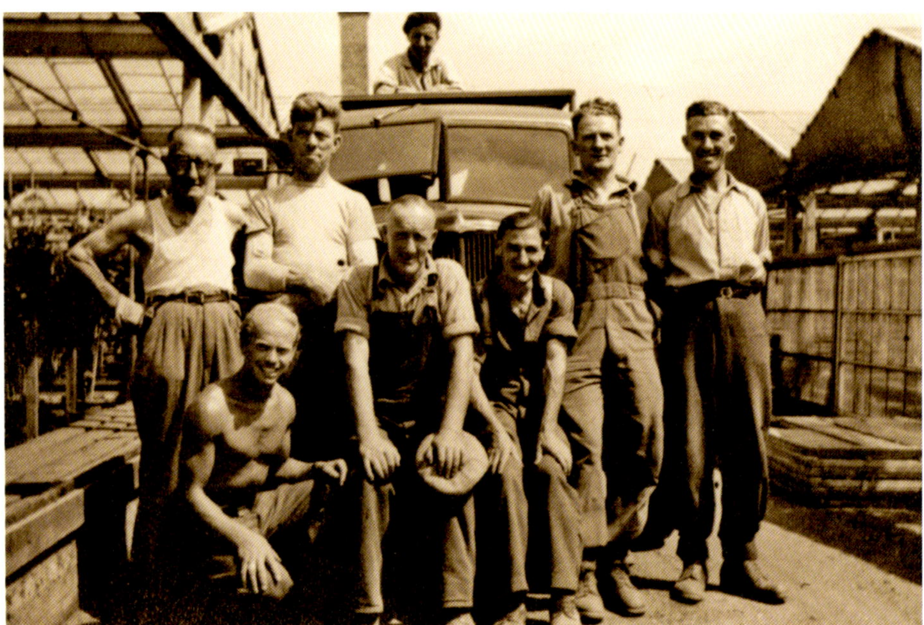

Tank track

The Berlin-born engineer Kurt Joachim Sommerfeld escaped to England in 1938, and moved into The Cedars in the High Street.

He invented a portable metal track that could be rolled out over soft sand, and would bear the weight of heavy military vehicles. Sommerfeld was assisted in this project by Try's workforce, and it was manufactured in a factory in Iver Lane. The newspaper picture shows King George VI and Field Marshal Montgomery, standing on some Sommerfeld track on a Normandy beach.

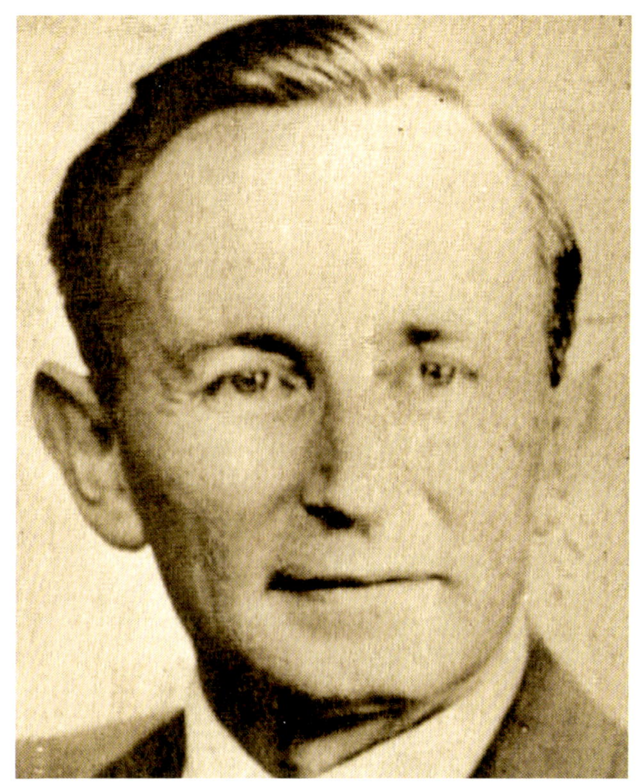

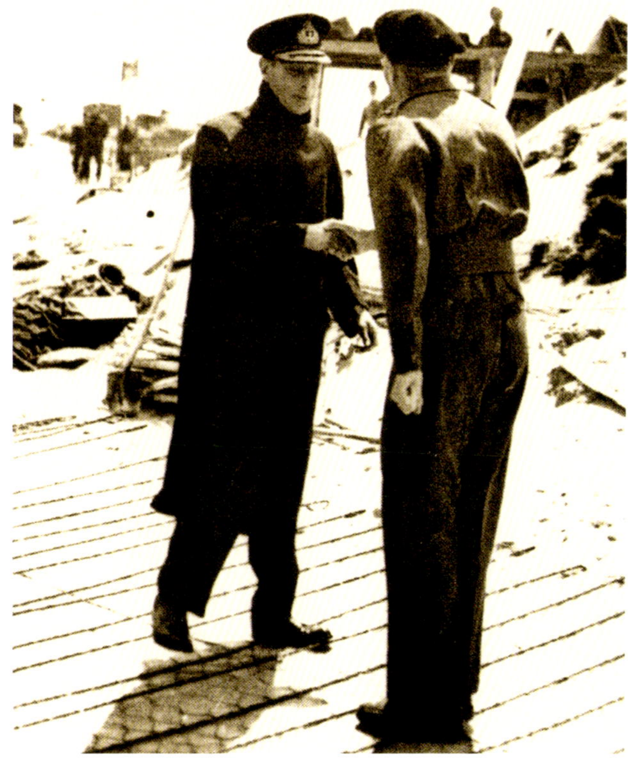

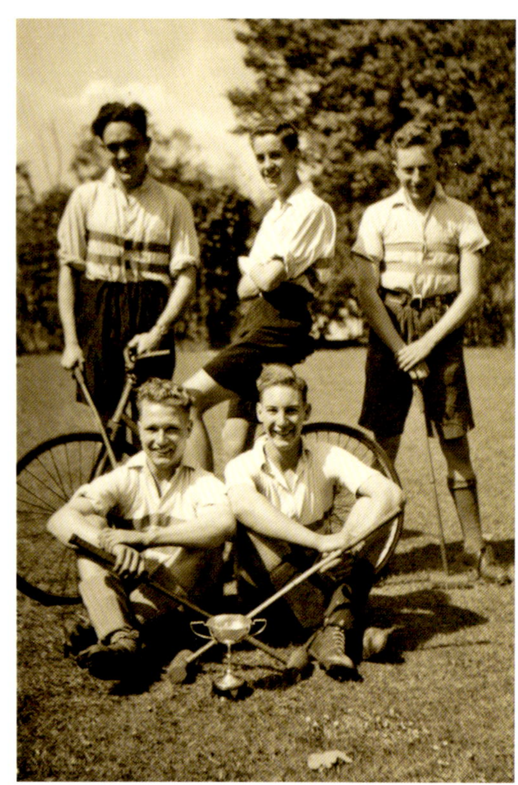

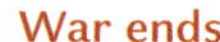

War ends

Bicycle polo gained popularity in the war years, and here are the Cowley Youth Club team celebrating their victory in the League Division II cup. They are (clockwise from top left) Peter Nutchey, ?, Ron Edlin, Gerald Bird, Dennis Snapes.

The street party in Clammas Way was held to celebrate Victory in Europe in May 1945. Food and drink were conjured up from somewhere, despite rationing.

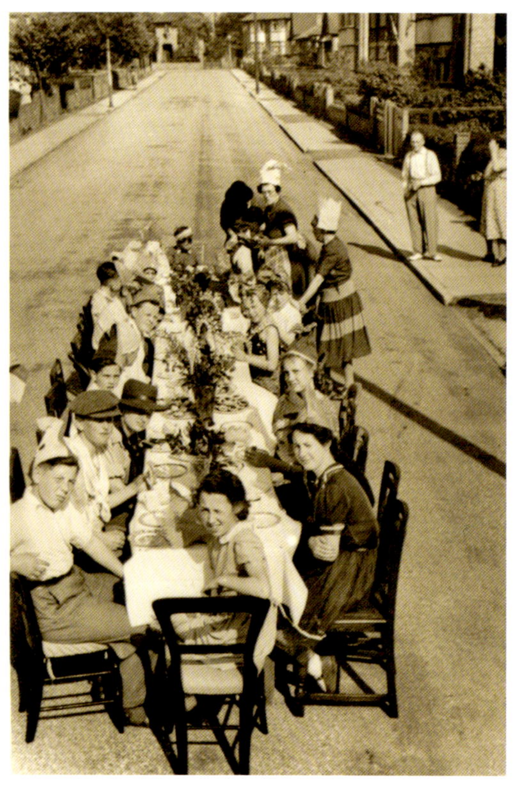

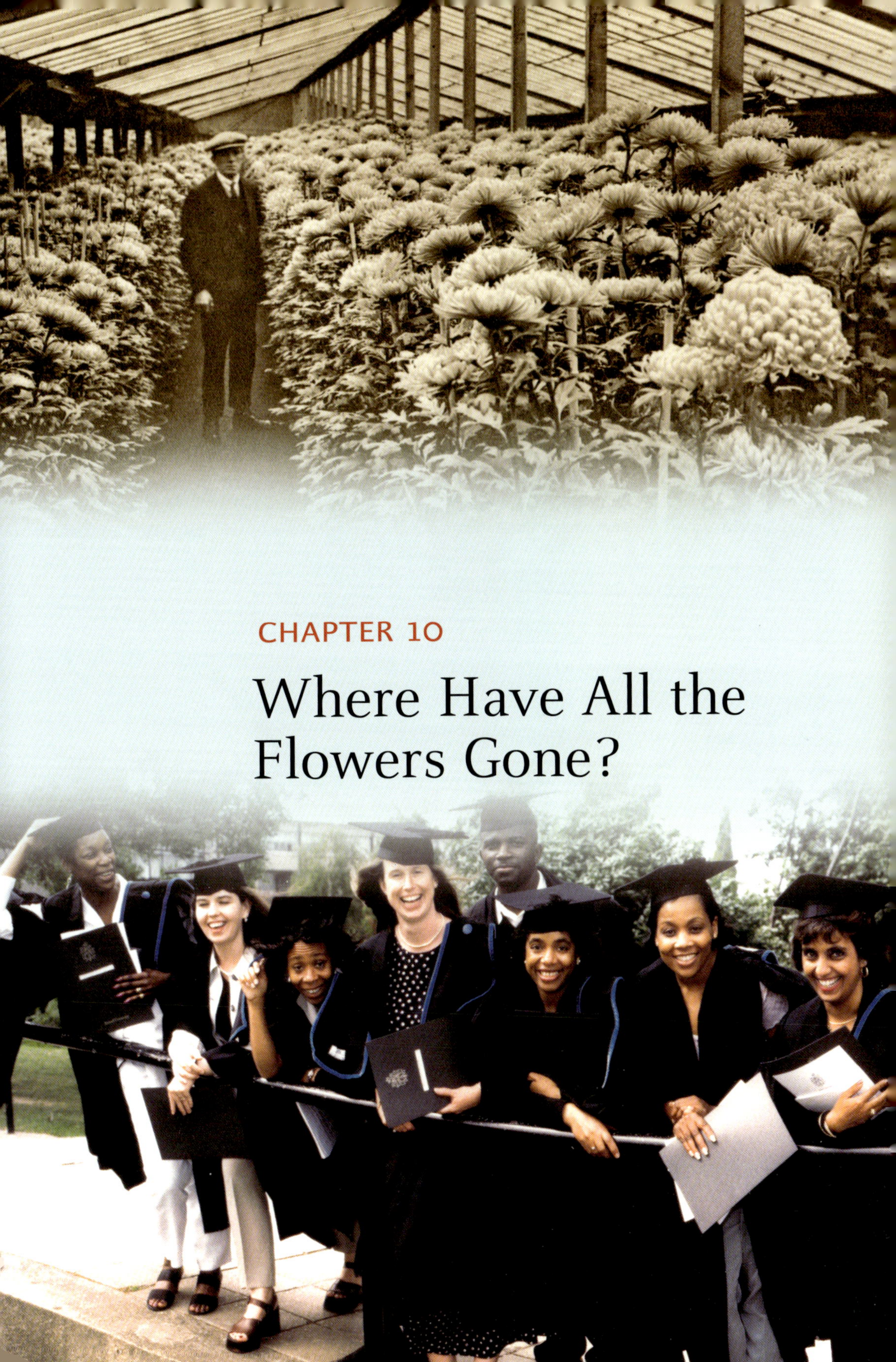

CHAPTER 10

Where Have All the Flowers Gone?

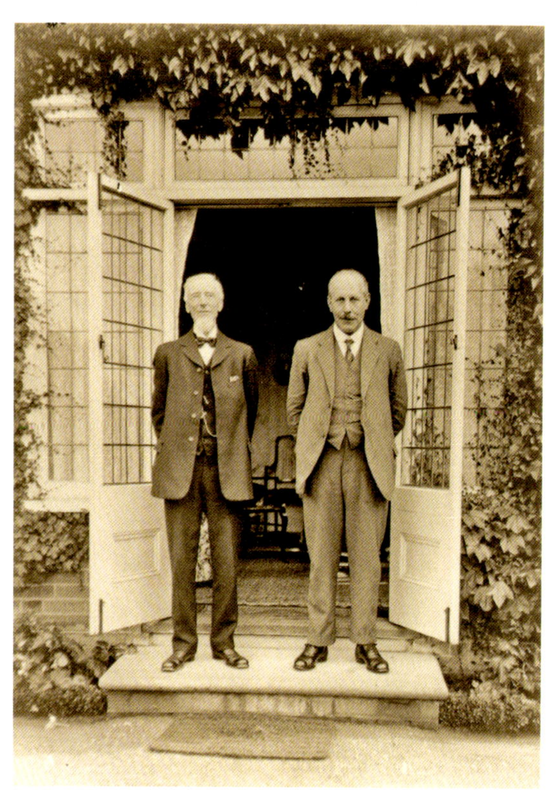

Joseph Lowe and George Shawyer
Lowe started a cut-flower nursery in Kingston Lane in 1868, specialising in roses and chrysanthemums. His business prospered, and additional land was purchased. In 1897 George Shawyer was taken into partnership, and even greater success followed. Lowe died in 1929, but by 1936 over 800 people were employed on an area of nearly 200 acres.

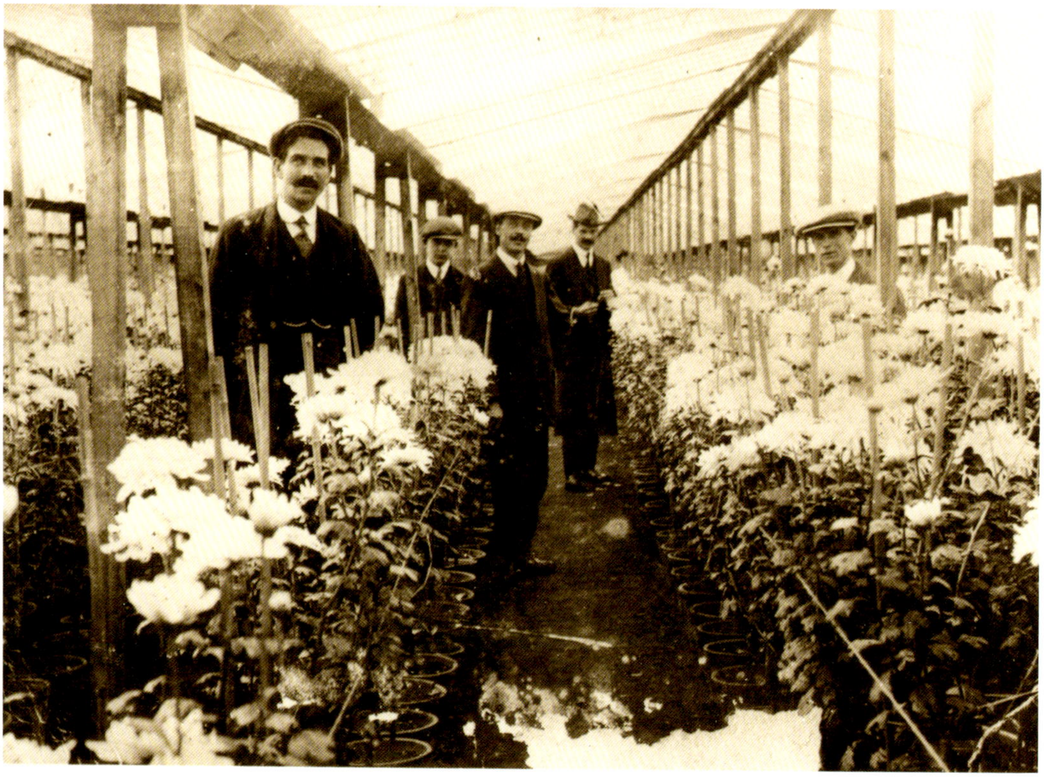

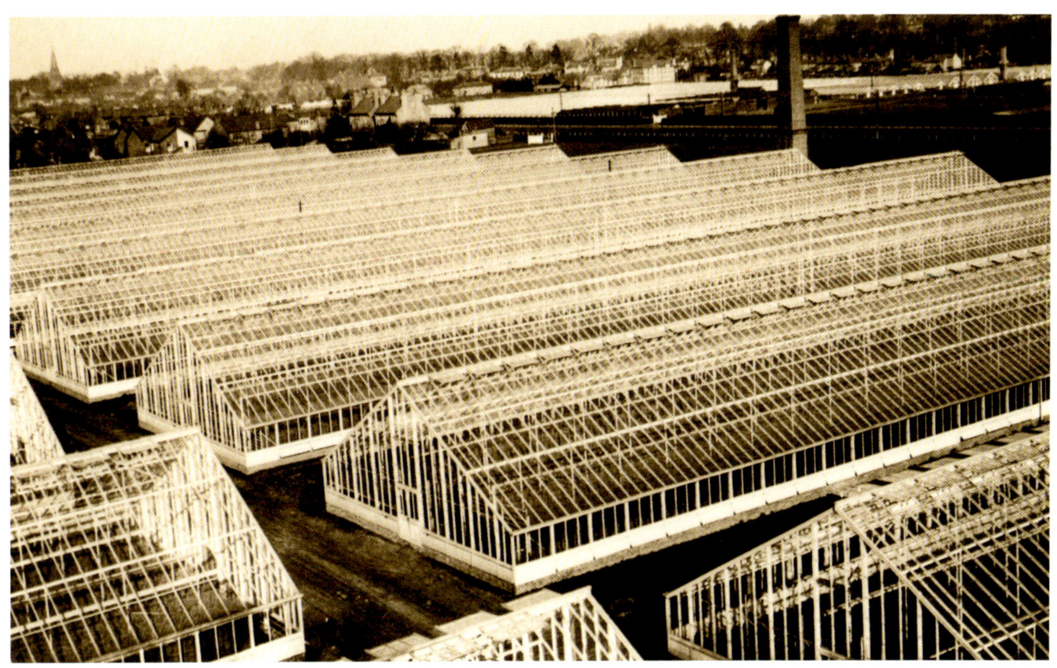

A gigantic enterprise

New greenhouses in 1929, built to grow carnations. In 1934 Queen Mary and her granddaughter Elizabeth (now HM The Queen) toured the site. In the peak summer period over a thousand people were employed. 18 million gallons of water were used per annum, and over six thousand tons of fuel were needed to feed the fourteen furnaces.

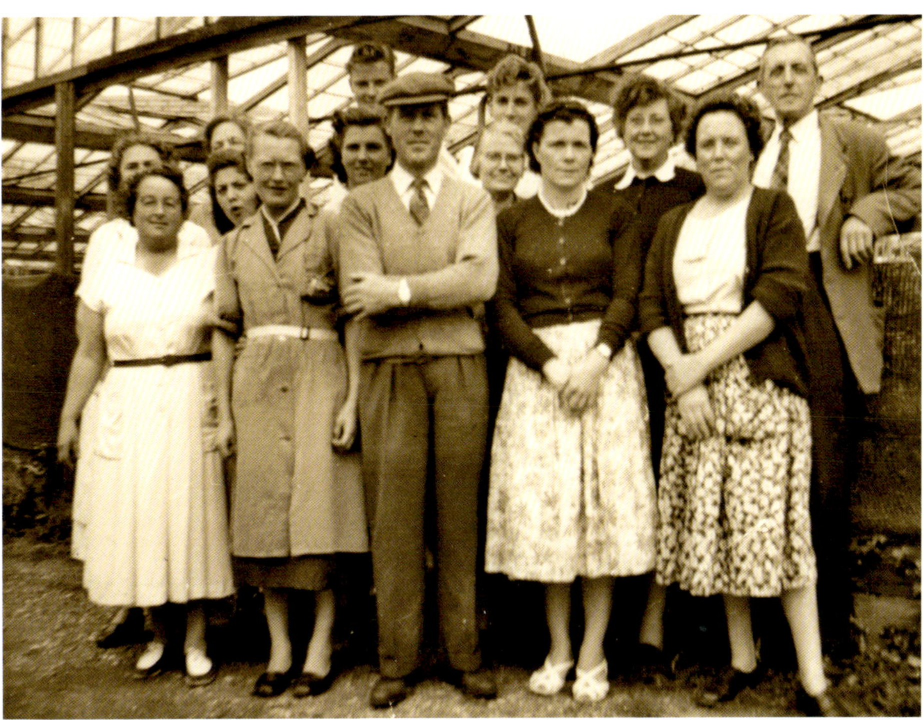

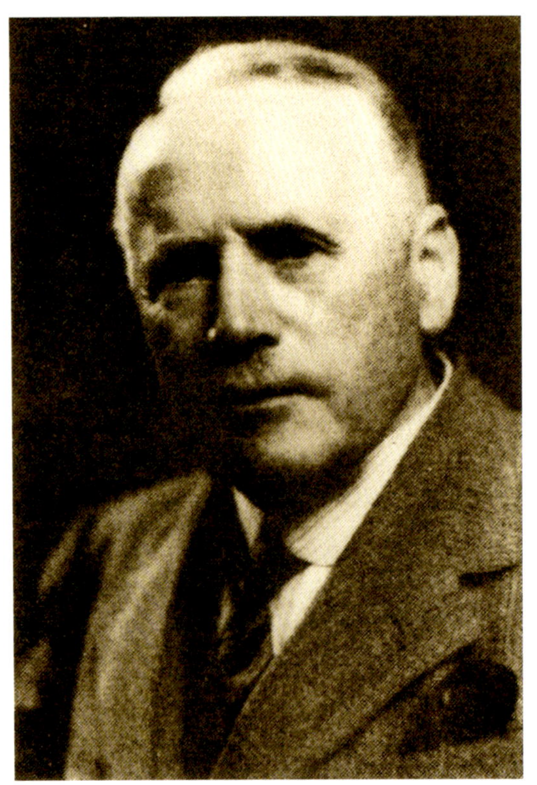

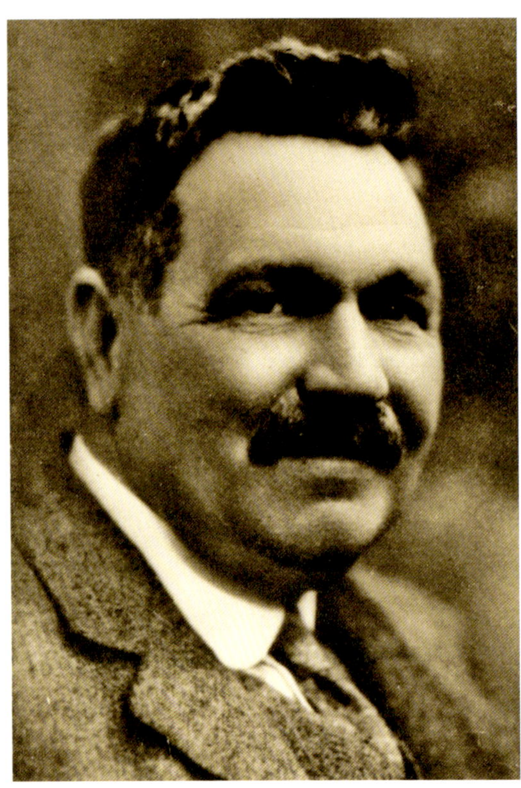

Offshoots

Milton Hutchings (1872-1939) was born in Cowley, and went to work for Joseph Lowe on leaving school. In 1894 he left to set up his own nursery in Pield Heath Road, and the company became well known for growing Cape Erica hybrids. The nursery has now evolved into the Wyevale garden centre.

In 1917 Thomas Stevenson, an expert on chrysanthemums and sweet peas, joined Lowe and Shawyer. One of his first tasks was to arrange work for German prisoners-of-war, who were marched up from their camp at Denham to work on the nursery. He left in 1928 to establish the Colham Green nursery in Chapel Lane, Hillingdon.

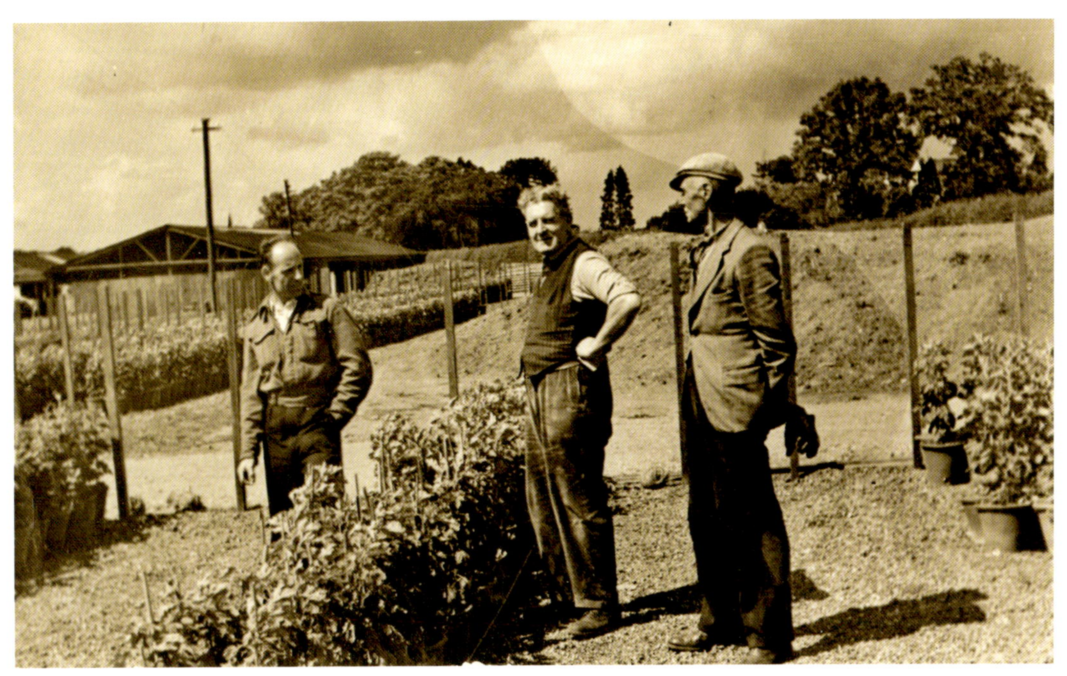

The Workforce

Women and girls were employed in the nursery, for the first time, during the 1914-1918 war. Many were employed packing the flowers into boxes, which were then sent to market. The lower picture shows an Annual Dinner for employees, held in Uxbridge in the early '30s. Company carnations are in evidence, but it seems to have been a 'men only' occasion.

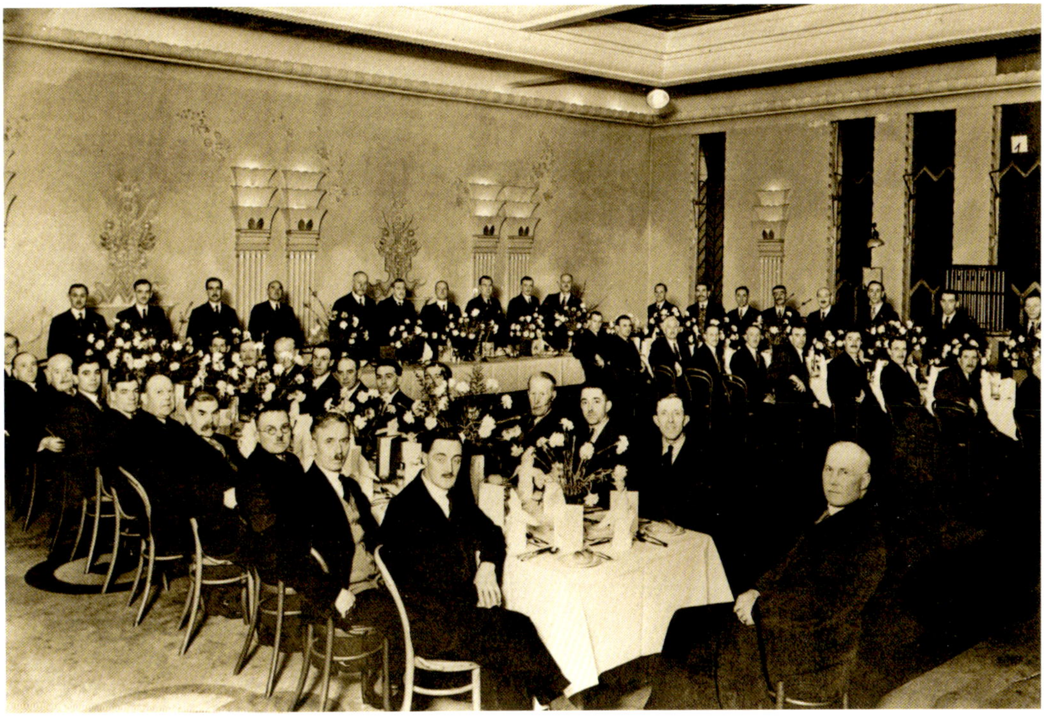

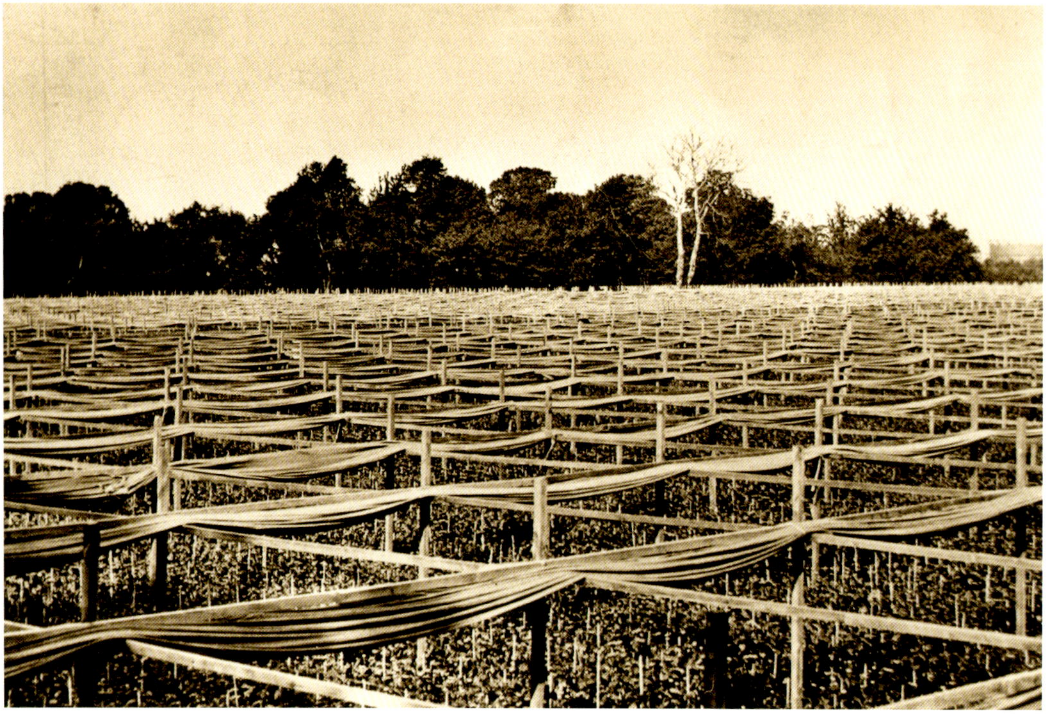

Fox Field, Station Road

A late frost in Spring could destroy the chrysanthemums, so men were called out at night to pull canvass over the blooms. In the post-war years employees were reluctant to do this, and it was one of the many problems that led to the end of the nursery, by voluntary liquidation in 1958. Below is Fox Field today, full of student residences.

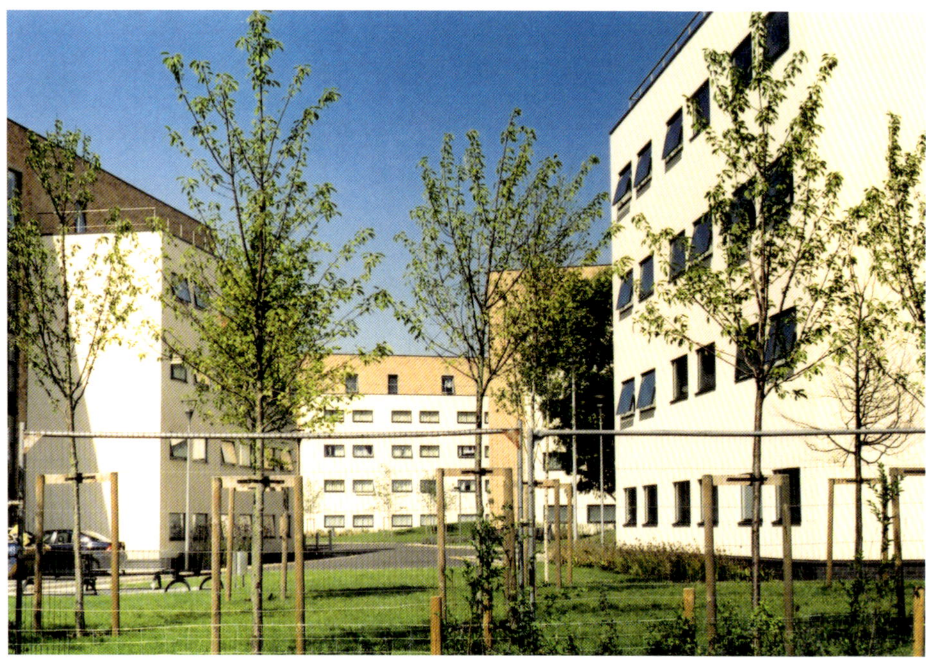

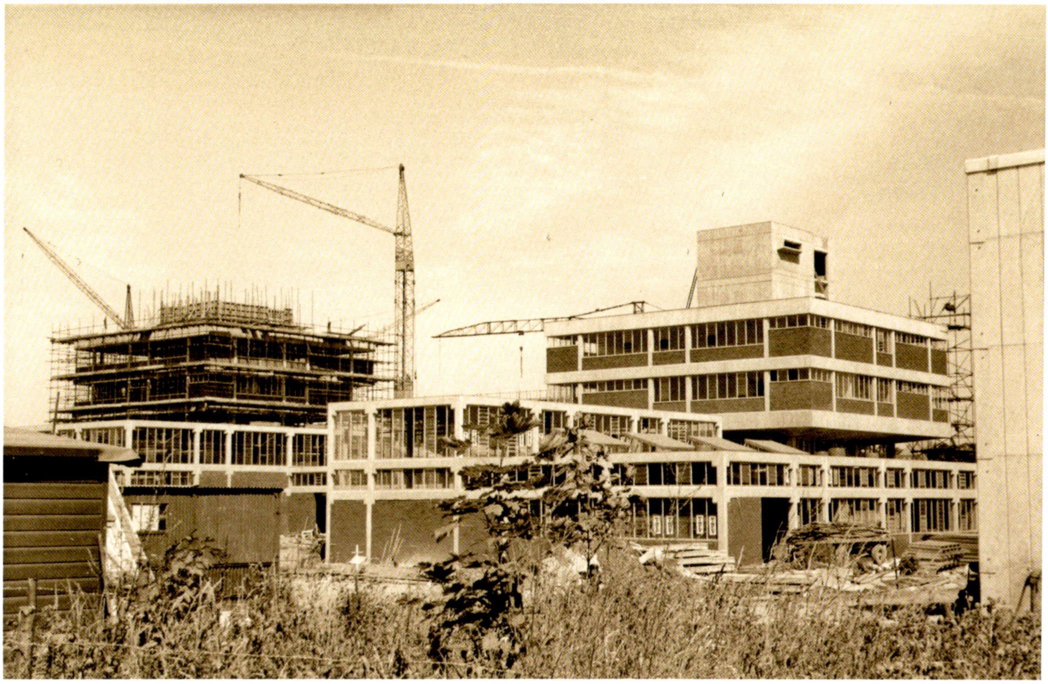

Brunel College

By 1958 the Brunel College of Advanced Technology at Acton was looking for larger premises, and most of the nursery land was destined to become its new home. By the time the first students appeared on campus the College had acquired its Charter as a university. Early buildings, like the Engineering block, were built using concrete, but in more recent times there has been something of a return to traditional materials.

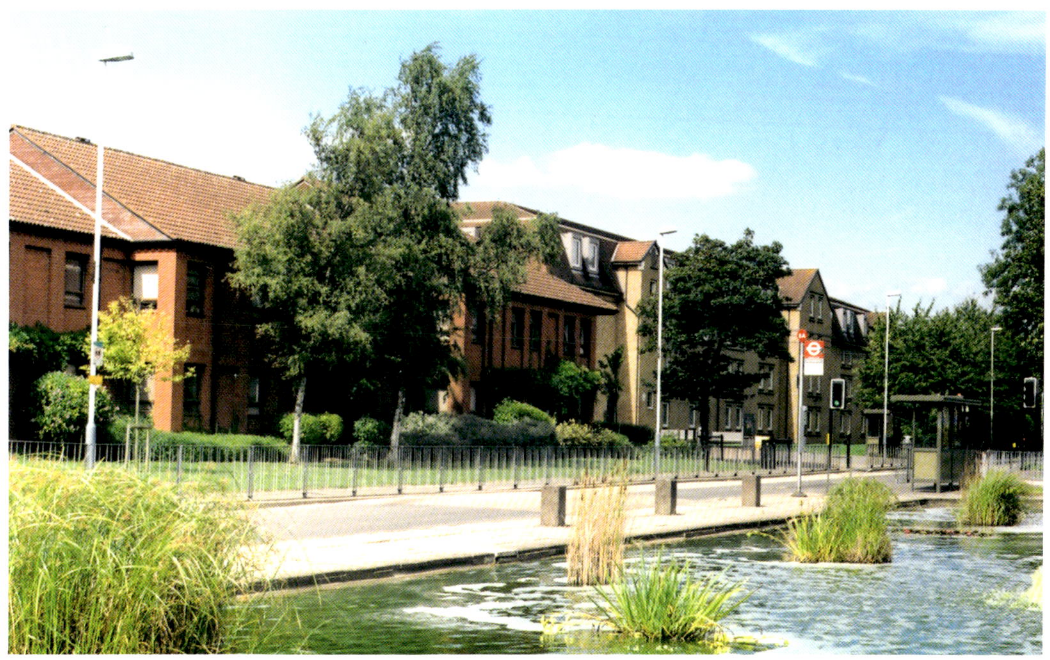

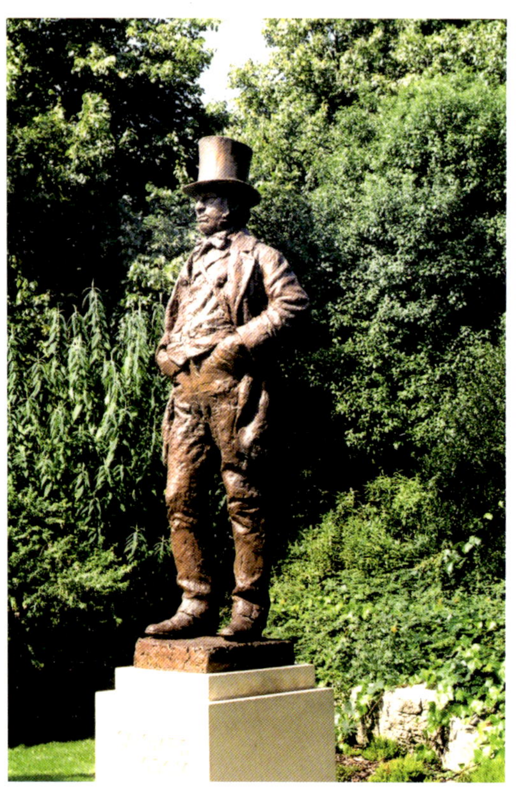

Isambard Kingdom Brunel

One feature of the campus is this statue of Isambard Kingdom Brunel, created by sculptor Anthony Stone. The figure is based on a famous photograph of the great engineer standing in front of the launching chains of his ship the *Great Eastern* in 1857. Fifty years ago the idea of buses passing along Cleveland Road would have been unthinkable. This bus, taken in 1995, soon proved to be too small for the increasing number of student passengers.

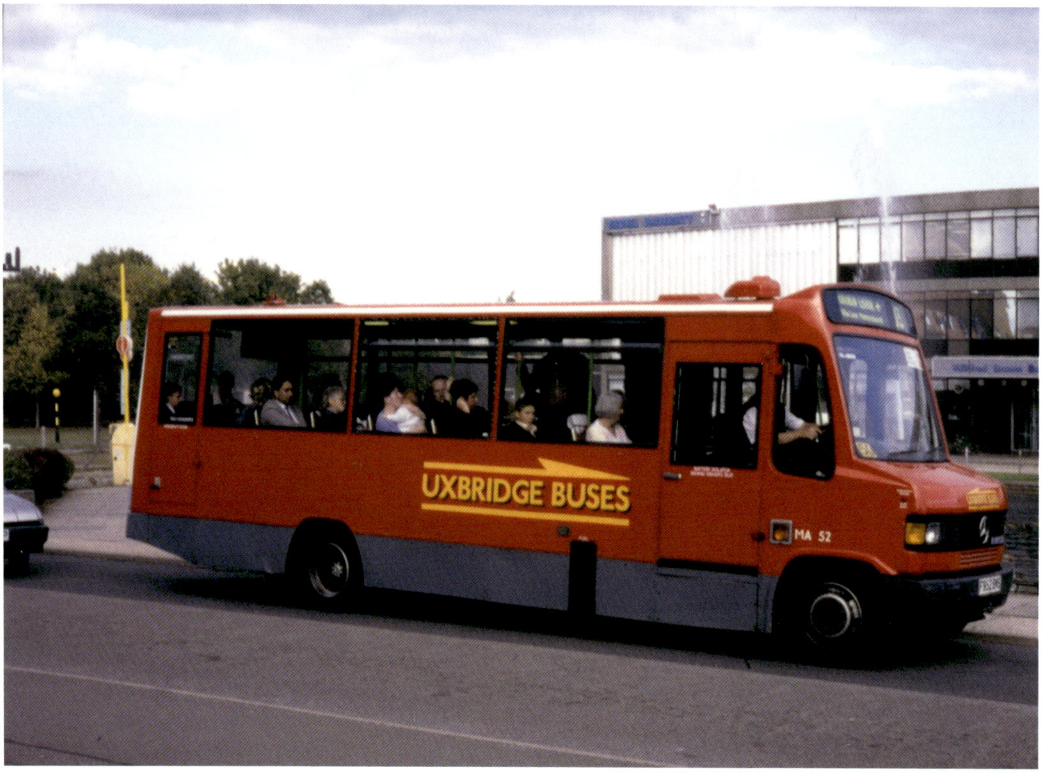

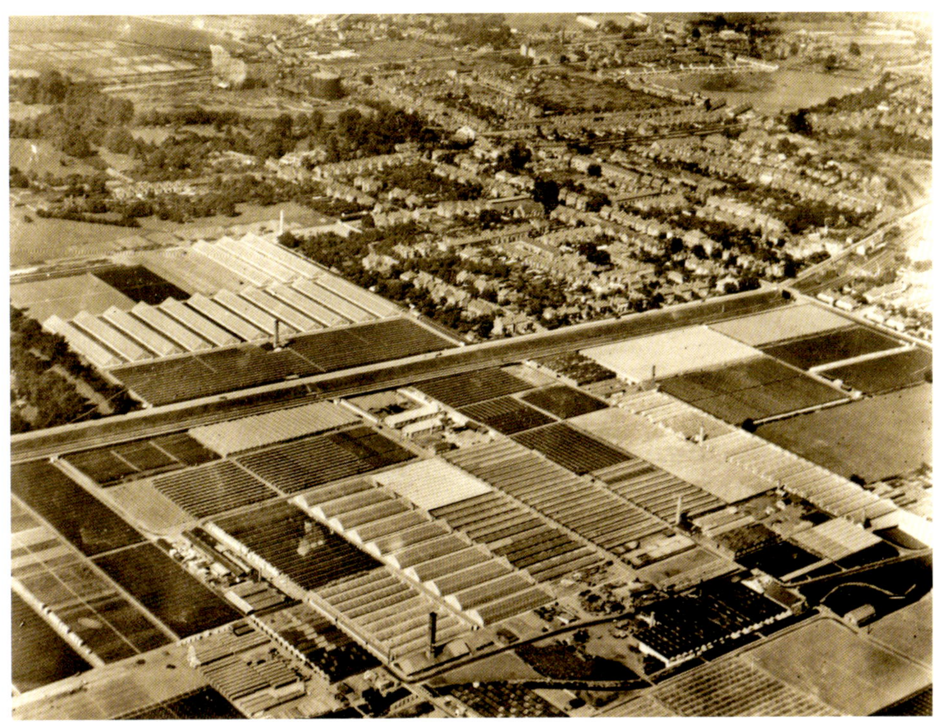

Aerial views

The Lowe and Shawyer nursery in 1929. Running across the middle of the photograph is Cleveland Road and the GWR branch line, with the Greenway bridge on the right. Greenhouses were being built on the far side of the road. This is in stark contrast with the aerial picture of the University taken from the east in 2008, with the white roof of the Sports Centre prominent in the foreground. (Photo. Commission Air/Brunel University.)

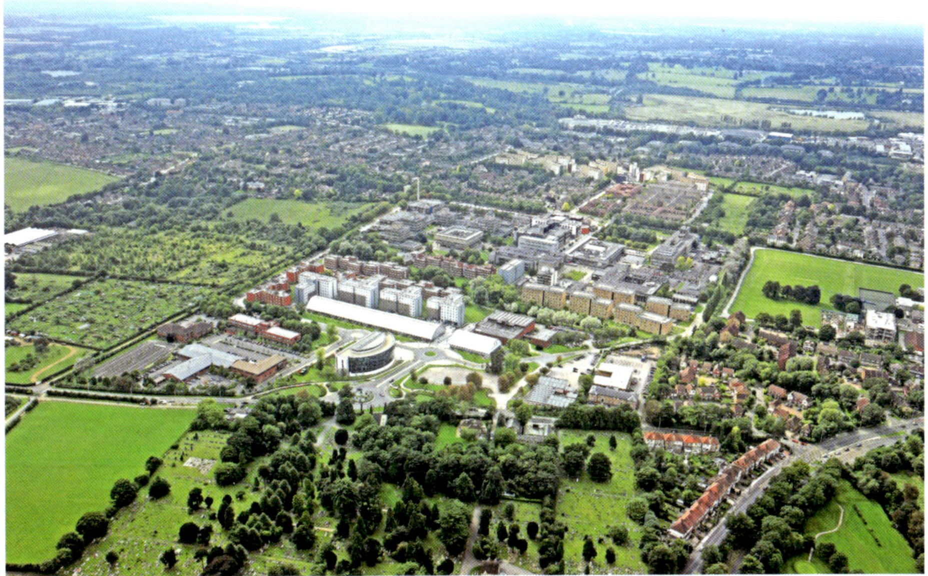

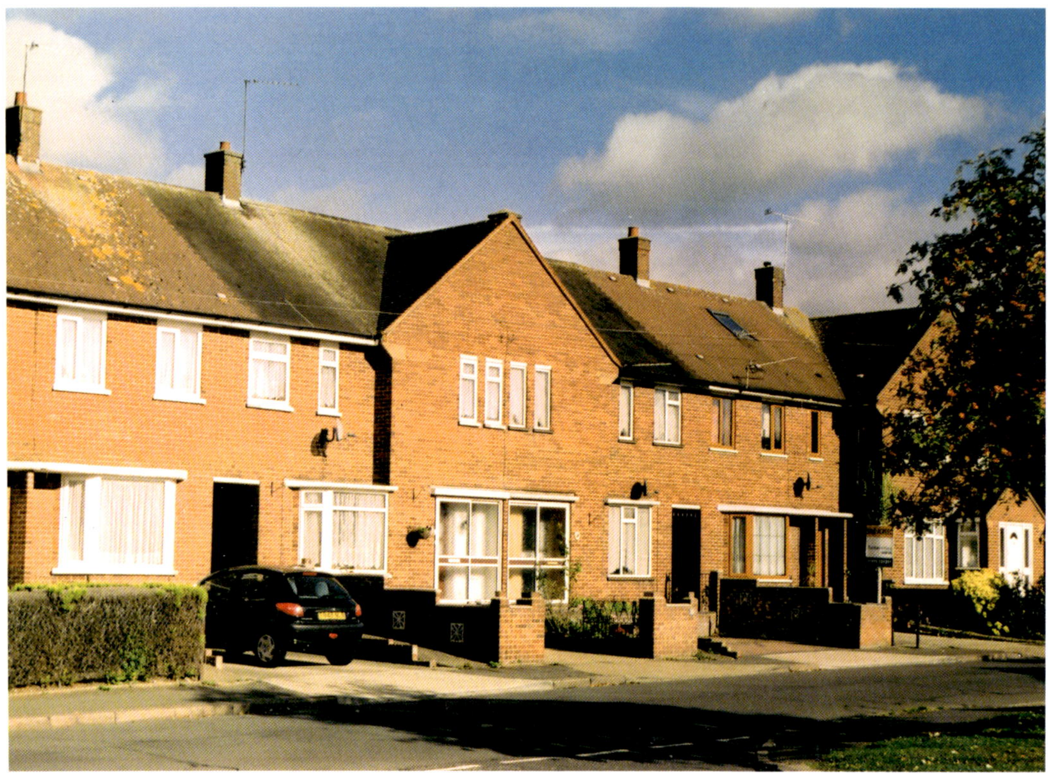

Post-war Council housing.

Acknowledgements

The author extends his sincere thanks to the following friends, who have helped him in the preparation of this book. They are Paul and Valerie Bourton, Peter Buckland, Sheila Field, Peter and Elizabeth Grimes, Steve Hardwicke, Beryl Holder, Hilda Hookham, David Keen, David Lewis, Brenda Mothersole, Pat North, Peter Nutchey, Helena Plowright, Joyce Randall, Stella Rowlands, Joy Saunders, Muriel Sims, Sally Trussler and Richard Try. He is also greatly indebted to his daughter, Gill Clark, who prepared all his material for the publishers.